MEMOIRS (1630–1680)

The Other Voice in Early Modern Europe:
The Toronto Series, 25

The Other Voice in Early Modern Europe: The Toronto Series

SERIES EDITORS Margaret L. King *and* Albert Rabil, Jr.
SERIES EDITOR, ENGLISH TEXTS Elizabeth H. Hageman

Previous Publications in the Series

The Other Voice in
Early Modern Europe:
The Toronto Series

SERIES EDITORS Margaret L. King *and* Albert Rabil, Jr.
SERIES EDITOR, ENGLISH TEXTS Elizabeth H. Hageman

Previous Publications in the Series

Enchanted Eloquence: Fairy Tales by Seventeenth-Century French Women Writers
Edited and translated by Lewis C. Seifert and Domna C. Stanton
2010

Gottfried Wilhelm Leibniz, Sophie, Electress of Hanover and Queen Sophie Charlotte of Prussia
Leibniz and the Two Sophies: The Philosophical Correspondence
Edited and translated by Lloyd Strickland
2011

In Dialogue with the Other Voice in Sixteenth-Century Italy: Literary and Social Contexts for Women's Writing
Edited by Julie D. Campbell and Maria Galli Stampino
2011

Sister Giustina Niccolini
The Chronicle of Le Murate
Edited and translated by Saundra Weddle
2011

Liubov Krichevskaya
No Good without Reward: Selected Writings: A Bilingual Edition
Edited and translated by Brian James Baer
2011

Elizabeth Cooke Hoby Russell
The Writings of an English Sappho
Edited by Patricia Phillippy
With translations by Jaime Goodrich
2011

Lucrezia Marinella
Exhortations to Women and to Others if They Please
Edited and translated by Laura Benedetti
2012

Margherita Datini
Letters to Francesco Datini
Translated by Carolyn James and Antonio Pagliaro
2012

The Other Voice in Early Modern Europe: The Toronto Series

SERIES EDITORS Margaret L. King *and* Albert Rabil, Jr.
SERIES EDITOR, ENGLISH TEXTS Elizabeth H. Hageman

Previous Publications in the Series

DELARIVIER MANLEY AND MARY PIX
English Women Staging Islam, 1696–1707
Edited and translated by Bernadette Andrea
2012

CECILIA DEL NACIMIENTO
Journeys of a Mystic Soul in Poetry and Prose
Introduction and prose translations by Kevin Donnelly
Poetry translations by Sandra Sider
2012

LADY MARGARET DOUGLAS AND OTHERS
The Devonshire Manuscript: A Women's Book of Courtly Poetry
Edited and introduced by Elizabeth Heale
2012

ARCANGELA TARABOTTI
Letters Familiar and Formal
Edited and translated by Meredith K. Ray and Lynn Lara Westwater
2012

PERE TORRELLAS AND JUAN DE FLORES
Three Spanish Querelle *Texts:* Grisel and Mirabella, The Slander against Women, *and* The Defense of Ladies against Slanderers: *A Bilingual Edition and Study*
Edited by Emily C. Francomano
2013

BARBARA TORELLI BENEDETTI
Partenia, a Pastoral Play: A Bilingual Edition
Edited and translated by Lisa Sampson and Barbara Burgess-Van Aken
2013

FRANÇOIS ROUSSET, JEAN LIEBAULT, JACQUES GUILLEMEAU, JACQUES DUVAL AND LOUIS DE SERRES
Pregnancy and Birth in Early Modern France: Treatises by Caring Physicians and Surgeons (1581–1625)
Edited and translated by Valerie Worth-Stylianou
2013

MARY ASTELL
The Christian Religion, as Professed by a Daughter of the Church of England
Edited by Jacqueline Broad
2013

Memoirs (1630–1680)

SOPHIA OF HANOVER

~

Edited and translated by

SEAN WARD

Iter Inc.
Centre for Reformation and Renaissance Studies
Toronto
2013

Iter: Gateway to the Middle Ages and Renaissance
Tel: 416/978–7074   Email: iter@utoronto.ca

Fax: 416/978–1668   Web: www.itergateway.org

Centre for Reformation and Renaissance Studies
Victoria University in the University of Toronto
Tel: 416/585–4465   Email: crrs.publications@utoronto.ca
Fax: 416/585–4430   Web: www.crrs.ca

Iter and the Centre for Reformation and Renaissance Studies gratefully acknowledge the generous support of James E. Rabil, in memory of Scottie W. Rabil, toward the publication of this book.

Library and Archives Canada Cataloguing in Publication

Sophia, Electress, consort of Ernest Augustus, Elector of Hanover, 1630–1714
[Memoiren der Herzogin Sophie nachmals Kurfürstin von Hannover. English]
Memoirs (1630–1680) / Sophia of Hanover ; edited and translated by Sean Ward.

(Other voice in early modern Europe. The Toronto series ; 25)
Translation of Memoiren der Herzogin Sophie nachmals Kurfürstin von Hannover, originally published: Leipzig : Hirzel, 1879.
Translated from the French.
Includes bibliographical references and index.
Issued in print and electronic formats.
Co-published by: Iter Inc.
ISBN 978-0-7727-2148-8 (pbk.). ISBN 978-0-7727-2149-5 (pdf)

1. Sophia, Electress, consort of Ernest Augustus, Elector of Hanover, 1630–1714.
2. Princesses—Germany—Hannover (Province)—Biography—Early works to 1800.
3. Mothers of kings and rulers—Great Britain—Biography—Early works to 1800.
4. Hannover (Germany : Province)—History—Sources. 5. Hannover (Germany : Province)—Politics and government—Sources. I. Ward, Sean, 1963–, editor, translator II. Victoria University (Toronto, Ont.). Centre for Reformation and Renaissance Studies, issuing body III. Iter Inc, issuing body IV. Title. V. Title: Memoiren der Herzogin Sophie nachmals Kurfürstin von Hannover. English. VI. Series: Other voice in early modern Europe. Toronto series ; 25

| DD190.3.S67A313 2013 | 943'.59044092 | C2013-905358-1 |
| | | C2013-905359-X |

Cover illustration:
Princess Louisa Hollandina of the Palatinate (1622–1709): Princess Sophia of the Palatinate [later duchess and electress of Hanover] dressed as an Indian (detail). Fürst Salm-zu-Salm, Anholt, Germany.

Cover design:
Maureen Morin, Information Technology Services, University of Toronto Libraries.

Typesetting and production:
Iter Inc.

Contents

Acknowledgments

A number of friends and colleagues (some of whom are both) generously read all or part of the manuscript and provided me with detailed feedback: Bill Brooks, Jeff Connaughton, Carolyn Lougee, Sarah Nelson, Renée Schell, and Lisa Shapiro. Their expertise, erudition, and encouragement made the book better (and me smarter). My sincere thanks to them all. An anonymous reader assigned by the press also provided helpful comments and suggestions. I am grateful to the copyeditors, Sharon Brinkman and Tracee Glab, for seeing things I no longer could and, in some cases, never would have; to the typesetter, Anabela Carneiro, for graciously implementing my many changes to the page proofs; and to the project manager, Margaret English-Haskin, for skillfully shepherding the book to press. In the early stages of this project I was fortunate to have my own Bergstrasse Irregulars—Benedikt Bader and Johanna Best—to hunt down long-forgotten people and places in Heidelberg and Hanover. In the later stages I had the benefit, thanks to the generous support of professors Eric Rentschler and Judith Ryan, of two years as an associate of the Department of Germanic Languages and Literatures at Harvard University, which enabled me to do research for this book at Widener and Houghton libraries. Finally, I would like to thank the series editors, Albert Rabil and Margaret King, for giving Sophia a home.

SEAN WARD

Introduction

The Other Voice

The sky above Herrenhausen palace and garden portended rain, but the eighty-three-year-old chatelaine, Dowager Electress Sophia of Hanover, was determined to take her early evening walk. She set out, still somewhat weak from the malady (severe stomach pain) and remedy (two enemas) she had endured the day before. She was accompanied by two good friends, the countess of Bückeburg and Princess Caroline, her grandson's wife. The melodic lines of the trio's conversation rose and fell above the delicate percussion of their steps on the garden's gravel paths. The coin struck to commemorate the day—June 8, 1714—describes their pace as brisk ("vegeto et strenuo passu deambulans").[1] As they approached a fountain in the middle of the garden, the rain came, and Sophia, overcome by renewed stomach pain, began to totter. With her friends' support she managed a few more steps but then collapsed, unconscious, in their arms. They laid her on the ground, loosened her bodice, removed her hairpiece, kneeled next to her, and prayed. They watched as Sophia's face reddened, then paled. The countess of Bückeburg called it the most peaceful, beautiful death imaginable.[2]

In Sophia's case, beginning with the end is appropriate. Death is never timely, but Sophia's was particularly untimely. This, in fact, is the main reason why her voice has gone largely unheard in the English-speaking world. For just seven weeks later, on August 1, 1714, Queen Anne of Great Britain and Ireland, Sophia's first cousin once removed, died in her sleep in Kensington Palace, London. Had Sophia lived just two months longer, she would have succeeded Anne as queen (in the event, it was Sophia's son George Lewis who, as George I, became Britain's first Hanoverian monarch). Had she lived long enough to be queen for just a year or two, she would occupy a much

1. Johann Georg Heinrich Feder, *Sophie Churfürstin von Hannover im Umriß* (Hanover: Hahn, 1810), 181.

2. *Correspondance de Leibniz avec l'électrice Sophie de Brunswick-Lunebourg*, ed. Onno Klopp (Hanover: Klindworth, 1874), 3: 457–62.

more prominent place in the English cultural landscape. Her life, from penurious youth to august senectitude, would be a much more familiar story (and likely would have been accorded one of popular culture's highest forms of ennoblement: serving as the subject for a BBC miniseries). But having never acceded to the throne, Sophia gradually receded from memory.

Sophia's memoirs can help recall her to a modern readership. They appear here in English for the first time in their entirety.[3] They recount the first fifty years of Sophia's life: her childhood and teens in Leiden and The Hague; her years as a young woman at her brother's court in Heidelberg; her married life in the north German towns of Iburg, Osnabrück, and Hanover; and her trips to Italy in 1664–65 and to France in 1679. A contemporary declared Sophia, a German princess, to be France's greatest *bel esprit*.[4] It is no surprise, therefore, that her memoirs (which Sophia wrote in French) abound with insightful, entertaining, and occasionally acerbic accounts of her meetings with prominent leading men and ladies (a young Charles II, a middle-aged Louis XIV, Pope Alexander VII, Queen Christina of Sweden) and with long-forgotten bit players (cavaliers, concubines, clerics, coachmen, and quacks). As such, they offer detailed insights into the public and private lives of early modern European nobles (their codes of etiquette, habits of dress, entertainments, fights, and amours) and of these nobles' small army of attendants, servants, and hangers-on. They complement, and indeed serve as a prequel to, Lloyd H. Strickland's fine translation of letters between Sophia, her daughter, and Gottfried

---

3. The translator of the only previous English edition expurgated about one-tenth of the text as "distasteful to our modern ideas." *Memoirs of Sophia, Electress of Hanover, 1630–1680*, trans. H. Forester (London: Richard Bentley & Son, 1888), xiv.

4. Urbain Chevreau (1613–1701), author, personal secretary to Queen Christina of Sweden, and tutor to the duke of Maine (one of Louis XIV's natural children). He added that Sophia's sister Elizabeth was France's greatest savant (quoted in Feder, *Sophie*, 8). The translator of the German edition of the memoirs conceded that Sophia could express herself more felicitously in French than in German but felt compelled to add that this did not detract in the least from her innate Germanness. *Die Mutter der Könige von Preußen und England. Memoiren und Briefe der Kurfürstin Sophie von Hannover*, trans. and ed. Robert Geerds (Munich: Langewiesche-Brandt, 1913), 7–8.

Wilhelm von Leibniz, which was recently published in this series.[5] The memoirs cover the period 1630–80; the letters, 1691–1713. Together, they give us a fairly complete picture of Sophia's life in her own words.

Throughout much of her life Sophia was among the highest-born Protestant princesses in continental Europe. Throughout all her life she was a true celebrity, feted and fussed over wherever she traveled. Among the roughly fifty other women in this series, there are only three—Margaret of Navarre, the duchess of Montpensier, and Sophia's own sister Elizabeth—who held similarly stratospheric positions in the social hierarchy of early modern Europe. This position—and the experiences and personalities to which it gave her access—makes Sophia something of an other voice among the other voices. It is a voice worth hearing, both for the remarkable story it tells and for the remarkably entertaining way it tells it.

Historical Background and Biography

Sophia's parents—the Lady Elizabeth, daughter of King James I of England, and Frederick V, palsgrave of the Rhine and elector Palatine—were married in London on Valentine's Day in 1613. Frederick was the sovereign of the Lower Palatinate (situated along the Neckar and Rhine rivers in southwestern Germany, with Heidelberg as its residence) and the Upper Palatinate (situated north of the Danube and west of Bohemia in what is today northern Bavaria).[6] Several nuptial masques and hundreds of epithalamia celebrated the union of two of Europe's most important Protestant families, the houses of Stuart and Palatine, as the marriage of Thames and Rhine.[7] In April 1613 the newlyweds—accompanied by a retinue of more than seven hundred

5. *Leibniz and the Two Sophies: The Philosophical Correspondence*, trans. and ed. Lloyd H. Strickland (Toronto: CRRS, 2011).

6. It has become a historiographical bromide to assert that, prior to the nineteenth century, Germany is an anachronism and that the proper term is the Holy Roman Empire of the German Nation. Although not a political entity in Sophia's day, Germany was common parlance for that part of Central Europe where German was spoken. Sophia's mother, for example, refers repeatedly to "Germanie" in her English correspondence. *The Letters of Elizabeth of Bohemia*, ed. L. M. Baker (London: Bodley Head, 1953), 24, 100, 133, 138, 167, and 197.

7. Some of the music from the masques is available on I Ciarlatani, *Fly Cheerful Voices: The Marriage of Pfalzgraf Friedrich V & Elizabeth Stuart*, recorded June 13–15, 1997,

courtiers and attendants—sailed to Holland, continued up the Rhine, and installed themselves in the grand pink Renaissance palace overlooking Heidelberg and the Neckar.

Frederick was the leader of the Union, an alliance, formed in May 1608, of German Protestant principalities and free imperial cities. Its purpose was to check what it saw as the erosion of Protestant rights by the emperor (a Catholic from the House of Habsburg) and by the empire's legislative and judicial institutions (in all of which Catholics held a clear majority). In August 1619 the predominantly Protestant estates of Bohemia, as part of their revolt against Habsburg rule, elected Frederick to be their king, a crown that had perennially gone to a Catholic Habsburg prince. Against the advice of the majority of his councilors and most allied Protestant princes (who saw that the Palatinate lacked the military power to defend itself against the inevitable Habsburg riposte), Frederick accepted and was crowned in Prague on November 4, 1619.

His undoing was swift. In August and September 1620 a Spanish army captured Heidelberg and occupied the Lower Palatinate west of the Rhine. Ten weeks after losing Heidelberg, Frederick lost Prague. On November 8, 1620, an imperial army routed Frederick's forces on White Mountain outside the city. The emperor had won the first major battle of what would become the Thirty Years War. Frederick, whose reign as king of Bohemia lasted almost exactly one year, had spent just one winter in Prague Palace, whence his epithet: the Winter King.

Sophia's parents fled Prague in such disarray that they almost left behind one of her siblings. Parents and children—Frederick Henry (born in 1614), Charles Lewis (1617), Elizabeth (1618), Rupert (1619), and Morris (1621, born while they were on the run)—sought, with little success, refuge at allied courts in Germany. Finally, in April 1621, they found a warm welcome and secure exile in The Hague, where they had ties familial (Frederick's mother was a princess of the House of Orange) and religious (Calvinism). In the beginning they received generous subsidies: 10,000 guilders a month from the States General

Christophorus, 77214, 1998, compact disc. For an example of the epithalamia, see Thomas Heywood, *A Marriage of Triumph* (1613; repr., London: Percy Society, 1842).

and £26,000 from England. Over time the welcome grew cooler and the subsidies scantier.

In their Dutch exile Frederick and Elizabeth continued to style themselves king and queen of Bohemia and continued to have children at a nearly annual rate: Louisa Hollandina (1622), Lewis (1624), Edward (1625), Henrietta (1626), Philip (1627), Charlotte (1628), Sophia (1630), and Gustavus Adolphus (1631). To judge from the couple's steadfastly adoring letters to one another, their fecundity was as much a product of an enduring erotic enthusiasm as of dynastic duty.[8] It was partially offset by childhood illness and mishap: Lewis and Charlotte died as infants, Gustavus Adolphus as a child, and Frederick Henry (the oldest) as a teenager. The Winter King himself died, probably of bubonic plague, in 1632. He was only thirty-six, his daughter Sophia at the time only two. On Frederick's death, Sophia's brother Charles Lewis became palsgrave of the Rhine and elector Palatine—if he could ever win back his territory and titles, which the emperor, as punishment for Frederick's Bohemian adventure, had transferred to Duke Maximilian of Bavaria in 1623.

Sophia was born in The Hague on October 14, 1630, and soon moved to the private boarding school in Leiden that the exiled Palatines had established for their sizeable brood and the hundred-strong staff of governesses, teachers, valets, and other servants who attended to the children's schooling and other needs. The standard of the children's education, for both the boys and the girls, was extremely high, and all became prodigious polyglots. Sophia spoke French, German, and Dutch fluently, could converse in English and Italian, and had rudimentary knowledge of Spanish and Latin. On reaching their midteens the children were retrieved from the school, the boys to travel and the girls to keep their mother company.

The Hague in the 1640s, a place of exile for Sophia's family and for royalists chased from England by the parliamentarians, was a hotbed of spying, scheming, and skullduggery. Sophia found herself in the middle of it. The scheme (cherished by her mother) was for Sophia to marry the Prince of Wales, the future Charles II. The skullduggery (cherished by Princess Amalia of Orange-Nassau) was for a

---

8. *A Collection of Original Royal Letters*, ed. Sir George Bromley (London: John Stockdale, 1787), 1–66.

prince of Orange-Nassau to seduce Sophia so that, with her reputation tarnished, one of Amalia's own daughters could marry the Prince of Wales. To escape the intrigue and gossip Sophia moved to Heidelberg, the residence of her brother Charles Lewis, to whom the Lower Palatinate had recently been restored by the Treaty of Westphalia. She arrived in the late summer of 1650, two months before her twentieth birthday.

The eight years Sophia spent in Heidelberg centered around marriage: the arrangement of a suitable one for her and the unraveling of Charles Lewis's. The first serious suitor (a mere Portuguese duke had been rejected out of hand) was the recently widowed Prince Adolphus John of Zweibrücken. He had a prognathous face and a pugnacious temperament (he was rumored to have beaten his wife). Sophia did not like him. It was Sophia's good fortune that the prince made promises regarding her future income that his older brother, King Charles VI of Sweden, was unwilling to keep and that the next, much more desirable suitor was already on the scene.

In 1657 Sophia became engaged to Duke George William of Brunswick-Lüneburg (1624–1705). But the groom, realizing that he was too wedded to his sybaritic bachelor lifestyle to actually wed, soon rued his decision. Although the marriage contracts had already been signed, George William hoped to extricate himself by making a novel proposal: what if his favorite brother, Duke Ernest Augustus (1630–98), married Sophia in his place? George William would simply sign a document in which he pledged to remain a bachelor, to leave his demesne to Ernest Augustus on his death, and to support Ernest Augustus and Sophia financially in the interim.

Charles Lewis, who negotiated on Sophia's behalf, told her that he considered the younger brother to be more amiable and sensible than the elder but left it up to her to decide. Sophia, who had met Ernest Augustus several times, told Charles Lewis that all she wanted was a financially solid arrangement suitable to her rank and that if the proposed match would achieve this she would not mind swapping grooms. In April 1658, George William signed a renunciation of marriage; in June, Ernest Augustus and Sophia signed their marriage contract; and in October, their wedding was celebrated in Heidelberg.

The newlyweds moved into George William's palace in Hanover. At times George William seemed to regret ceding Sophia to his younger brother. Indeed, the early years of Sophia's marriage were marred by her brother-in-law's continued flirtatiousness and her husband's jealousy. This tense situation was resolved in 1661 when Ernest Augustus was made secular bishop of Osnabrück, and he and Sophia established their own court at Iburg castle, located eight miles south of Osnabrück.

A few months after the wedding Sophia wrote to Charles Lewis that, "miracle of the century, I love my husband."[9] Perhaps she was just trying to reassure her brother about the marriage he had arranged for her. But the memoirs and her correspondence suggest that she remained passionately devoted to her husband, despite his serial infidelity.[10] Nearly two decades into Sophia's marriage, her sister Elizabeth writes of her: "the world and her husband do still possess her heart. God will in his due time touch us both."[11]

Ernest Augustus had two other older brothers besides George William. Their father's will stipulated that as long as two of the brothers (or their male heirs) were alive, the family domains—the duchies of Lüneburg and Calenberg in what is today the federal state of Lower Saxony in north-central Germany—were not to be united under a single sovereign. Instead, the oldest brother would get the duchy he preferred, the next oldest would get the duchy that was left over, and

9. *Briefwechsel der Herzogin Sophie von Hannover mit ihrem Bruder, dem Kurfürsten Karl Ludwig von der Pfalz, und des Letzteren mit seiner Schwägerin, der Pfalzgräfin Anna*, ed. Eduard Bodemann (Leipzig: Hirzel, 1885), 9; letter dated February 6, 1659.

10. Ernest Augustus at times wrote for—and received—Sophia's permission for his adultery. "Briefe des Kurfürsten Ernst August von Hannover an seine Gemahlin, die Kurfürstin Sophie," ed. Anna Wendland, *Niedersächsisches Jahrbuch* 7 (1930): 234; letter dated October 8, 1671. But Sophia was not above *Schadenfreude* in her dealings with her husband's bedmates. She would sometimes require Countess von Platen, her husband's official mistress, to accompany her on long walks in hot weather, leaving the corpulent countess bathed in sweat, her heavy makeup streaming down her face. See Georg Schnath, *Geschichte Hannovers im Zeitalter der neunten Kur und der englischen Suzsession 1674–1714*, 4 vols. (Hildesheim: Lax, 1938–82), 2: 487.

11. *The Correspondence between Princess Elisabeth of Bohemia and René Descartes*, trans. and ed. Lisa Shapiro (Chicago: University of Chicago Press, 2007), 203; letter dated July 16, 1677.

the rest would have to wait their turn (when Sophia married Ernest Augustus he was one of the latter: a domainless duke). The tax revenues in Lüneburg were much higher, so it was always the first choice. The two sovereign dukes were customarily referred to by the name of their duchy's principal town: the duke of Celle (for Lüneburg) and the duke of Hanover (for Calenberg).

What had seemed unlikely at the time of Sophia's marriage actually transpired. Two of her brothers-in-law died without male issue, and her husband became, in 1679, duke of Hanover. The other surviving brother was none other than George William, her erstwhile fiancé. In the interim he had finally given up bachelorhood and entered into a civil union with Eleanor Desmier d'Olbreuse (1639–1722), a former lady-in-waiting who came from a minor noble family in Poitou in western France. In keeping with the pledge to Ernest Augustus, this union was not, until 1676, a marriage. George William and his mate had one child, Sophia Dorothea (1666–1726).

The two surviving brothers sought to consolidate the House of Brunswick-Lüneburg's political power by ending its choose-your-duchy policy and establishing primogeniture over all its domains. To seal this deal they arranged a marriage to unite their families. The bride was Sophia Dorothea, the groom George Lewis, Ernest Augustus and Sophia's oldest son (and the future King George I of Great Britain and Ireland). It was a mésalliance with a capital *M*.[12] George Lewis was the great-grandson of King James I of England and related to the royal houses of France and Denmark and to the premier princely houses of Germany and Holland. Sophia Dorothea was the love child (later legitimated) of a German duke and a complete nobody. The marriage contract was signed on October 24, 1682. Sophia and Ernest Augustus

---

12. Some might say it was also endogamy with a capital *E*, since Sophia Dorothea and George Lewis were first cousins. But first-cousin marriages were common in early modern Europe. Sophia herself was briefly courted by her first cousin Charles Stuart (the future Charles II of England), a courtship enthusiastically supported by her mother. Brunswick consanguinity was intensified in 1706 when Sophia Dorothea and George Lewis's daughter (also named Sophia Dorothea, 1687–1757) married her first cousin, Frederick William (1688–1740), the future king of Prussia. Their oldest son, and the result of two generations of endogamy, was Frederick the Great (1712–86).

grinned and bore it as the most effective way to ensure their son's eventual inheritance of both duchies.[13]

But Sophia did not know all. Her husband had kept the primogeniture law, which received imperial sanction in 1683, a secret from her until the documents had been signed and sealed. When she found out, she was heartbroken. The new arrangement effectively disinherited all her other sons: Frederick Augustus (1661–90), Maximilian William (1666–1726), Charles Philip (1669–90), Christian (1671–1703), and Ernest Augustus (1674–1728). Now it was highly unlikely that any would ever become sovereign dukes. Unlikelihood became something close to impossibility when, in 1683, George Lewis's wife bore him an heir.[14]

Enemy fire solved the primogeniture problem for two of Sophia's sons. Charles Philip died in combat in 1690 in Albania, Frederick Augustus in 1691 in Transylvania. Christian died on active service in 1703, drowning while attempting to ford the Danube. But primogeniture had created a rift between Sophia and her husband, one that never closed. When a plot by Maximilian William to overthrow primogeniture was thwarted, he was put on trial for treason and Sophia briefly under house arrest for not revealing her foreknowledge of the plot. On a happier note, in the interim a good match had been found for Sophia's beloved daughter Sophia Charlotte (1668–1705), who married Prince Frederick of Brandenburg (1657–1713), the future King Frederick I of Prussia, in October 1684.

The purpose of consolidating Brunswick-Lüneburg's power was to achieve a stature that would enable the house to obtain a higher dignity in the empire; namely, for the duke of Hanover to become an elector.[15] This purpose was achieved in March 1692 when the emperor,

---

13. Their grins were perhaps rendered slightly less forced by the contract's financial provisions. George William agreed to pay Ernest Augustus an annuity of fifty thousand imperial dollars, a balloon payment of one hundred and fifty thousand dollars within six years of the marriage, and the entire amount of the subsidy payments owed to Ernest Augustus by Spain and Holland. *Memoiren der Herzogin Sophie nachmals Kurfürstin von Hannover*, ed. Adolf Köcher (Leipzig: Hirzel, 1879), 190.

14. George Augustus, the future King George II of Great Britain and Ireland (1683–1760).

15. To all but the specialist, the workings of the Holy Roman Empire are as opaque as those of the European Union. A good primer on the empire, its institutions, and politics in the

in exchange for Brunswick money and troops to use in the war against the Ottoman Empire, conferred the electorship on Ernest Augustus.[16] Sophia was now an electress, the highest female dignity in the empire after empress.

But upwardly mobile Brunswick-Lüneburg was soon embarrassed by a scandal. Ignored by her husband, Sophia Dorothea took a lover, Count Philip Christoph von Königsmarck, colonel of the Hanover guards regiment. They were eventually found out, Königsmarck was murdered by overzealous courtiers, and Sophia Dorothea was placed under house arrest in perpetuity. She spent the rest of her life (from September 1694 to November 1726) in a small, moated palace in Ahlden, about twenty-five miles north of Hanover.[17] Sophia, never fond of her daughter-in-law, did not lift a finger to help her.

There was little she could have done anyway. At this or any other time, she had neither access to the Hanover privy council nor knowledge of its deliberations. Women with real political power were rare in seventeenth-century Germany. Sophia had none.[18] But she did have connections, which she used when she could. For example, she helped negotiate a number of politically motivated marriages (her daughter's, for instance); she arranged for her husband to send a small

early modern period is Peter H. Wilson's *The Holy Roman Empire 1495–1806* (London: MacMillan, 1999); on the emperor and electors specifically, 34–45.

16. Because several existing electors steadfastly opposed the conferral, the duke of Hanover's representative did not officially join the college of electors until 1708. The correct nomenclature would actually be "elector of Brunswick-Lüneburg," not "elector of Hanover." But the latter was common usage by the early eighteenth century and has become the standard title. See Georg Schnath, *Streifzüge durch Niedersachsens Vergangenheit: Gesammelte Aufsätze und Vorträge* (Hildesheim: Lax, 1968), 112.

17. Now mostly forgotten, the story of Sophia Dorothea's love affair and punishment was repeatedly retold, in fictional form, from the late eighteenth to the mid-twentieth century. For an overview of the affair itself, see Schnath, *Geschichte*, 2: 121–204; for its literary and filmic echo, see 2: 206–12.

18. Schnath says that Countess von Platen, Sophia's husband's official mistress, did not have any either, despite suggestions that she was a sort of Madame de Pompadour *avant la lettre* (Schnath, *Geschichte*, 2: 484). In her memoirs Sophia briefly mentions two women who did wield real political power as regents during their respective sons' minority: Landgravine Hedwig Sophia of Hesse-Kassel (regent from 1663 to 1670) and Princess Christina Charlotte of East Friesland (regent from 1665 to 1690).

contingent of troops to support her brother Charles Lewis in one of his conflicts with neighboring principalities; she asked for Charles Lewis to lobby the emperor on matters affecting her husband and brothers-in-law; she wrote letters (included verbatim in the memoirs) to her brother-in-law George William to complain about him allowing his low-born wife to be styled "duchess"; she did a little PR for her husband with Louis XIV while she was at the French court; and she intrigued, insubstantially and unsuccessfully, with several courts on behalf of her younger sons in the primogeniture dispute. But Sophia never influenced a significant domestic or foreign policy during the reign of her husband or of her son George Lewis. The latter, for example, frequently ignored her in his negotiations with English diplomats regarding the Protestant succession, even though it was she who was first in line.

The death of Sophia's husband, on February 2, 1698, inaugurated the final stage of her life. In 1694 her future widow's income had been increased to twelve thousand imperial dollars a year, making her financially secure. Her dower residence was Herrenhausen palace and its garden, a few miles northwest of Hanover's wall-enclosed old town. The large, rectilinear Dutch garden was her joy and her ongoing project.[19] She spent many hours walking in it and improving it. Her other chief occupation was her correspondence, mostly notably with her niece Elizabeth Charlotte at the French court (Sophia's half of the correspondence is, unfortunately, lost) and Gottfried Wilhelm von Leibniz, who was in the Brunswick dukes' service in various capacities (librarian, historian, councilor, and envoy) from 1675 to his death in 1716. Several thousand of Sophia's letters have been published.[20] Her letters to Charles Lewis and Leibniz certainly constitute the

---

19. Herrenhausen looked like a classical French garden to me on my visit (regrettably on a chilly, blustery October afternoon). But Schnath states that mine is a common misconception and that the style is actually Dutch (Schnath, *Streifzüge*, 107–108).

20. Sophia, *Briefwechsel; Briefe der Königin Sophie Charlotte von Preussen und der Kurfürstin Sophie von Hannover an hannoversche Diplomaten*, ed. Richard Doebner (Leipzig: Hirzel, 1905); *Briefe der Kurfürstin Sophie von Hannover an die Raugräfinnen und Raugrafen zu Pfalz*, ed. Eduard Bodemann (Leipzig: Hirzel, 1888); Leibniz *(Sophie)*; Bromley *(Collection)*, Feder *(Sophie)*; and *Die Briefe der Kinder des Winterkönigs*, ed. Karl Hauck (Heidelberg: G. Koester, 1908).

richest mine of anecdote and wit. Regrettably, only a small selection of Sophia's letters exists in English.[21]

The Protestant succession arrived in Hanover—symbolically anyway—on August 14, 1701, when the earl of Macclesfield, the son of a royalist cavalry commander who had fought alongside Sophia's brother Rupert in the English Civil War, appeared to present Sophia with an illuminated copy of the Act of Settlement. The act, which had been passed on June 12, 1701, stipulated that

> the most excellent Princess Sophia, electress and duchess of Hanover, daughter of the most excellent Princess Elizabeth, late queen of Bohemia, daughter of our late Sovereign Lord King James the First of happy memory, be and is hereby declared to be the next in succession in the Protestant line ... after his Majesty [King William III] and the Princess Anne of Denmark and in default of issue of the said Princess Anne and his Majesty respectively.[22]

There had been no default of issue of Princess Anne. Sadly for Anne, however, her issue was ill-fated. Although she had seventeen pregnancies in the first seventeen years of her marriage, many ended in miscarriage, and only one child survived infancy: William Henry, duke of Gloucester, born in 1689. His death, on July 30, 1700, set in motion the legislative process that resulted in the Act of Settlement. When King William III died on March 8, 1702, Anne became queen. Sophia, now seventy-one years old, was next in line to the throne. By order of Queen Anne's council, Sophia's name was inserted into the Book of Common Prayer. But as already stated at the start of this introduction, Sophia died seven weeks before Anne. In the words of the Act of Settlement, it was therefore one of the "heirs of her body," her

21. Lloyd Strickland includes about two dozen of Sophia's letters (most of them to Leibniz) in Sophia, *Leibniz*. Josephine Duggan includes several of Sophia's letters in their entirety and quotes extensively from more than twenty in her biography, *Sophia of Hanover: From Winter Princess to Heiress of Great Britain, 1630–1714* (London: Peter Owen, 2010).

22. *English Historical Documents, 1660–1714*, vol. 8, ed. Andrew Browning (New York: Oxford University Press, 1953), 132.

oldest son George Lewis, who acquired "all the honours, styles, titles, regalities, prerogatives, powers, jurisdictions, and authorities" belonging and appertaining to the monarch of Great Britain and Ireland.[23] When the court moved from Hanover to London, Sophia's favorite place, Herrenhausen garden, was made open to the public, as it remains today.

The Memoirs

1680, in which Sophia turned fifty, was to be a year of loss. Her sister Elizabeth died in February, followed in August by Charles Lewis, her brother, surrogate father, and closest friend. Sophia called her correspondence with him, which began in 1658 when she left Heidelberg after her wedding, one of the greatest pleasures in her life. In late October 1680 Sophia experienced another loss when her husband Ernest Augustus left Hanover for one of his many extended stays in Italy. It was in the four months following his departure that Sophia wrote her memoirs, the last page of which is dated February 21, 1681. In a way, Sophia's memoirs and Descartes's method were created under similar circumstances. Like Descartes, Sophia was in Germany at the beginning of winter, had no conversation to divert her (Charles Lewis was gone permanently, Ernest Augustus temporarily), stayed alone all day, and had the leisure to entertain herself with her own thoughts.[24] Deprived of epistolary dialogue with Charles Lewis, she turned to the monologue of life-writing. She asked for her letters to him to be returned to her and used them to refresh her memory as she wrote. Yet what was so personal for Sophia—a time of mourning and relative isolation—in fact constituted fairly common circumstances under which early modern nobles (both male and female) drafted

---

23. *Historical Documents*, 8: 132.

24. René Descartes, *A Discourse of a Method for the well guiding of Reason, and the Discovery of Truth in the Sciences* (London: Thomas Newcombe, 1649), 15. Of isolation, the duchess of Montpensier writes: "Alone is of course relative for a duchess." We can assume that even while writing her memoirs Sophia had one or more of her ladies-in-waiting in the room with her. "Not only is this state highly conducive to recalling events in order, but one finds the necessary leisure to write them down" (Anne-Marie-Louise d'Orléans, duchess of Montpensier, *Memoirs*, trans. Philip J. Yarrow, ed. William Brooks, London: MHRA, 2010, 1).

their memoirs. Henri de Campion (1613–63), for example, had recently lost his granddaughter; Catherine de La Guette (1613–76), her husband, two daughters, and a son.[25] Although Sophia would survive her brother and sister by thirty-four years, in the last paragraph of the memoirs she writes that a chronic pain in her spleen suggests she might soon follow them to the grave. The proximity of death and, concomitantly, a more intense awareness of one's own mortality were (and likely are) typical triggers for life-writing. Bernard Beugnot describes memoir writing as a response to loss and lack as the expression of a "will to reconstruct."[26] This, I think, can be taken in two senses: the will to reconstruct one's past life as a text and, by doing so, to begin the process of constructing a new life under altered circumstances.

It is hardly surprisingly, therefore, that Sophia saw the practice of life-writing as life-preserving. She states at the beginning of the memoirs that her aim is to "amuse myself during my husband's absence, to fend off melancholy, and to buoy my spirits. For I am convinced that cheerfulness preserves health as well as life, which is very dear to me."[27] The act of recalling and transcribing the past is a form of self-prescribed mood therapy and, ultimately, self-preservation. Yet this seemingly intensely personal justification is itself a topos. For self-diversion (*se divertir*) and self-amusement (*s'amuser*) are typical stated aims of the early modern memoirist (the first paragraph of Henri de Campion's memoirs reads much the same as that of Sophia's).[28] Frédéric Briot points out that the verb "divert" should be read to some degree literally. Life-writing marks a caesura in the early modern memoirist's life, a point at which it diverts from its previous path and takes a new direction.[29] In the case of Sophia and a number of other contemporary life-writers, this change is brought on by the death of close family members.

25. Frédéric Briot, *Usage du monde, usage de soi: Enquête sur les mémorialistes d'Ancien Régime* (Paris: Seuil, 1994), 227–28.

26. Bernard Beugnot, "Livre de raison, livre de retraite," in *Les valeurs chez les mémorialistes français du XVIIᵉ siècle avant la Fronde,* ed. Noemi Hepp and Jacques Hennequin (Paris: Klincksiek, 1979), 51.

27. Page 33.

28. Henri de Campion, *Mémoires,* ed. M. C. Moreau (Paris: Jannet, 1857), 1.

29. Briot, *Usage,* 237.

As a rule, early modern memoirs were not written for a wide readership and certainly not for publication. They were by nature private and intended for a small, select group—until a member of this group ignored the author's wishes and gave the manuscript (or a copy) to a publisher.[30] Henri de Campion and Théodore Agrippa d'Aubigné (1552–1630), for example, intended their memoirs for their children. In Sophia's case there was no intended readership. She states in the first paragraph that her memoirs are for herself alone. Admittedly, this statement is to some degree posturing (if one is writing only for oneself then why state that fact?) and to some degree a disavowal of liability (potential readers should know that they are reading something not meant for them). But she was also drawing a distinction between her memoirs and writing intended for publication. And, with a single exception, she seems to have meant it. She never mentions the memoirs in her correspondence and is known to have shown them to only one person: Leibniz. He made a copy in his own hand (the original in Sophia's hand is lost), and it was this copy that was found in the Hanover archives in 1850.[31] The evidence therefore suggests that after writing her memoirs Sophia gave little thought to them. So in this sense the project was what she said it was: a four-month antidote to melancholy.

With self-amusement the putative purpose of Sophia's project, it may therefore seem curious that she is so anxious to set the historical record straight on a whole range of issues relating to herself and the houses of Palatine and Brunswick-Lüneburg. On some, she goes to the trouble of providing documentary evidence: she painstakingly transcribes the entire text of letters and contracts that support her contentions. On others, the memoirs serve as her own deposition. In

30. Briot, *Usage*, 33 and 31.

31. Here are Leibniz's somewhat pedantic, but ultimately complimentary, "Reflections on the duchess's memoirs": "1. The orthography is irregular, although in truth this hardly matters and can be remedied by a [corrected] copy being made. 2. The style seems simple but has a wonderful power and, despite its apparent nonchalance, has something of what Longinus calls the sublime. Even when the subject matter seems ordinary, it is rendered in a certain admirable way … 3. The tenses (for example, the perfect tense and the imperfect tense) are often mixed up" (Sophia, *Memoiren*, 3; my translation). Van der Cruysse contends that Sophia's orthography was generally better than Leibniz's (Sophia, *Mémoires et lettres de voyage*, ed. Dirk Van der Cruysse. Paris: Fayard, 1990, 19).

one sense, the gesture of providing documentary evidence is an index of how important an issue is to Sophia (for example, the contract under which her one-time fiancé pledged to remain unmarried for the rest of his life and to allow his younger brother to marry Sophia in his place). In a broader sense, however, correcting the historical record is a central motive of early modern (and many present-day) memoirs: I was there; I know the truth.[32] Yet if Sophia is writing for herself alone, why not just assert her point of view and refer to documents instead of dutifully (obsessively?) transcribing them verbatim? After all, before 1850 no one besides Leibniz benefited from her high evidentiary standards. One possible explanation is that Sophia, in her desire to shape posterity's (or at least a potential reader's) opinion, is like other early modern female memoirists, whose "private musings" may not seem to be "destined for public consumption" but who "clearly inscribe a public into their works and advance them as additions to the collective memory."[33]

Scholars have identified a greater focus on the private sphere as one of the defining—and innovative—characteristics of early modern female memoirists:

> They situated the roots of personhood in the experiences of childhood (a phase of existence that men memoirists almost never described). They delved into their relationships with parents and siblings, the physical and psychological changes of adolescence, and the pivotal significance of marriage. Abandoning the pursuit of history that characterized masculine memoirs,

32. Briot, *Usage*, 86; Patricia Francis Cholakian, *Women and the Politics of Self-Representation in Seventeenth-Century France* (Newark: University of Delaware Press, 1990), 37–38.

33. Faith E. Beasley, "Altering the Fabric of History: Women's Participation in the Classical Age," in *A History of Women's Writing in France*, ed. Sonya Stephens (Cambridge: Cambridge University Press, 2000), 76–77. As Briot points out, however, memoirs by both men and women were in most cases intended as "private musings" and not for publication (Briot, *Usage*, 33).

they turned from the public sector to the private, creating a new kind of life-writing.[34]

This characterization also applies to Sophia, although, in my view, with some restrictions. Yes, she writes about her childhood and youth, about her relationship with her mother and siblings, and about private matters like her physical suffering during childbirth, her miscarriages, and her husband's infidelity. Yet I can discern no self-analytical moment in which Sophia asserts, or even hints, that she is including an anecdote because it shaped her personality (or personhood). Rather, her principle for selecting an anecdote for inclusion would seem to be its dramatic or entertainment potential; her reminiscences of her childhood in particular amount to one humorous scene after another. Also, it would be incorrect to infer that writing about private (and even extremely private) matters was unique to early modern women. Like Sophia's own letters, those of her brothers (particularly those of Charles Lewis to Sophia, his mother, and his second wife) are filled with the minutiae of family and private life.[35] And although it is indeed unlikely that Charles Lewis would have included these intimate details in his memoirs, the distinction loses some of its precision when one considers that early modern memoirs (typically written for a restricted social group, such as the author's children) constituted an only marginally more public type of writing than letters (typically written for one person, although often read by several; Sophia, for example, likely shared at least portions of her personal correspondence with her husband, ladies-in-waiting, and possibly other courtiers). In this sense, Sophia's letters—which at least had a readership during her lifetime—were more public than her memoirs.

At the beginning of her memoirs Sophia describes each move in the ornate choreography of bows and curtsies that she and her

34. Cholakian, *Women*, 43. See also Beasley, "Altering," 76: "In contrast to previous examples of the genre, women's memoirs have a more interiorized perspective, are occasionally introspective, and focus on aspects of life considered unimportant for the historical record—women's activities in the 'private' and public realm."

35. Charles Lewis's letters to Sophia are printed in Sophia, *Briefwechsel*; to his mother, in Bromley, *Collection*; to his second wife, in *Schreiben des Kurfürsten Karl Ludwig von der Pfalz und der Seinen*, ed. Wilhelm Ludwig Holland (Tübingen: Litterarischer Verein, 1884).

sibling princesses and princes performed every day before dinner at their boarding school in Leiden. She even announces her cumulative curtsy count—nine—for this ritual. Although the dinner hour provided Sophia with a break from her lessons, it also drilled her, relentlessly, in court etiquette and protocol. It is not surprising, then, that protocol—precedence and deference—is a central theme in her memoirs. Just as her description of the children's preprandial ritual is a catalog of curtsies given and received, the memoirs as a whole are a catalog of the honors Sophia gives (or refuses to give) and those she receives (or is denied). Briot finds early modern memoirists' preoccupation with matters of precedence to be "the most impersonal" sections of their writing.[36] I disagree. Such matters are central to, and in a real way constitutive of, a noble's identity. To paraphrase Norbert Elias: a duchess who is not treated like a duchess is almost no longer a duchess.[37] In the case of Sophia and other female memoirists, the preoccupation may even be more pronounced. Unlike her husband, Sophia cannot achieve glory as a soldier or statesman. But she can—and does—revel in the glory of her rank and the honors she receives at courts across Germany and Europe. Owing to the centrality of rank and honor to Sophia's sense of self, it is worthwhile, I believe, taking a closer look at some of the nuances of protocol (and its temporary suspension), which might otherwise escape a modern reader's notice.

When Sophia writes that a duke or other noble anticipated her arrival in a town by riding (usually with a large entourage) some distance outside the town to meet her, she is not just narrating events in the order they occurred. She is drawing attention to the fact that her host exceeded the requirements of protocol in order to demonstrate esteem or affection for her.[38] The same applies to a range of other

36. Briot, *Usage*, 117.

37. "Ein Herzog, der nicht wohnt, wie ein Herzog zu wohnen hat, der also auch die gesellschaftlichen Verpflichtungen eines Herzogs nicht mehr ordentlich erfüllen kann, ist schon fast kein Herzog mehr." Norbert Elias, *Die höfische Gesellschaft: Untersuchungen zur Soziologie des Königtums und der höfischen Aristokratie* (1969; repr., Frankfurt: Suhrkamp, 1994), 99.

38. The duchess of Montpensier announces proudly in her memoirs that her father, Gaston of Orleans, "came as far as Chambord, ten miles from Blois, to meet me" (Montpensier, *Memoirs*, 7).

symbolic acts that Sophia recounts with precision and pride: when nobles of superior rank rise and cross a threshold to receive her, when they accompany her to her room when the audience is finished, or when they refuse to allow her to accompany them back to their room (which would normally be her duty). The degree of meticulousness with which Sophia catalogs these details correlates to the renown of the court she is visiting and reaches its apogee in the account of her visit to the French court in 1679. Among the highlights were Sophia being allowed to take precedence over—that is, walk ahead of—royalty and higher-ranking nobles during a tour of St. Cloud palace and gardens; the queen of Spain (the duke of Orleans's daughter) sitting on a simple taboret in Sophia's presence instead of on the armchair due her rank; and the king of France entering a room, brushing aside members of the royal family, and announcing that it is Sophia he has come to talk to.[39] Each rule of protocol purposely suspended, each prerogative purposely foregone, adds to Sophia's glory and is therefore proudly recalled and documented.

Two other suspensions of protocol are frequent features of Sophia's memoirs: the court game known as *Wirtschaft* (the German word for "inn") and the practice of traveling incognito. In a *Wirtschaft*, the host and hostess at a court (for example, the duke and duchess of Württemberg at a gathering in Stuttgart in 1651 that Sophia describes) pretend to be an innkeeper and his wife, and their guests pretend to be travelers who have stopped at the inn. For the time and space circumscribed by the game, no one takes precedence, no one shows deference, and everyone can sit, stand, or circulate where and as they like. Indeed, the game temporarily inverts the symbolic order: the host and hostess personally serve the guests their drinks, something they would of course never do under normal circumstances. A *Wirtschaft* provided welcome relief from the constraints of court

---

39. For a detailed explanation—including a helpful matrix—of who had the right to sit in what type of chair (and who had to remain standing) in the presence of the different members of the French royal family and ranks of nobility, see Henri Brocher, *À la cour de Louis XIV. Le rang et l'étiquette sous l'Ancien Régime* (Paris: Félix Alcan, 1934), 24–34.

etiquette through a fiction—travelers meeting at an inn—that clearly marked the relief as temporary.[40]

If fictional travel offered relief from etiquette, actual travel often made it prudent to seek relief. Outside Germany Sophia usually traveled incognito. This does not mean she was wearing a disguise (although during carnival in Italy she, like everyone else, was often masked). It meant she was traveling not as what she was (a duchess of the Holy Roman Empire) but simply as a person of quality. This was sensible for several reasons. First, it saved money by obviating the need for taking along an entourage commensurate with one's rank or dignity. Second, it simplified encounters with other nobles by eliminating potential sources of affront. Third, it prevented precedents from being set. For example, German princes saw the king of France and the Holy Roman emperor as rough equivalents and therefore believed they ought to receive the same honors from the king that they received from the emperor, such as the right to sit in an armchair in the king's presence. But the king of France did not recognize titles conferred by another sovereign and therefore did not grant the honors that appertained to them.[41] The solution, chosen by Sophia and hundreds of other foreign nobles, was to visit France incognito. By not claiming their title they could avoid the insult of not receiving the honors they believed they were due. Conversely, the king of France could grant an honor—as he did to Sophia—without setting a precedent, since he was granting it to an individual person of quality rather than to a certain rank of foreign nobility.

Something else Sophia frequently did while traveling was to attend the seventeenth-century equivalent of a beauty pageant. Then, no less so than today, women's faces and bodies were continually the objects of a variety of gazes: aesthetic appraisal, aesthetic appraisal combined with (or serving as an excuse for) sexual stimulation,

---

40. A similar, but more narrowly circumscribed game was played at the royal court of Denmark, which Sophia visited several times. Here, the guests drew lots to determine the seating order at supper, which otherwise would have been determined by rank. The queen drew a lot like everyone else, but the king did not and always took his place at the head of the table. Perhaps he was uncomfortable with the symbolism of his divinely ordained place being occupied by someone else.

41. Brocher, *À la cour de Louis XIV*, 18–19.

undisguised sexual stimulation, and so forth. But in an era that did not have the technology to mass-produce and mass-distribute images of women, would-be gazers (unless they were content with a painting or drawing) sought out places where gazing opportunities were maximized through aggregation: dances and convents. Sophia recounts her participation in women-watching rituals in Rotterdam, Osnabrück, Milan, Vincenza, Bologna, and Venice. Arriving in Milan, for example, she learns that a ball is being held at which she might appraise the beauty of the town's female nobility; curiosity winning out over fatigue, she attends the ball and finds the ladies worth the exertion. In Bologna a ball is organized for the express purpose of mustering the town's ladies for Sophia's inspection.[42] In Venice she is taken to a convent to see several girls who, in their parents' opinion, are too beautiful to be seen by men before they are married.[43]

On a smaller scale than a dance or a convent, Sophia's own entourage is a gaze-attracting aggregation of young women. For although her ladies-in-waiting also fulfilled other functions (like serving as entertaining conversational partners for Sophia and as a pool of potential wives for senior Hanoverian ministers and military officers), one of their main functions was to look good. At the start of Sophia's trip to Italy, for example, her husband tasks her with hiring two new and comely ladies-in-waiting in order to upgrade the pulchritude of her entourage so that it will make a bigger splash in Italy. The noble tourist, then, avidly views local large-scale displays of female beauty and also travels with her own small-scale display.

If such an entourage and ritualized gazing imply competition with other women, such competition was explicit from the beginning of Sophia's life and is a prominent theme of her memoirs. It started within her own family when she was retrieved from their boarding school in Leiden to join her mother's court in The Hague. She asserts that she was "not at all disconcerted to take my place beside three older sisters, all prettier and more accomplished than myself," although she reports a few paragraphs later that she was highly gratified to overhear English noblemen say that she would, when grown up,

42. This also serves to indicate Sophia's celebrity: when she arrives, the local nobility organizes the equivalent of a beauty pageant for her entertainment.

43. Sophia, *Mémoires*, 187.

"eclipse all my sisters."[44] When she moves to Heidelberg in 1650 she finds herself, unwillingly, in a competition for her brother's attention with her older sister Elizabeth and her sister-in-law. And her marriage involved a competition—or a tacit arrangement of sharing—with her husband's many lovers, which is perhaps why she is somewhat acerbic about Italian women, whose beauty she considers overrated by her husband.

A recurring concern Sophia expresses in her correspondence with her brother Charles Lewis and her mother is that her life, particularly when she is residing at the comparatively small and remote courts of Iburg and Osnabrück (1661–79), does not provide her with a ready supply of entertaining anecdotes.[45] The memoirs are animated throughout by a will to entertain, both their author and, despite Sophia's protestations that she is writing for herself alone, a potential readership. This is an obvious reason for the weight she gives to her travels to Italy and France, which made up about one-hundredth of her life as a fifty-year-old but about one-third of her memoirs.

Siblings

Below I provide brief biographical sketches of Sophia's many sisters and brothers, several of whom are important characters in her memoirs. For the cumulative magnitude of their accomplishments, failures, celebrity, notoriety, intellect, wit, good looks, and eccentricity, they—Sophia included—had few rivals among noble siblings of the early modern era. Translated to the twentieth century, it would be as if the Mitford girls and Kennedy boys had formed a single family.

The Palatines' court in The Hague, in tribute to the four highly accomplished and attractive princesses, was dubbed the "mansion of the muses and graces."[46] Sophia's oldest sister, Elizabeth (1618–80), was known in the family as "La Greque" ('The Greek') and "Signora Antica" ('Madam Antiquity') for her mastery of languages and learning. She corresponded with Huygens, Malebranche, Leibniz, William

44. Pages 39 and 42.

45. See Sophia, *Briefwechsel*, 91, 101, 130, 367, and Bromley, *Collection*, 226–27 and 203.

46. Elizabeth Ogilvy Benger, *Memoirs of Elizabeth Stuart, Queen of Bohemia, Daughter of King James the First*, 2 vols. (London: Longman, 1825), 2: 356.

Penn, and, most famously, Descartes. She is the dedicatee of the *Principia Philosophiae*, in which Descartes states that Elizabeth is "the only person I have so far found who has completely understood all my previously published works."[47] Although Elizabeth's suitors were all A-list (King Vladislav IV of Poland, the electoral prince of Brandenburg, and Duke Bernard of Saxe-Weimar), none of these knots was tied. In 1661 Frederick William of Brandenburg, Elizabeth's former suitor, appointed her coadjutrice and in 1667 abbess of the Protestant convent at Herford in north Westphalia, a position that also made her chief magistrate of the convent's environs.[48]

Louisa Hollandina (1622–1709), whose family nickname was "Mademoiselle sans façon" ('Miss Casual') for the lack of attention she paid to her appearance, was a skilled artist whose many drawings and paintings—one of which is reproduced on the cover of this book—provide glimpses of life at the exiled Bohemian court. Plans to marry off Louisa fell through as well (and in the case of one suitor, fell through the trap door of a scaffold: James Graham, marquis of Montrose, was hanged in Edinburgh in 1650). In December 1657 Louisa snuck away from her mother's court and went to France, where, to her family's dismay, she converted to Catholicism. Supported by a pension from Louis XIV, in March 1659 Louisa entered the Cistercian abbey of Maubuisson, located northwest of Paris. After a novitiate of

---

47. *The Philosophical Writings of Descartes*, trans. John Cottingham, Robert Stoothoff, and Dugald Murdoch (Cambridge: Cambridge University Press, 1985), 1: 192. See also Elizabeth, *Descartes*.

48. William Penn added a memorial to Elizabeth, whom he visited in 1667, to the 1682 edition of *No Cross, No Crown*:

> She chose a single life as freest of care, and best suited to the study and meditation she always inclined to … She had a small territory which she has governed so well, that she shewed herself fit for a greater. She would constantly, every Last Day in the week, sit in judgment, and hear and determine cases herself; where her patience, justice, and mercy were admirable … [H]er mind had a noble prospect. Her eye was to a better and more lasting inheritance than can be found below; which made her often to despise the greatness of courts, and the learning of the schools, of which she was an extraordinary judge. (*No Cross, No Crown: A Discourse Shewing the Nature and Discipline of the Holy Cross of Christ.* Philadelphia: Collins, 1853, 403–404).

eighteen months she took vows in September 1660 and was appointed abbess in August 1664.

Sophia describes Henrietta Maria (1626–51), known by her siblings as Nennie, as the prettiest Palatine—and says little else about her except that she was the chief beneficiary of Nennie's favorite pastime: making jams and jellies. Of Sophia's sisters who survived childhood, Henrietta had the shortest life; she died three months after her marriage in 1651 to Prince Sigmund of Transylvania.

The sibling who played the biggest role in Sophia's life was her oldest brother, Charles Lewis (1617–80). Like their sister Elizabeth, he was impressively polyglot (he spoke and wrote Latin, German, French, English, Dutch, and Italian with complete fluency) and erudite (particularly in law and theology). Charles Lewis was frequently in England during the 1630s and 1640s to gather support for the liberation of the Palatinate, which was occupied by Spanish and Bavarian troops. In 1637 he used English funds to purchase the fortress town of Meppen in northwest Germany to serve as a base for military operations against the Habsburgs. The campaign was unsuccessful, however, and in 1638 he narrowly escaped capture. In 1648 the Peace of Westphalia restored to Charles Lewis the Lower Palatinate along the Rhine and Neckar rivers and created a new, eighth electorship for the House of Palatine; the Upper Palatinate and the original electorship were ceded to Duke Maximilian of Bavaria and the House of Wittelsbach. In October 1649 Charles Lewis returned to Heidelberg to take possession of the Lower Palatinate, which the Thirty Years War had left severely damaged, depopulated, and indebted.[49] For the next three decades his energies would be devoted to rebuilding it and solidifying its finances.

Sophia's other brothers—Rupert, Morris, Edward, and Philip—receive little mention in her memoirs. Rupert (1619–82) accompanied Charles Lewis to England in 1634–35, fought with him in Germany

---

49. The Lower Palatinate's population was nearly 75 percent lower than before the war. The elector's annual commodity revenues, which he used in large-scale barter transactions or sold to generate cash, had declined even more precipitously, from 300,000 to 35,000 gallons of wine and from 240,000 to 45,000 bushels of rye. See Volker Sellin, "Kurfürst Karl Ludwig von der Pfalz: Versuch eines historischen Urteils," *Schriften der Gesellschaft der Freunde Mannheims und der ehemaligen Kurpfalz* 15 (1980): 6.

in 1638, but did not elude capture and was interned for three years in Linz, Austria. In the first phase of the English Civil War, Rupert commanded Charles I's cavalry and, briefly, all royalist ground forces. In honor of Rupert's victories in 1643 and 1644, Charles created him earl of Holderness and duke of Cumberland. In the second phase of the war, beginning in 1648, Rupert took to the sea with a small squadron, seizing and sinking parliamentary shipping for five years, from the coast of Africa to the West Indies. In 1654 he came to Heidelberg with the hope of obtaining an appanage from Charles Lewis; his hope was not fulfilled, and in 1657 an angry Rupert left the Palatinate for good. After the Restoration, in 1660, Rupert returned to England, where Charles II appointed him to his privy council, among other offices. A natural scientist and prolific inventor, Rupert was the third founding member of the Royal Society. He remained on active service as an admiral until 1673.

Morris (1621–52) was also a senior royalist cavalry officer. In 1648 he joined Rupert at sea, serving as his vice admiral. Morris died when his ship sank in a storm in December 1652.

Edward (1625–63), known in the family as Ned (and less flatteringly as Willful Ned), was the first sibling to break Protestant ranks. While in Paris in 1645 he converted to Catholicism and married a wealthy heiress, Anna Gonzaga (1616–84), the second daughter of the recently deceased Charles Gonzaga, duke of Nevers, Montferrat, and Mantua. Edward's letters match those of his siblings for wit and surpass them for smut, often simultaneously.[50] One of Edward's daughters, Benedicta (1652–1730), later married one of Sophia's brothers-in-law, Duke John Frederick of Brunswick-Lüneburg.

Philip (1627–50), who is mentioned just once in Sophia's memoirs, was notorious for murdering, in 1646, a young French marquis named d'Espinay who had publicly boasted of bedding not only one of Sophia's sisters but also her mother. Philip died as a colonel in the Lothringen cavalry at the siege of Rethel, a fortified town twenty-five miles northeast of Reims, France.

---

50. Hauck, *Kinder*, 67–163.

Publication and Reception

Sophia's memoirs, not seen by anyone since Leibniz had read them in the late seventeenth century, were discovered in the royal archives in Hanover by Georg Heinrich Pertz in 1850. Prior to their publication in 1879 they were used as a primary source for a history of Brunswick-Lüneburg and mined for biographical gems for the introduction to the first volume of Sophia's correspondence with Leibniz.[51] Their reception in France, Britain, and Germany was essentially identical: they received lengthy reviews—ten, thirty, and sixty pages, respectively—that fall somewhere between précis and paraphrase.[52] The memoirs have continued to incite paraphrase among Sophia's biographers. This is partly because Sophia's anecdotes are simply too good to resist retelling and partly because the memoirs are the principal primary source for information about her childhood, teens, and young adulthood. The result is that anyone who has read Sophia's memoirs can safely skip the sections of her biographies that deal with the period 1630–80. They are all, predominantly, paraphrases of her memoirs, and Sophia tells the story better herself.[53]

An English translation appeared in 1888. Regrettably, this prim rendering omitted as "distasteful" approximately 10 percent of the text. Although some of the expunged material may not be noteworthy (Sophia's lurid description of the findings of her brother's autopsy, for example), much is. This is particularly true of Sophia's observations on the amorous behavior of her fellow nobles (chief among whom: her husband), which was a very real part of both Sophia's personal life and milieu. A German translation, which includes more than one hundred

51. Wilhelm Havemann, *Geschichte der Lande Braunschweig und Lüneburg*, 3 vols. (Göttingen: Dieterich, 1853–57); Leibniz, *Sophie*, 7–11.

52. Arvède Barine, "Une princesse allemande au XVIIe siècle," *Revue des deux mondes* 50 (1882): 203–13; Anonymous, "The Electress Sophia," *Quarterly Review* 161 (1885): 172–203; Eduard Bodemann, "Herzogin Sophie von Hannover. Ein Lebens- und Culturbild des 17. Jahrhunderts," *Historisches Taschenbuch* 7 (1888): 27–86.

53. Duggan, *Sophia*; Karin Feuerstein-Praßer, *Sophie von Hannover (1630–1714): "Wenn es die Frau Kurfürstin nicht gäbe"* (Regensburg: Pustet, 2007); Maria Kroll, *Sophia, Electress of Hanover: A Personal Portrait* (London: Gollancz, 1973); Mathilde Knoop, *Kurfürstin Sophie von Hannover* (Hanover: Lax, 1964).

letters, was published in 1913; a modern French edition, which also includes a selection of letters, in 1990.

A Note on the Translation

Sophia wrote her memoirs in seventeenth-century French. I believe the translation that would make them most present to us is one that replicates the syntax, vocabulary, punctuation, and even the orthography of seventeenth-century English. It would be like an original-instruments recording of an early modern musical composition. The English of such a translation might read something like this:

> Right understanding is the most equally divided thing in the World; for every one beleevs himself so well stor'd with it, that even those who in all other things are hardest to be pleas'd, seldom desire more of it than they have; wherein it is not likely that all Men are deceived: But it rather witnesseth, That the faculty of right-judging and distinguishing truth from falsehood (which is properly call'd, Understanding or Reason) is naturally equal in all Men.[54]

This famous passage, from the 1649 translation of *Le discours de la méthode*, is immeasurably better known to scholars and students in the version from the standard English edition of Descartes's works:

> Good sense is the best distributed thing in the world: for everyone thinks himself so well endowed with it that even those who are the hardest to please in everything else do not usually desire more of it than they possess. In this it is unlikely that everyone is mistaken. It indicates rather that the power of judging well and of distinguishing the true from the false—which is what we properly call "good sense" or "reason"—is naturally equal in all men.[55]

54. Descartes, *Method*, 2–3.

55. Descartes, *Philosophical*, 1: 111.

Although in a couple cases the standard Descartes translation is actually less idiomatic (it prefers, for example, "the true and the false" to "truth and falsehood"), it is easier for us to follow without stumbling. But a little stumbling can be a good thing. Call it a welcome alienation effect, an unfamiliarity that forces us to pause frequently and make certain we have right-judged the text.

I concede, however, that a seventeenth-century replication probably would not serve to increase Sophia's popularity in the twenty-first century. So my aim has been to produce a sprightly, readable translation in modern, idiomatic English. This, I believe, is the second-best approach. Unlike H. Forester's 1888 translation, mine does not try to stay close to the original French syntax or prefer cognates to other, more idiomatic renderings. Nevertheless, Forester's version was my starting point, and I kept the bits I liked. Briot identifies a conversational tone as one of the defining characteristics of all early modern memoirs.[56] That is the tone I have tried to strike in the hope of capturing both Sophia's skills as a raconteuse and the verve of the French original.

Over the last century it has become common practice in English to refer to German nobles by the German version of their names (with some exceptions, such as Frederick the Great). Thus Sophia's oldest brother is best known today as Karl Ludwig. This was not the case in the seventeenth century and, indeed, through the end of the nineteenth century. The contemporary English translation of the Treaty of Westphalia refers to Sophia's brother as Charles Lewis; other early modern English variants included Charles Louis, Charles Ludovic, and Charles Lodowicke (but never Karl Ludwig). Lewis XIV—the French king we know as Louis XIV—was a common designation in

---

56. Briot, *Usage*, 38. Perhaps I (and Briot) simply wish we were talking to Sophia and other memoirists:

> [I]n different ways, all philological practices generate desires for presence, desires for a physical and space-mediated relationship to the things of the world (including texts), and that such desire for presence is indeed the ground on which philology can produce effects of tangibility (and sometimes even the reality thereof). (Hans Ulrich Gumbrecht, *The Powers of Philology. Dynamics of Textual Scholarship.* Urbana and Chicago: University of Illinois Press, 2003, 6).

It is noteworthy that the title of this series, The Other Voice in Early Modern Europe, invokes Western metaphysics' privileged index of presence: the human voice.

the early modern period and can still be found in texts from the late nineteenth century.[57]

Despite the prevalence of the current practice, I chose to anglicize most names and all titles, for three reasons. First, it reflects early modern practice. Second, it is analogous to Sophia's practice of frenchifying all names (she refers, for example, to her brother-in-law not as Georg Wilhelm or George William but as Georges Guillaume); what is French in Sophia's French should presumably be English (and not German) in an English version. Third, I think prose in a single language—where there are no *ducs* or *Herzöge*, no Guillaumes or Wilhelms—flows better. I have not been wholly consistent, however. The names of titled nobles are anglicized, but those of minor figures (attendants, servants, and so forth) are not. I also made an exception in the case of Louis XIV, which I concede is unshakably established.

There are a number of other nomenclatural issues. First, to help the reader to keep track of who is who, I have made names more uniform than they are in the original. What I have rendered as Duke George William may have been *le duc d'Hanovre, le duc Georges Guillaume,* or *Monsieur le duc.* Second, precisely because the text is a duke-intensive zone (Sophia's husband and three brothers-in-law are all dukes, and she mentions dozens of others), I chose to simplify matters by having her refer to her husband Duke Ernest Augustus as "my husband." This solution enhances readability but clearly lacks the stateliness of Sophia's designation for him in the original: *Monsieur le duc.* "My husband" is, however, closer to Sophia's less formal designation for him in her letters to her brother Charles Lewis: *Monsieur mon mari.*

The manuscript has no paragraph or chapter breaks. Those in the translation are adopted from earlier French and German editions or are my own.

Finally, a note about the footnotes. There are a lot of them. Readers who have progressed this far in the introduction have already met most of the main figures in Sophia's life. Readers who do not care about the identity of every duke, landgravine, earl, or marchioness

---

57. The late nineteenth century is the onomastic transition period, as evidenced by the 1888 review of Sophia's memoirs, which refers to the Sun King as both Lewis XIV and Louis XIV (Anonymous, *Quarterly Review,* 173 and 191).

may safely ignore the small print; they know enough members of the cast to follow the action. For the more curious, I have tried to identify nearly every person, place, or thing Sophia mentions. In this effort I have benefited considerably from the annotations of earlier editions but have also succeeded in identifying a score of figures whom previous editors had not been able to track down. My principle for citation is to give a previous editor credit for an item of information in a footnote only if it is the result of extra detective work; that is, if it goes beyond the information about a figure—such as birth year, death year, parents, children, titles, significant accomplishments, posts held—that is readily available in a general reference work.

MEMOIRS (1630–1680)

Hanover, 1680
At my age I have no better pastime than to recall past times.
I believe I may indulge this inclination without wishing to
appear in these memoirs (which are for myself alone) as a fic-
tional heroine or to emulate those ladies whose celebrity is due
to their extravagant conduct worthy of a novel. My only aims
are to amuse myself during my husband's absence, to fend off
melancholy, and to buoy my spirits. For I am convinced that
cheerfulness preserves health as well as life, which is very dear
to me.[1]

---

1. Köcher speculates, probably correctly, that the ladies known for their extravagant conduct are Marie Mancini (Cardinal Mazarin's niece, Louis XIV's adolescent amour, and a
favorite companion of Sophia's husband during his frequent trips to Italy) and Eleanor
d'Olbreuse (the morganatic wife of Sophia's brother-in-law Duke George William). See
Sophia, *Memoiren*, ed. Adolf Köcher (Leipzig: Hirzel, 1879), 20. Mancini's memoirs were
printed in 1676 and 1677; d'Olbreuse's ghost-written memoirs, in 1679.

Chapter 1
Leiden, The Hague (1630–50)

I am told that I was born on October 14, 1630. I was the twelfth issue of my parents' marriage. Consequently, if my father the king and my mother the queen felt any elation at my birth it was only because I had vacated the place I had been occupying.[2] They even had trouble choosing a name and finding godparents for me, since all of the illustrious kings and princes had already performed this duty for my older siblings. So they decided it would be a good idea to write different names on slips of paper and draw one. It was therefore chance that bestowed on me the name Sophia.[3] The king chose the princess Palatine of Birkenfeld (the countess of Hohenlohe), the countess of Culenbourg, and Madam de Brederode (the countess of Nassau) as my like-named godmothers and the States of Friesland as my godfathers.[4]

As soon as I was strong enough to be transported, my mother the queen sent me to Leiden, which is only three hours from The Hague. Preferring the company of her pet monkeys and dogs to that of her offspring, Her Majesty had all her children raised well out of her sight.[5]

2. For information about Sophia's parents, Frederick V (elector Palatine and deposed king of Bohemia) and Elizabeth Stuart (daughter of King James I of England), see pages 3–5.

3. Sophia was likely short-listed because it was the name of the queen of Bohemia's youngest sister, who died twenty-four hours after birth in 1606; she, in turn, had been named after her grandmother, the queen mother of Denmark. Sophia was baptized in the Klosterkirk in The Hague on January 27, 1631, three days after her family had held funeral services there for her sister Charlotte (1628–31).

4. The godmothers are Sophia, daughter of Charles I, palsgrave of Birkenfeld, and wife of Count Crato of Hohenlohe-Neuenstein; unidentified; Sophia Hedwig, daughter of Henry Julius of Brunswick and wife of Count Ernest Casimir of Nassau-Dietz. Sophia Hedwig was already the godmother of Sophia's sister Louisa Hollandina, evidence that new godparents were indeed hard to find. See Carola Oman, *Elizabeth of Bohemia*, 2d ed. (London: Hodder and Stoughton, 1964), 311. According to Green, the States of Groningen and the palsgrave of Neuburg were also Sophia's godfathers. See Mary Anne Everett Green, *Elizabeth, Electress Palatine and Queen of Bohemia* (London: Methuen, 1909), 279.

5. At Leiden, which is approximately ten miles from The Hague, the Palatine children lived in the Prinsenhof, a former convent of St. Barbara that had been converted into a residence for the prince of Orange (Oman, *Elizabeth*, 277). The queen of Bohemia was candid about

Our court at Leiden was very much in the German style. Our schedules were as regimented as our bows and curtsies. My governess, Madam von Plessen, had held the same post for my father when he was a child, which gives an indication of her age.[6] She was assisted by her two daughters who looked even older than she. Their conduct was upstanding in the eyes of God and man: the former was well pleased with them, and the latter never tempted by them, for their appearance was horrible and apt to terrify little children. They taught me to love God, fear the Devil, and be profoundly pious according to Calvin's good doctrine. They also taught me the Heidelberg Catechism in German, and I soon knew the whole thing by heart without understanding a word of it.[7]

Each morning I rose at seven and, while still in my nightgown, was obliged to go to Miss Marie von Quadt, one of Madam von Plessen's daughters, to say my prayers and read the Bible. The next part of my lesson was to learn Pibrac's *Quatrains*.[8] Miss von Quadt would use this time to rinse out her mouth and clean her teeth, which always needed it. Her grimaces during this ritual are more firmly fixed in my memory than anything she tried to teach me. By half past eight I was dressed and ready to endure the daily succession of teachers, who kept me busy until ten o'clock (unless the good Lord was kind enough

her pedophobia, remarking in 1659 to her son Charles Lewis, "[Y]ou know I care not much for children" (*The Letters of Elizabeth of Bohemia*, ed. L. M. Baker. London: Bodley Head, 1953, 290). The Palatines' residence in The Hague consisted of the Wassenaer Hof and the adjacent Naaldwijk Hof. The Wassenaer Hof, located at Kneuterdijk 22, is now occupied by the Dutch Ministry of Finance (Oman, *Elizabeth*, 248).

6. Possibly Kunigunde Charlotte von Plessen (1575–?), wife of Wollrad von Plessen (1560–1632), a Palatine councilor.

7. Written at the direction of Sophia's great-great-grandfather Frederick III, the *Heidelberger Katechismus* was published in 1563 and first translated into English in 1591. A modern English translation is available at crcna.org and other websites affiliated with the Christian Reformed Church.

8. Guy du Faur, seigneur de Pibrac (1527–84), was a Protestant jurist, ambassador, royal councilor, and author of moral poetry. First published in 1573, *Les quatrains du S. de Pybrac, contenans preceptes, & enseignemens utiles pour la vie de l'homme*, was reprinted scores of times and remained, into the nineteenth century, a popular educational tool in francophone families.

to grant me a respite by giving one of them a cold). At ten, welcome relief came in the form of the dancing master, who put me through my paces until eleven, which was our dinner hour.

This meal always took place with great ceremony at a long table. On entering the room I would find all my princely brothers drawn up in front, with their governor and their respective gentlemen-in-waiting arrayed side by side behind them. Court etiquette demanded that I first make a very deep curtsy to the princes, a shallow one to the others present, another deep one on placing myself opposite them, then another little one to my governess, who on entering the room with her daughters curtsied very deeply to me. I had to curtsy again when I gave them my gloves to hold, then again when I turned back around to face my brothers, once more when the gentlemen-in-waiting brought me a large basin in which I washed my hands, again after grace was said, and for the last and ninth time just before I sat down at the table.

Everything was so rigidly organized that we knew what we were going to eat by what day of the week it was, just like in a convent. Two pastors or two university professors were invited to dine with us on Sundays and Wednesdays. They thought I was going to become very learned because I was a fast study. But my only real aim was to master everything they wanted me to learn so that I could be done with my tiresome lessons as quickly as possible. After dinner I rested until two o'clock, when my teachers renewed their assault. I supped at six and went to bed at half past eight after reading a few chapters in the Bible and saying my prayers.[9]

I led this life until I was nine or ten years old. I shall pass over in silence the tricks I used to play on my governess (whom old age had

---

9. Sophia's description of her daily schedule is confirmed, down to the hour, by a report written in 1632 by one of the children's tutors in Leiden. Interestingly, the princesses and princes had largely the same curriculum. The main difference was that the princes had no hour of rest after dinner and received military training in the late afternoon (fencing, musketry, riding, and fortification studies). The tutor's report is printed in Friedrich Schmidt, *Geschichte der Erziehung der pfälzischen Wittelsbacher* (Berlin: A. Hofmann, 1899), 328–29.

since deprived of sight), fearing that my story might resemble that of Lazarillo de Tormes.[10] I shall only say that as my brothers and sisters grew up, the queen retrieved them from Leiden, the princes to travel and the princesses to live with her in The Hague.

I was left at Leiden with my little brother Gustavus, who was a year younger than I and who died when he was eight years old. The sad news of the king her husband's death was brought to the queen at the time of Gustavus's birth.[11] The poor child suffered from kidney stones from an early age. In his case one could ask the same question the disciples asked in the Gospel: who did sin, this boy or his parents, that he was born so sickly?[12] Still, he was a very fine-looking boy. I remember one afternoon when the queen had the two of us brought to The Hague to be shown to her cousin the princess of Orange-Nassau. As the queen paraded us like prize stallions, Lady Goring appraised us both and said, "He's very handsome, but she's skinny and ugly. I hope she doesn't understand English."[13] But I understood it only too well. Her words hurt my feelings and left me profoundly sad, for I believed my ill fortune to be beyond remedy.[14] Yet mine was not so great as that

10. Sophia's reference to *La vida de Lazarillo de Tormes*, an anonymous picaresque novel first published in 1554, is more specific than previous editors of her memoirs have noted. For in the first chapter Lazarillo recounts the tricks he played on an older person deprived of sight: a blind mendicant whose alms and wine Lazarillo steals through various stratagems. *La vie de Lazarillo de Tormès, La vida de Lazarillo de Tormes*, trans. Alfred Morel-Fatio (Paris: Aubier, 1988), 86–103.

11. Sophia's memory is faulty: her brother Gustavus was born on January 14, and her father died on November 29, 1632.

12. John 9: 1–3: "And as Jesus passed by, he saw a man which was blind from his birth. And his disciples asked him, saying, Master, who did sin, this man, or his parents, that he was born blind? Jesus answered, Neither hath this man sinned, nor his parents: but that the works of God should be made manifest in him."

13. The manuscript's "Mme Gorin" is Lady Lettice Goring (1610–57), the wife of Lord George Goring (1608–57), who at the time held a colonelcy in the Dutch army and later fought alongside Sophia's brother Rupert in the English Civil War.

14. Some twenty years later Sophia committed the same gaffe as Lady Goring while visiting The Hague with her niece Elizabeth Charlotte, known as Liselotte. In a letter to Charles Lewis dated February 2, 1660, the queen of Bohemia writes, "There was last night a sad business betwixt your sister [Sophia] and Lisslotte. She [Sophia] said in English, that her [Liselotte's] brother had a better face than she had, which she [Liselotte] vnderstood and

of my little brother, who soon afterward died a horrible death, which both moved and upset me. The autopsy revealed five stones (one the size of a pigeon egg surrounded by four pointed ones) in his bladder. He also had a kidney stone shaped like a large tooth, root and all. It makes one shudder to think of it. It also reveals the ignorance of physicians, a great many of whom had examined my brother during his life.

His end was also that of our court at Leiden, for to my great joy it was deemed inappropriate to leave me there alone. Still, I felt some regret at being separated from my governess and her two daughters, venerable ladies who were too old for a change of residence or routine. My affection for them was more a product of habit and gratitude than of affinity, which is rare between young and old. They were respected by everyone for their goodness; and having lived as saints, they died in the same manner.

I was nine or ten years of age when I came to live at my mother the queen's court in The Hague. In my ignorance I was awestruck by all I beheld. It was heavenly to see so much variety, so many people—and none of my teachers. I was not at all disconcerted to take my place beside three older sisters, all prettier and more accomplished than myself and universally admired. It was enough that my cheerfulness and jokes served to amuse them. Even the queen took pleasure in my antics and liked people to tease me so that I might sharpen my wits and learn to hold my own.[15] I made it my business to make fun of everyone. Clever people enjoyed this game, whereas others dreaded it. Among the latter was the prince of Tarentum, who did not have

manie a teare was shed for it, but I maintained that she had the better face, which much rejoiced her" (Elizabeth, *Letters*, 297). So similar are the incidents that one wonders whether Sophia remembers Liselotte's tears as her own.

15. Aristocratic children capable of witty remarks "found this kind of speech admired and encouraged by adults, for it seemed to show the 'natural' grace thought to be typical of nobles, as opposed to those whose 'eloquence' was based on long years of study ... Jokes were therefore a serious business and were a powerful means of socializing children to the underlying values and structures of aristocratic society" (Mark Motley, *Becoming a French Aristocrat: The Education of the Court Nobility, 1580–1715*. Princeton: Princeton University Press, 1990, 74–75).

the wit to defend himself and so fled from me as from the plague.[16] Among the former were Mr. de Zulestein and Mr. Marigny.[17]

Zulestein was the natural child of Prince Frederick Henry of Orange-Nassau, and his Flemish sense of humor was sometimes less than refined.[18] One day when his jokes became too crude, I resolved to avenge myself by giving his head a good dousing. I went to wet my handkerchief in the drinking bowl used by the queen's pet dogs, but Her Majesty had so many of them that the bowl was empty. So instead I soaked my handkerchief in a chamber pot (which contained a less lucent liquid) and threw it in Zulestein's face. My brother Morris, having seen that the queen's seat of ease had been instrumental in my revenge, did not hesitate to tell everyone, which increased the general mirth and left our Flemish friend quite disconcerted.

Marigny, a Frenchman, had more wit and better manners. To amuse the queen, he wrote me a letter on behalf of Her Majesty's pet monkeys, in which they elected me their queen. The letter was handed to me at a large gathering so that everyone could see how I would take the joke. Much too amused to be angry, I laughed with everyone else.

16. Henry Charles de la Tremouïlle, prince of Tarentum (1620–72), whose paternal and maternal grandmothers were princesses of Orange-Nassau, was raised in Holland. In 1648 he married Princess Emilia of Hesse-Kassel (1626–93), the older sister of Princess Charlotte of Hesse-Kassel (1627–86), who married Sophia's brother Charles Lewis in 1650. As a distant relation of the defunct royal house of Aragon, Henry Charles styled himself prince of Tarentum, the title of the crown prince of Naples. See Adolf Köcher, "Denkwürdigkeiten der zellischen Herzogin Eleonore, geb. d'Olbreuse," *Zeitschrift des historischen Vereins für Niedersachsen* (1878): 28.

17. "Marigny" is Van der Cruysse's emendation for the manuscript's "Marigné." See Sophia, *Mémoires et lettres de voyage*, ed. Dirk Van der Cruysse (Paris: Fayard, 1990), 41.

18. Born in 1584, Prince Frederick Henry was stadtholder of The Netherlands from 1625 to his death in 1647. He was the half-brother of Sophia's paternal grandmother, Princess Louisa Juliana of Orange-Nassau (1576–1644). Louisa Juliana and Frederick Henry were the children of Prince William I of Orange-Nassau (1533–84) by his third and fourth wives, respectively. Frederick Nassau de Zulestein (1608–72) was Frederick Henry's natural child by an Englishwoman named Mary Killegrew.

They tried to play another trick on me involving the Venetian ambassador's son, a very handsome boy and my frequent playmate.[19] An Englishman named Vane, who was always being teased about his long chin, wrote me a letter in the little Venetian's name in the hope of eliciting a response that he could then taunt me with.[20] But I saw through his plan and, knowing the importance of counter-battery fire, I entrusted him with a letter for the little Venetian along with a small box which I said contained a ring (it actually contained a turd from one of the queen's dogs). In the letter I had written:

This little present I intend	Pour Mr. le Confident
For Mr. Confidential Friend;	Je lui donne ce présent;
It's long, and what he finds within	Il est long et de la forme
Will match his own misshapen chin.[21]	De son menton si diforme.

There were many more jokes of this kind, unworthy of recollection. I prefer instead to turn my thoughts to a later period of my life when I began to become somewhat more reasonable.

The queen usually spent her summers at a hunting palace in Rhenen.[22] On one occasion when Her Majesty was there, my sisters decided to perform Corneille's *Medea* to entertain her.[23] At first they refused to

19. The son of ambassador Alvise Contarini (1597–1651).

20. Knighted by James I in 1611, Sir Henry Vane (1589–1655) was at various times a member of parliament, privy councilor, and secretary of state. He served as Charles I's envoy on a number of diplomatic missions to Holland and Germany whose aim was to restore the Palatinate to Sophia's father Frederick V and, after Frederick's death, to her brother Charles Lewis.

21. The English translation of Sophia's poem is by Forester (*Memoirs of Sophia, Electress of Hanover, 1630–1680*, trans. H. Forester. London: Richard Bentley & Son, 1888, 11).

22. "A little promenade just outside [Rhenen's] north wall is known as the Queen's Walk … The palace, already decaying, was converted into a barracks for French troops in 1789, and destroyed in 1812" (Oman, *Elizabeth*, 305). An inn built later on the same site was called *De Koning van Bohemen* ('The King of Bohemia') until 1855 and now bears the name *De Koning van Denemarken* ('The King of Denmark'). It is located at Utrechtsestraatweg 2 and at dekoningvandenemarken.nl.

23. *Médée*, by the French dramatist Pierre Corneille (1606–84), was first performed during the 1634–35 Paris season and appeared in print in 1639, two years before the Palatine princesses, whose tastes in drama were clearly *au courant*, performed it for their mother.

let me play a part, saying that I would not be able to memorize so many verses. Feeling that my honor had been impugned, I learned the whole play by heart, although in the interim they had relented and allowed me to play Nerine which was the only part I really needed to know. The queen was quite satisfied with my performance, although it was chopines that gave me the proper stature and an actress who had taught me the proper gestures, for I understood none of the lines I spoke. This was hardly surprising, since I was only eleven years old.

Some time after our play the queen returned to The Hague, where the queen of England arrived with her daughter the Lady Mary, who was betrothed to the young prince of Orange.[24] My mother the queen went to Honselersdijk to meet them, and I was selected from among my sisters as being the fittest companion for the little princess, who was only slightly younger than I.[25] The fine portraits by Van Dyck had given me a lofty idea of the beauty of all English ladies. I was therefore surprised to discover that the queen, so beautiful on canvas, was actually a short woman (despite the extra high heels of her Liège-style chopines) with long wizened arms, crooked shoulders, and teeth protruding from her mouth like ravelins from a fortress.[26] On more careful inspection I found that she had very beautiful eyes, a well-formed nose, and a lovely complexion. She did me the honor of saying that I looked a little like her daughter the Lady Mary. This so pleased me that henceforth I considered the queen a great beauty. I also heard the English lords say to each other that I would, when grown up, eclipse all of my sisters. This remark gave me a liking for the entire English nation, so charming is it to be thought pretty when one is young.

24. Queen Henrietta Maria (1609–69), sister of King Louis XIII of France and wife of King Charles I of Great Britain (1600–49), left England in February 1642 for The Hague, where she was active for the royalist cause. Her daughter Mary (1631–60), Sophia's first cousin, subsequently married William II of Orange-Nassau (1626–50).

25. Actually, Sophia and her mother were stand-ins for the princess of Orange, whose advanced pregnancy rendered her unable to make the journey to Honselersdijk (Oman, *Elizabeth*, 354–57).

26. Henrietta Maria sat for Sir Anthony Van Dyck (1599–1641) nine times. If Sophia's description is accurate, the queen's likeness in Van Dyck's *Queen Henrietta Maria with Sir Jeffrey Hudson* (1633), which hangs in the National Gallery of Art in Washington, D. C., is indeed flattering.

My sister Princess Elizabeth, who was already renowned for her looks, had black hair, a fresh complexion, brown sparkling eyes, large black eyebrows, a well-shaped forehead, beautiful cherry lips, a good set of teeth, and an aquiline nose that had a tendency to turn red. She had a thirst for learning, but all her philosophy could not save her from vexation when her mischievous circulation sent blood rushing to her nose. At such times she hid herself from everyone. I remember that my sister Princess Louisa, who was frank to a fault, asked her on one such unlucky occasion to come upstairs to our mother's room, as it was the usual hour for visiting Her Majesty. Princess Elizabeth asked, "Would you have me go with this nose?" To which Princess Louisa replied, "Do you intend to wait until you get another?"

Louisa was lively and unaffected; Elizabeth, very learned. She knew every language and every science under the sun and corresponded regularly with Mr. Descartes.[27] Her erudition, however, made her somewhat absentminded, which was often a source of our mirth. Louisa was not as pretty as Elizabeth but had, in my opinion, a more amiable disposition. She completely devoted herself to painting, and so great was her talent that she could capture peoples' likeness without them having to sit for her. In painting other people, however, she neglected her own appearance. Her clothes looked like they had been thrown on her, which caused Mr. Harrington to compose verses comparing her to an artist who, angry at being unable to paint the lather

---

27. In the mid-1640s Elizabeth moved to the Brandenburg court to live with her paternal aunt. During this period Sophia served as intermediary between Elizabeth and Descartes. The correspondence includes three accompanying letters, written in the second half of 1646, that Descartes addressed directly to Sophia (*The Correspondence between Princess Elisabeth of Bohemia and René Descartes*, trans. and ed. Lisa Shapiro. Chicago: University of Chicago Press, 2007, 144, 150, 154). From the final accompanying letter it can be inferred that Sophia had written one to Descartes in which she had wittily rejected his assertion that she has an angelic face. To which Descartes, ever the smooth-tongued courtier, replies, "Rather than diminishing the opinion I had, on the contrary, it [Sophia's letter] assures me that it is not only the face of Your Highness that merits being compared with that of angels. For just as painters can draw a model from your face with which to represent angels well, so too the graces of your mind are such that the philosophers have reason to wonder at them" (Elizabeth, *Descartes*, 154).

on a horse, hurls the brush at the canvas and, by this lucky stroke, achieves a perfect rendering of the horse's frothy coat.[28]

My sister Princess Henrietta bore no resemblance to the other two. She had flaxen hair, a complexion of lilies and roses, and a pale, well-chiseled nose that, unlike Elizabeth's, was able to resist the cold. She had soft eyes, black well-arched eyebrows, an admirably shaped face and forehead, a pretty mouth, and hands and arms as perfect as if they had been turned on a lathe. She had a pair of legs and feet worthy of the House of Palatine, which is ample praise. Her two favorite pastimes were needlework and making preserves; of the latter I was the chief beneficiary.

I must also mention that, since the von Quadt sisters had been unable to accompany me to The Hague, they had wished to provide me with an attendant after their own hearts. They recommended an old maid named Galen. I found her highly disagreeable and was not alone in this opinion. I often hid behind the bed curtains or a tapestry to make her have to search the entire house for me.

I became friends with an English girl named Carey who waited on my sister Henrietta. She was a modest young creature, not pretty, but fresh faced and well dressed. Her older sister, one of the queen's maids of honor, was a girl of remarkable prudence and discernment.[29] The younger sister's affection for me came from genuine feeling, whereas the elder's was supplemented by self-interest, for she saw that my stock was beginning to rise and that I might someday be useful in furthering her fortune. She desired her younger sister to take charge of my

28. Sir James Harrington (1611–77), author of *The Common-Wealth of Oceana* (1656), served in Lord Craven's regiment in Germany (see footnote 30) and was often at The Hague and the queen of Bohemia's court. Harrington's uncle, Sir John Harrington, had been the queen's guardian when she was a child in England; he died in 1613 in Germany after accompanying her to Heidelberg.

29. The older is Mary, the younger is Anne, daughters of Sir Robert Carey, who had done military service in Holland under Sir Horace Vere in the 1620s, and Alice Hogenoke. See George Charles Moore Smith, *The Family of Withypoll: With Special Reference to Their Manor of Christchurch, Ipswich and Some Notes on the Allied Families of Thorne, Harper, Lucar, and Devereux* (Letchworth: Garden City Press, 1936), 78–79.

wardrobe and to make sure I looked my best. The task was an easy one, for youth itself is one of the loveliest ornaments.

I had light brown, naturally curly hair, a cheerful and easy manner, a good figure (though I was not very tall), and the bearing of a princess. Other charms, now no longer reflected in my mirror, I do not care to recall. I prefer the pleasure of looking at the portraits of me in my youth to the task of penning a portrait of things that are past and gone.

In those years The Hague was rife with malicious gossip. It was fashionable for the local wits to sit in judgment on everyone's actions. My manners and behavior had been so carefully watched over by my two older girlfriends that I was more commended for my conduct than for my looks. An old English gentleman, Lord Craven, took up my cause.[30] The idea was that I might someday marry the Prince of Wales, who was only a year older than I.[31] This plan was deemed infallible because the English wanted their prince to marry a coreligionist, and at that time there was none whose birth was superior to mine.

My good friends were not the only ones to eye this tasty morsel. The wife of Prince Frederick Henry of Orange-Nassau had formed the same plan for one of her daughters and considered it feasible because

30. At the time he took an interest in Sophia, the "old English gentleman," William Craven, earl of Craven (1606–1697), was in his late thirties and extremely wealthy. Knighted by James I in 1627 for exemplary military service on the Continent under the princes of Orange-Nassau, Craven later helped finance, and commanded elements of, two English expeditionary forces dispatched to Germany to help restore the Palatinate to Sophia's father Frederick V (in 1632) and her brother Charles Lewis (in 1637). Craven was a fixture at the queen of Bohemia's court. Some contemporaries suspected the two were lovers. After the Restoration, Craven returned to England and recovered his estate, which had been confiscated under Cromwell. He provided a residence, Drury House in London, for the queen of Bohemia when she returned in 1661; he may have intended Ashdown House, his Dutch-style hunting lodge in Berkshire on which construction began in 1661, to be a rural retreat for her. On the staircase walls at Ashdown House hang twenty-eight portraits (most of them of the Palatines, including one of Sophia by Gerard van Honthorst) purchased from the Craven family by the National Trust in 1968. The portraits, which are in superb condition, may be viewed two afternoons a week from April through October (nationaltrust.org.uk/main/w-ashdownhouse).

31. The future Charles II (1630–85); he married Catherine of Breganza (1638–1705) in 1662.

they were coreligionists too. She judged that I was the only obstacle to her ambition (to satisfy which she was usually ready to sacrifice anything). After discussing the matter with her husband, she resolved to do her utmost to destroy my reputation, well aware that the world is easily deceived by appearances. Her scheme called for her son, who was already married, to try to compromise me, believing that I would welcome the amorous attention of so worthy a prince.[32] While she was hatching this plot, a German valet named Fritz got wind of the whole thing. A principled youth, Fritz was shocked by their wickedness and at once informed Streithagen, the court chaplain of my brother Charles Lewis, the elector Palatine, of all that he had heard.[33] It soon became apparent that he was telling the truth, for the young prince, heeding his mother's orders, appeared every evening in my mother's antechamber. But his efforts were in vain, for whenever he appeared I left the room. Driven to seek some other means of spreading rumors, the conspirators resolved to put on a ballet in which my brother Prince Philip could not refuse to participate nor derogate from his rank by allowing the rehearsals to be held at the court of Orange instead of in his own apartments. My brother, who saw through their scheme, foiled it by declaring that his apartments were too small. For he easily perceived that their object was simply to gain freer access to our court, so as to make people talk. They then employed the rhinegrave, who dared to tell me that I could rule all Holland and follow the example of the duchess of Chevreuse, whose charms had gained her considerable power.[34] I replied that he ought to give such advice to his wife,

---

32. Frederick Henry's wife, Princess Amalia of Solms-Braunfels (1602–75), had been raised in Heidelberg where her father served in the electoral household as head tutor during the reigns of Sophia's father and grandfather. Prior to her marriage, Amalia had been one of the queen of Bohemia's ladies-in-waiting, whence, doubtless, Sophia's ire at her disloyalty to the Palatine House. Amalia's son, William II (1626–50), was married to Mary Stuart (1631–61).

33. Peter Streithagen (1591–1653) had served as the king of Bohemia's court chaplain from 1631 until the king's death in November 1632. After a brief period as pastor of the Church of St. Peter in Heidelberg, Streithagen became Charles Lewis's court chaplain in late 1635 and in 1649, on Charles Lewis's restoration, his councilor for church affairs. *Allgemeine Deutsche Biographie* (Leipzig: Duncker & Humblot, 1875–1910), 36: 568–69; cited from deutsche-biographie.de.

34. Marie de Rohan-Montbazon (1600–79) was married to the duke of Luynes and later to the duke of Chevreuse. The rhinegrave is perhaps Leopold Philip of Salm (?–1663).

though I believed her too sensible to follow it, for she was much more distinguished than he.

[1647–49]

Meanwhile, I was much courted by the entire English nation, which went to great lengths to please me, and all for the mere wisp of a chance, for the affairs of King Charles I were then in a desperate state. The king was a prisoner on the Isle of Wight, and his son the Prince of Wales, for whose sake they made such a fuss over me, had taken refuge in The Hague. We saw that he was a prince whose soundness in mind and body was not matched by the kind of good fortune that would allow him to think of marriage. Several of the English, however, thought of it for him, even after his father's terrible death, which had made him king. The leaders of an insurrection against Cromwell were also among the supporters of my marriage to the prince. Like the late king, however, it was their misfortune to be betrayed and beheaded.

Among those who sought their own fortune in my service was the marquis of Montrose. Being a valiant military commander and a man of great ability, he believed everything to be attainable through bravery and talent. He was certain that he could restore young King Charles II if His Majesty would appoint him Lord-Lieutenant of Scotland. And after rendering so great a service, he thought His Majesty would bestow on him the hand of my sister Princess Louisa. The king granted him the commission for Scotland, despite the opposition of a hostile Presbyterian faction headed by the duke of Hamilton and Lord Lauderdale.[35] The princess of Orange, seeing that they opposed Montrose, believed they must also be my enemies. She plotted to such good effect that the Scottish Presbyterians turned against me in favor of one of her daughters, having been persuaded by the princess that I

35. In 1632 James Hamilton, third marquis and first duke of Hamilton in the Scottish peerage, second earl of Cambridge in the British peerage (1606–49), led the English expeditionary force to Germany to which Sophia's father and Lord Craven were attached. John Maitland, second earl and first duke of Lauderdale (1616–82).

was not a good Presbyterian because I went to Common Prayer with the king.[36]

[April–May 1650]

Montrose, meanwhile, went to Scotland, and parliament, fearing his influence and valor, sent deputies to the king at Breda (where my mother the queen and I were also residing) to offer him the crown of Scotland on the condition that he renounce Montrose, swear to the Covenant, and acknowledge parliament's legitimacy.[37] His Majesty let Montrose's enemies persuade him to agree to all these terms in order to obtain the crown. I was deeply shocked, the more so when I heard that the gallant Montrose had been drawn and quartered, as may be read in the histories of England.[38]

I had noticed other signs of weakness on the king's part. He and I had always been on the best of terms, as cousins and friends, and he had shown a liking for me with which I was much gratified. One day, however, his friends Lord Gerard and Somerset Fox, who were short of money, persuaded him to pay me compliments while we walked together in the Lange Voorhout.[39] The king told me, among other things,

36. The modern French edition omits the words that correspond to "She plotted … her daughters" (Sophia, *Mémoires*, 48).

37. First signed in 1638, the National Covenant was an oath that criticized James VI and Charles I's changes to the Scottish kirk and that engaged its signers to defend the kirk against foreign and domestic enemies. Sophia refers here to the Scottish parliament, not the English.

38. Originally a covenanter, James Graham, fifth earl and first marquis of Montrose (1612–50), became a royalist in May 1641. After being commissioned a lieutenant-general by Charles I in February 1644, Montrose entered Scotland in April and, between September of that year and August 1645, won six battles against the covenanters. Montrose returned to Scotland in March 1650 as Charles II's nominal lieutenant-governor. He and about two hundred fighters were defeated on April 27, 1650, at Carbisdale in Ross-shire. Montrose was sentenced to death by the Scottish parliament (more for his troops' marauding in the 1644–45 campaign than for his failed invasion in 1650). He was hanged in Edinburgh on May 21, 1650; his corpse was quartered and displayed publicly in four Scottish cities.

39. The manuscript's "Milord Gerit" is probably Charles Gerard, baron of Brandon in Suffolk, viscount Brandon, and first earl of Macclesfield (1618–94), a royalist cavalry commander who fled England with Sophia's brother Prince Rupert in 1646 and served as gentleman of the bedchamber to Charles II. In 1701 Gerard's son was chosen as the emissary to present Sophia with her copy of the Act of Settlement. Van der Cruysse may be correct to

that I was prettier than Mrs. Barlow and that he hoped to see me in England.[40] I was surprised by his words and learned afterward that Somerset Fox's aim was to induce me to ask Lord Craven for money for the king, which Somerset Fox intended to share with his good friend Lord Gerard. I was offended, but my mother the queen was delighted by the attention I was paid by His Majesty and reproved me for not promenading in the Lange Voorhout the following evening. I excused myself by saying I had a corn on my foot which made walking painful. The real reason, however, was to evade the king, for I had sense enough to know that this is not how royal marriages are made. At Breda I also noticed that the king avoided my company in the presence of the Scottish deputies, although he had sought it before their arrival. Taken together, all these circumstances proved to me that my friends' plan would come to nothing and that if I remained in Holland I would be subjected to the mortification of losing the esteem in which I was held. For those persons who now paid court to me would do so no longer when they came to perceive that I would not be in a position to reward them.

I remember with pleasure the folly of the people who sought to advance their fortunes by vying with each other to insinuate themselves into my good graces. Chief among the ladies were Lady Herbert, Lady Staunton, and Mrs. Barlow.[41] They belonged to different factions and were rivals for my favor, and I often used to laugh at their expense

interpret the manuscript's "Somerset Fox" as a conflation of Robert Carr, earl of Somerset (1590–1645), and Sir Stephen Fox (1627–1716) (Sophia, *Mémoires*, 49). However, Charles II refers to a "Somerset Fox" in an undated letter to Rupert, suggesting that there was a courtier by this name. See *A Collection of Original Royal Letters*, ed. Sir George Bromley (London: John Stockdale, 1787), 277. The Lange Voorhout is a tree-lined square in the center of The Hague.

40. Lucy Walter (1630–58), Charles II's mistress, went by the name Mrs. Barlow. Charles recognized her son James Scott (1649–85), despite doubts about the boy's paternity, and later created him duke of Monmouth.

41. Lady Herbert is probably not, as Van der Cruysse proposes, the wife of Edward Herbert, third Baron Herbert of Cherbury, but rather Lady Margaret Herbert (née Smith), the wife of Sir Edward Herbert (1591–1657). Sir Edward, a member of parliament and attorney general to Charles I, went to sea with Rupert in 1648 and was afterward in The Hague as Charles II's attorney general. Van der Cruysse amends the manuscript's Stenton to Staunton and

with my faithful friends the Careys and the good Lord Craven, who was frequently a party to our conversations.

Lord Craven was a very valuable friend, for he had money, which I lacked, to dispense presents to my partisans. He always had refreshments standing ready and handed out numerous gewgaws to delight the younger crowd. He needed all these devices to render himself agreeable and to enable us to tease him a little in private. In order to shine in conversation he used to say the oddest things. One day he declared that he could will himself to think of nothing. So, shutting his eyes, he said, "Now I'm thinking of nothing." On another occasion he maintained that French ought to be spelled like Latin. I told him that for the most part the words in these two languages were utterly dissimilar and asked him how he would spell *l'huile*. He replied, "With an *o* because *oglio* is Latin for 'oil,'" at which we all laughed heartily.[42]

At that time I had such a sunny disposition that everything amused me. The misfortunes of the House of Palatine had no power to depress my spirits, although at times we were obliged to enjoy feasts as rich as Cleopatra's, since at our court we often had nothing to eat but diamonds and pearls.[43] But as the English deliberately bring up princes in

identifies her as Lady Philippina Staunton. The manuscript reads Waler not Barlow; but Sophia likely means Walter, Mrs. Barlow's maiden name (Sophia, *Mémoires*, 49).

42. Despite the holes in Lord Craven's Latinity (*oleum*, not *oglio*, is the Latin for "oil"), the orthographic principle the younger crowd find so risible resembles remarks made by Antoine Arnauld and Claude Lancelot in their *Grammaire générale et raisonée* of 1660: "[I]t often occurs, especially in the case of languages derived from other languages, that there are certain letters which are not pronounced, and which thus are useless as far as sound is concerned, but which nonetheless help us perceive what the words signify. For example, in the words *champs* (fields) and *chants* (songs), the *p* and the *t* are not pronounced, but are nevertheless useful for signification, since through them we understand that the former comes from the Latin *campi* and the latter from the Latin *cantus* ... And from this it can be seen that those who complain so much about what is written deviating from what is pronounced, are not always right, and that what they call abuse is sometimes not without utility" (Antoine Arnauld and Claude Lancelot, *General and Rational Grammer: The Port-Royal Grammer*, trans. and ed. Jacques Rieux and Bernard E. Rollin. The Hague: Mouton, 1975, 57).

43. Here, Sophia may be distinguishing herself from her sister Elizabeth, whom in May 1645 Descartes diagnosed as suffering from a Palatinate-induced fever: "The most common cause

ignorance of money matters so that they can control them more easily, it is not surprising that our poverty did not trouble me. The merchants furnished all that I required, and I left to Providence the matter of payment. My cheerfulness was interrupted only by paroxysms of piety. I remember one day composing some very bad poetry that at least serves to show my feelings during this period:

Lord, can one, as a child of thine,	Seigneur, peut-il qu'un tien enfant
Forever beat the castanet;	Batte toujours la castagnette,
Or, figuring as arch coquette,	Ou bien s'adjuste en coquette
To dancing, time resign?	Et passe son temps en dansant?
And should the mind's whole study be	Peut-il que son esprit ne pense
The modulation of the voice,	Qu'à bien gouverner sa voix,
Or, making of some fool the choice,	Ou d'un niais faire le choix
Mock his simplicity?	Pour rire de son innocence?
If this could give thee pleasure, Lord,	Si tout cecy te pouvait plaire,
How happy might I ever be	Heureux serais-je de tout temps
To have, below, frivolity,	Avoir icy le passe-temps
And then, on high, reward.[44]	Et en l'autre monde le salaire.

of a low-grade fever is sadness, and the stubbornness of fortune in persecuting your house continually gives you [Elizabeth] matters for annoyance which are so public and so terrible that [they are] … the principal cause of your indisposition … ." (Elizabeth, *Descartes*, 86). In volume 9 of his *Natural History*, Pliny the Elder relates a story about Cleopatra betting Mark Antony that she could spend ten million sesterces on a single meal for just herself. She supposedly won the bet by dissolving a large pearl in dish of vinegar and drinking it.

44. The English translation of Sophia's poem is by Forester (Sophia, *Memoirs*, 28).

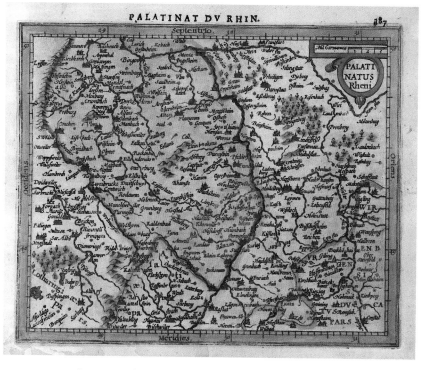

Seventeenth-century map of the Lower Palatinate

Chapter 2
Heidelberg (1650–58)

As I mentioned, at times I felt that my happiness in The Hague could not last. My good friends having come to the same conclusion, it was agreed that I should go to the Palatinate to visit my brother Charles Lewis, the elector Palatine. The elector had always favored me with his affection and even called me his daughter, for he was thirteen years older than I.[45] He had recently married a princess of the House of Hesse-Kassel.[46] Knowing the elector to be highly intelligent, I felt certain that in so important a matter he would not have allowed ardor to overrule good judgment and that in his young and beautiful wife I would find a delightful companion.

My mother the queen, who still clung to the idea of marrying me to the king of England, was reluctant to consent to my departure. But when it was pointed out to her that my trip to Heidelberg would not be an obstacle to her design, she permitted me to go and even insisted that I be accompanied by my two dearest friends, the Carey sisters, the older of whom was now married to Mr. Withypoll, a very accomplished and agreeable gentleman.[47] Lord Craven, as superintendent of our travel party, was responsible for all aspects of the journey.

45. Both Sophia and her next-older sister Henrietta called their brother Charles Lewis "papa."

46. The marriage was on February 12, 1650.

47. Sophia's departure was far less harmonious than she contends, as is evident in a letter from the queen of Bohemia to Charles Lewis dated August 29, 1650: "As for Sophies journey, I uill neuer keep anie that has a minde to leaue me, for I shall neuer care for anie bodies companie that doth not care for mine" (Elizabeth, *Letters*, 78). In May 1654 the queen was still chagrined, both at Sophia and Anne, the younger Carey sister: "[If Carey] say, she went uith Sophie by my order, she is much in the wrong, … for to tell you the truth, I was not verie well satisfied uith Sophies going, neither did I euer committ anie charge to her of Sophie for I think Sophie has as much uitt as she to gouuern her self …" (Elizabeth, *Letters*, 205). Mary Carey married Henry Withypoll (1602–70) sometime between 1646 and 1650 (Smith, *Withypoll*, 78–79).

Prior to this, I had ventured outside The Hague only once to go to Rhenen and occasionally taken a horse-drawn canal boat to Leiden or Delft. Apprehensive of a long and exhausting carriage ride, I asked the States General to loan me a pinnace in which I could float up the Rhine in comfort.

I had not intended to stop along the way, but as we went past Düsseldorf, the duke of Neuburg did me the honor of coming in person to welcome me and invite me to dinner.[48] With his wife away at Bad Ems, I was at first hesitant but finally decided that it was permissible to dine alone with a sexagenarian seigneur.[49] Although rumored to be extremely moody, on that day he was perfectly agreeable. He showed me his entire palace, which struck me as antiquated.[50] He went to the trouble of explaining in detail the more than one hundred little pictures that hung in his bedroom, representing stories from the Old and New Testaments and the lives of several saints. He next showed me his church, where I was introduced to a princess of Zweibrücken who had behaved badly by marrying a man named Pestacalda.[51] Having converted to Roman Catholicism, she enjoyed the duke's protection. He then took me to two convents, one of which was full of English girls who looked so happy and pretty that I felt tempted to stay with

48. Wolfgang William, palsgrave of Neuburg and duke of Jülich-Berg (1578–1653), was a close relative and a prominent Catholic convert. His son Philip William (1615–90), also a Catholic, became elector Palatine in 1685 when Charles II, the son of Sophia's brother Charles Lewis, died childless.

49. In August 1650, when Sophia decided that it was safe to dine alone with Wolfgang William, the supposed sexagenarian was in fact nearly seventy-two, though he was spry enough to marry for a third time, in May 1651, six weeks after the death of his second wife, Catherine Charlotte, born palsgravine of Zweibrücken (1615–51).

50. The Düsseldorf palace was destroyed by fire in 1872, with the exception of one corner tower, which now houses a museum of Rhine shipping history.

51. The Church of St. Andrews (*Andreaskirche*), built between 1622 and 1629, contains Wolfgang William's tomb. Princess Amalia Jacoba of Zweibrücken (1592–1655), married Jacobo Francesco, count of Pestacalda (?–ca. 1645), the Spanish military governor of Trier, in 1638. Amalia Jacoba's bad behavior consisted of entering into a marriage that was low (to a mere Iberian count), apostate (to a Catholic), unpatriotic (to an enemy officer), and undignified (she was forty-six at the time). Amalia Jacoba was an aunt of Wolfgang William's wife Catherine Charlotte.

them.[52] The duke read my thoughts and, being an avid proselytizer (for he himself was a convert), declared that he would not escort me out of the convent. I was thus compelled to walk back to the carriage alone, although the duke did join me for the drive back to my boat where I spent the night after thanking him for having been such a gracious host. His was the first court I had seen in Germany. I was impressed with the great civility shown to guests and the great respect shown to the duke. He was quite fastidious and changed clothes twice during my brief stay. His courtiers did not follow his example. As for the palace's furnishings, there were some fine and very old tapestries, but the beds and chairs, exhibiting the latter quality only, were not much to look at.

Continuing my journey, I reached Cologne, where I saw nothing to admire but the ramparts of its fortifications, for the skulls of the eleven thousand virgins and those of the Three Magi shown to me at the church were no more captivating than the wine presented to me by the burgomaster, for I never drank any. Madam Withypoll and Miss Carey, however, enjoyed it with gusto.[53]

The next place I reached was St. Goar, which belongs to Landgrave Ernest of Hesse-Rheinfels. The sight of Rheinfels castle perched on a promontory behind the town greatly excited my curiosity to see it. The landgrave honored me with a visit to my pinnace and granted my unspoken wish by inviting me to accompany him to the castle. He said that his wife was not there but would arrive shortly. She certainly lost no time and presently arrived in a post carriage accompanied by a young lady as disheveled as herself. Despite the disorder of her dress, she was attractive, although without the manners or grandeur of a princess. Everything I saw at this court had the air of a private home. The castle was comfortable enough but difficult to get to, particularly in the landgrave's carriage, a primitive and strange-looking conveyance. The honeyed discourse of its owner, however, smoothed

52. Neither convent, a Celestine completed in 1638 and a Carmelite completed in 1644, stands today.

53. After residing in Constantinople and Milan, the skulls venerated as those of the Three Magi were brought to Cologne in 1164 by Reginald of Dassel, archbishop of Cologne.

the difficulties of the way. Afterward, he and the landgravine escorted me back to my pinnace and took their leave of me.[54]

With the French still in garrison in Bacharach, we did not land there, although the military governor of the town was polite enough to ask whether he could be of any service to me. I went on to Oppenheim, where I first set foot in the Palatinate. The governor received me and then handed me into a rickety old carriage pulled by two uncooperative horses of different colors. Since there was no seat inside, I made myself as comfortable as possible on some cushions I had brought with me. The horses, however, refused to stir, and I was obliged to get out and walk through the mud, there being no paving stones as there are in Holland. The governor then took me to a windowless house where we stayed for awhile so that I might have some supper, which was the best part of my visit and tasted excellent after so unsavory a reception.

I arrived next at Mannheim, whither the elector and electress had most graciously come to receive me. The easy-mannered elector seemed delighted to see me. The electress, however, assumed a doleful air and hardly said a word the entire day, which gave me the opportunity to inspect her at my leisure. She was quite tall, with a compact torso and very long legs. She had a lovely complexion and the most magnificent bosom.[55] Her eyebrows, which she had dyed black, contrasted too sharply with her beautiful flaxen hair, and when she raised them she puckered her high brow in a very odd way. Although her features were irregular, she had beautiful, sparkling eyes, a large and

54. Landgrave Ernest (1623–93) and Landgravine Maria Eleanor (1632–89) of Hesse-Rheinfels. Maria Eleanor, who was not yet eighteen at the time Sophia met her, had been married to Ernest since the age of thirteen. The landgrave converted to Roman Catholicism in 1652 and is perhaps best known as the intermediary for the correspondence between Antoine Arnauld and Gottfried Wilhelm von Leibniz. Rheinfels castle was demolished by the French in 1797 during the War of the First Coalition.

55. It was a bosom Charles Lewis felt his wife was overly fond of displaying. At a social event during the imperial diet in 1657, he was reported to have groped her breasts in front of the emperor as a rebuke for her appearing in revealing clothes "as the most Public Coquet could do." See Anonymous, *The Life and Amours of Charles Lewis Elector Palatine* (London: Thomas Nott, 1692), 122.

expressive mouth, and a superb set of teeth. All in all, she could be called a fine-looking woman.

I got into a carriage with her and the elector to start for Heidelberg. After my experiences in St. Goar and Oppenheim, I was so pleased to ride in a well-built carriage that I praised its beauty. To my surprise, this praise caused the electress to grimace in displeasure. I was not then aware that this, her wedding carriage, was a sore subject with her, for in her opinion it was less magnificent than the one her sister the princess of Tarentum had received from their mother as a wedding gift.[56] The electress interpreted the perceived disparity as a sign that her mother had shown greater affection for her sister than for her.

We arrived at Heidelberg in the evening. The castle had suffered so severely during the Thirty Years War that the elector lived in the town in the building that had housed the Palatine finance commission.[57] The elector and electress did me the honor of accompanying me to the room prepared for me and then, in the German fashion, left me with my attendants. Once alone with them I could not help exclaiming, with true Dutch frankness, "My sister-in-law is a simpleton."

This impression was confirmed the next day. Since it was a Sunday, I went to find the electress in order to accompany her to church. When I entered her room, I saw that she had had all her fine clothes spread out on a table. She then began recounting where she had got them and how long she had owned them. I thought she must be joking, since the current fashion was to have a small number of dresses and to replace them frequently. After she had recounted the genealogy of her entire wardrobe, we went to church. On our return she confided to me that she had married the elector against her will, that she had been courted by several other princes, that her mother had chosen for her and made her marry a jealous old man, and that a Württemberg duke named Frederick had been infatuated with her, as had the dukes George William and Ernest Augustus of Brunswick-Lüneburg,

56. On the prince and princess of Tarentum, see footnote 16.

57. The building, known in German as the *Kommissariat*, formerly stood in Heidelberg's Kettengasse and was destroyed by the French army in 1693.

Palsgrave Philip of Sulzbach, and assorted counts.[58] These words took me aback, and I fervently wished I were back in The Hague, where it was considered a crime for a wife to complain about her husband and where such foolish creatures were held up to ridicule.

The elector also had grievances against his mate, which he likewise confided to me. He said that, although she had many fine qualities, she had been badly raised. He entreated me to cure her of her affectation and to explain to her how unbecoming it was in a person of her rank. In spite of the faults he found, I could see that he adored her, and I was often embarrassed to see him kiss her in front of everyone. Indeed, they canoodled continually, and I frequently saw her kneeling before him or him before her. At that time it seemed that their love would prove everlasting. But Jealousy, Love's meddlesome child, soon disturbed their peace.

The elector believed that the electress could not look at another man without it lessening her affection for him, and his passion for her often drove him to make accusations to which his wife responded with great indignation. She made little effort to allay his suspicions, although they were actually quite ill founded. It was from a certain weakness of character, and not from any evil design, that she wished to be the center of attention. Her actions were foolish rather than criminal. But the elector, who loved her with a quite delicate heart, wished to have her all to himself. The slightest word from him on this subject sent her into a frightful rage which usually lasted throughout the day, though the two antagonists would make peace at night. The elector employed a thousand endearing wiles to mollify her, but this made her even more fractious, for she took after her uncle, Landgrave Frederick, who was compliant only when ill-treated.[59]

---

58. Sophia's sister-in-law thus claims to have been courted by Sophia's future runaway fiancé (Duke George William of Brunswick-Lüneburg) and future husband (Duke Ernest Augustus of Brunswick-Lüneburg). The other supposed suitors are Duke Frederick of Württemberg-Neustadt (1615–82) and Palsgrave Philip of Sulzbach (1630–1703).

59. Possibly Landgrave Frederick of Hesse-Eschwege (1617–55), a high-ranking officer in the Swedish army during the Thirty Years War (Sophia, *Memoiren*, 48).

One can easily judge whether I was very happy during this period. The electress liked to hunt and play cards, whereas I was accustomed to neither pastime. I did not know how to shoot and had only played cards to entertain my mother the queen, who liked to watch us play a few hands after supper.

I was much relieved by the arrival of the princess of Tarentum, who understood how to make life pleasant. I greatly enjoyed her company, though she only stayed for two weeks. I wrote to our sister Princess Elizabeth, whom the elector had always greatly esteemed, and at my request she consented to undertake the journey to Heidelberg. Before starting out, however, she arranged the marriage of our sister Princess Henrietta to Sigmund Rákóczi, prince of Transylvania. It did not please the elector, who thought it harsh to send our sister all the way to Hungary for so poor a match.[60]

[Summer 1651]

Princess Elizabeth arrived in Heidelberg while our brother Prince Edward was also visiting. He had awaited her arrival impatiently, since they had not seen each other for a very long time. Her stay with our aunt at the court of Brandenburg had done her no good.[61] We thought her much changed, both in mind and body. Looking at her, Prince Edward whispered to me, "Where have her vivacious spirit and witty banter gone?" The electress also found her disagreeable, a sentiment soon adopted by the elector, who still bore Elizabeth a grudge for Princess Henrietta's marriage. The electress treated me very well

60. Letters from Elizabeth and Henrietta to Charles Lewis during the marriage negotiations make it clear that he was in fact furious about the match. See *Die Briefe der Kinder des Winterkönigs*, ed. Karl Hauck (Heidelberg: G. Koester, 1908), 43–63. To give Elizabeth some credit as a matchmaker, it should be noted that Prince Sigmund (1622–52) was at least a fellow Calvinist (as was his older brother George I Rákóczi, prince of Transylvania) and comfortably rich. The marriage, which took place in June 1651, was ill-fated. Princess Henrietta died in September 1651, Sigmund the following year.

61. Electress Elizabeth Charlotte (1597–1660), wife of Elector George William of Brandenburg (1595–1640), was the younger sister of Sophia's father Frederick V. Ward speculates that Princess Elizabeth may also have been saddened by the recent death, in February 1650, of her correspondent René Descartes (Adolphus William Ward, *The Electress Sophia and the Hanoverian Succession*. London: Goupil & Co., 1903, 61).

because she liked me better than my sister, whereas Elizabeth spoke to me with such an air of superiority that I began to prefer the company of the electress, who could be charming when she wished and was at times quite gracious to me. Still, I was much to blame for not submitting to a sister who was obviously more sensible than I. My good friends, on the other hand, were only too happy to encourage my ill humor toward Elizabeth in order to have me all to themselves.[62]

At about this time the duke of Württemberg invited the elector and all of us to visit him at Stuttgart. We went there and were received with great pomp outside the city's gates by the duke and his entire court. My uncle, the palsgrave of Simmern, was there with his sons, as were the margrave of Baden-Durlach and a young prince of Holstein. There were also a great many princesses, including the duchess of Württemberg, her daughters, two of her sisters-in-law (the princesses Antonia and Anna Johanna of Württemberg), and two of her cousins (the princesses Faustina and Floriana Ernesta).[63] There were also countless counts and countesses and innumerable lesser nobles.

Our cavalcade on entering Stuttgart was so large that it pleased the duke, despite the late hour, to have us parade through the streets two or three times. Our patience was further tried by a large and lengthy supper party that lasted till midnight. But this did not prevent our hosts from waking us early the next morning to go hunting. Just as we were nearly dressed it occurred to them that a hunt might not be advisable after the fatigues of our journey, and so it was cancelled. As compensation for this supposed disappointment we remained at table for almost the entire day. The men vied to outdrink each other, while the old princesses cracked open crayfish for us to eat. We spent the

---

62. The good friends are presumably Mary Withypoll and her younger sister, Anne Carey, who accompanied Sophia to Heidelberg.

63. In the order named, the party consisted of Duke Eberhard III of Württemberg (1614–74); Sophia's paternal uncle Palsgrave Lewis Philip of Simmern (1602–55); Margrave Frederick V of Baden-Durlach (1594–1659); Eberhard III's wife Duchess Anna Dorothea (1614–55); Eberhard III's sisters Princess Antonia (1613–79) and Princess Anna Johanna (1619–79); and Eberhard III's cousins Princess Faustina Marianna (1624–79) and Princess Floriana Ernesta (1623–81). The identity of the "young prince of Holstein" is unknown.

remainder of the time at Stuttgart dancing, listening to music, playing *Wirtschaft*, hunting, and going on walks.[64]

It was all very magnificent, but seasoned with little grace or charm and therefore not really to my taste. The gentlemen kept apart from the ladies, who were always very solemn. The prince of Holstein sought to demonstrate his gallantry by drinking to my health. As evidence of his supposed ardor for me, he drank an enormous glass of wine in a single gulp, spit it all back up, and downed it again. His display sparked jealousy in the two old princesses, Antonia and Anna Johanna, who envied me a conquest that I myself did not value. The prince of Holstein had a gentleman with him who bowed every time our eyes met. I endeavored to make the electress laugh at the man's curious behavior in order to distract her thoughts from her mother's death, the report of which had just arrived.[65] This news put an end to our stay in Stuttgart, by no means to my regret.

On our return to Heidelberg I found letters from Portugal written by Lady Dorothy Guzman, a friend of mine from Holland. She had written several times to persuade me to marry the duke of Aveiro.[66] Earlier that year I had had smallpox, which had considerably marred my looks. Nevertheless, after having considered marriage to a king, my ambition forbade me to descend to marrying a mere subject, although Lady Dorothy painted Portugal in the brightest colors imaginable.[67]

At about this time Duke Ernest Augustus of Brunswick-Lüneburg passed through Heidelberg on his return from Venice. I had met him

64. *Wirtschaft*, German for "inn," was a popular court entertainment in which the host and the hostess (in this case, the duke and duchess of Württemberg) dressed up as an innkeeper and his wife and served food and drink to their guests, who pretended to be customers. It offered a welcome suspension of protocol and court etiquette, which were otherwise strictly observed.

65. The electress's mother, Landgravine Amalia Elizabeth of Hesse-Kassel (1602–51), died on August 8, 1651.

66. Raimundo de Alencastro, duke of Aveiro (1627–55).

67. The king Sophia refers to is her cousin Charles II, although by her own testimony she did not really encourage his suit.

in Holland when he was very young. Now even more handsome, he was universally admired but, as the youngest of four brothers, was not a desirable match. We played guitar together, which served to show off his exquisite hands. He was also an excellent dancer. He offered to send me some of Corbetta's guitar music, and we began to exchange letters on this subject.[68] I broke off our correspondence, however, fearing that people might say I was being too friendly to him.[69]

[October 1652]

Some time after this my brother the elector set out for Prague, where he was to meet the emperor. His Imperial Majesty received the elector on White Mountain, where our father the king had been defeated by the emperor's father. This caused the emperor's courtiers to remark that my brother gained more on White Mountain than my father had lost.[70]

To console the electress for being left behind on the trip to Prague, the elector promised that she would accompany him to the imperial diet in Regensburg, though I strongly advised him against it. I saw that his jealousy combined with the electress's affectation and conceit could not fail to produce unpleasant results at so crowded a gathering. However, the elector's desire to have his adored wife always by his side caused us to undertake this journey in the middle of winter, attended

---

68. Francesco Corbetta (1615–81), an Italian guitar virtuoso, gave lessons to Louis XIV and was briefly a court musician in Hanover in the early 1650s. The music Ernest Augustus offered to send to Sophia was possibly the *Varii capricii per la ghittara spagnuola* (Milan, 1643) or the *Varii scherzi di sonate per la Chitara* (Brussels, 1648).

69. At the time, Sophia wrote to Charles Lewis, "It would have been discourteous not to reply to thank him [Ernest Augustus] for the music he sent. Not to do so would have smacked of pride, which is itself a great sin" (Sophia, *Briefwechsel der Herzogin Sophie von Hannover mit ihrem Bruder*, ed. Eduard Bodemann. Leipzig: Hirzel, 1885, 3, my translation; letter dated September 24, 1652). Judging from Sophia's defensive tone, Charles Lewis probably instructed her to break off the correspondence with Ernest Augustus.

70. The eight electors, or in some cases their representatives, met with Emperor Ferdinand III (1608–57) in Prague in the autumn of 1652. The symbolic reception on White Mountain (a sort of early modern photo op) was an important act of reconciliation by the emperor, who made every effort to show his esteem for Charles Lewis. See Karl Hauck, *Karl Ludwig, Kurfürst von der Pfalz (1617–1680).* (Leipzig: Breitkopf & Härtel, 1903), 104.

by a large retinue.[71] Escorted by numerous foot and horse guards, we made our solemn entry into Regensburg to the sound of trumpets and kettledrums. That evening the emperor and empress sent to welcome us.[72] After a few days' rest the elector had an audience with the emperor, and the electress with the empress, who did her the honor of walking through several antechambers to receive her at the head of the staircase, giving us her hand in the German fashion. We followed her to the audience chamber, where she seated herself in an armchair under a large baldachin. We sat across from her, the electress in an armchair and my sister and I in high-backed chairs. The profoundly deaf Count Fugger served as interpreter, and his infirmity rendered our conversation disconnected, although the empress was extremely bright and clever.[73] The next day Her Imperial Majesty honored the electress by returning the visit and was received at her carriage door and escorted back to it by the electress. On later occasions when we went to pay our respects, court etiquette was relaxed, and we played cards with Her Imperial Majesty. The emperor also entertained us with an opera, a carnival, and a *Wirtschaft* with Their Imperial Majesties serving as host and hostess. Everyone was splendidly dressed but danced like German peasants.

The electress, whose sole purpose during the trip was to dazzle this large gathering with her beauty, had sent to France for a hairdresser named La Prince. The electress did everything she could to cause a stir, though to her misfortune an untimely pregnancy had ruined her

71. Numerous imperial diets were held in Regensburg. This one lasted from early 1653 to early 1654. Sophia, her sister Elizabeth, her brother the elector, and her sister-in-law the electress arrived in Regensburg on January 8, 1653. Her brother stayed through the end of 1653; Sophia, Elizabeth, and the electress likely stayed at least until June 18, 1653, the day on which Ferdinand III's son, Ferdinand IV, was crowned king of the Romans, the title traditionally borne by the heir apparent to the emperorship. To finance the large retinue over the course of several months, the impoverished elector had to obtain loans from a number of towns in the Palatinate (Hauck, *Karl Ludwig*, 105).

72. The empress was Ferdinand III's third wife, Eleanor of Mantua (1630–86), whom he had married in 1651.

73. Presumably the empress was speaking Italian, which Count Fugger was translating into German or French, likely for the electress's benefit, since Sophia and Elizabeth were at least moderately competent in Italian.

figure.[74] This made her so ill-tempered toward her husband that he often sought refuge in my room. He liked to listen to the voice lessons I was taking from one of the emperor's musicians, a countertenor named Domenico del Pano.[75]

In the evenings the elector always supped in private with the electress, my sister Elizabeth, and me. At these meals we were served by our ladies-in-waiting, one of whom, my friend Miss Carey, by chance filled the elector's wine glass more often than the others did. This caused the electress to suspect that her husband was infatuated with Miss Carey and that this was the real reason he came to see me so often. The electress confided this suspicion to Elizabeth, who, jealous of the favor I enjoyed with the elector, persuaded the electress that he came to see me not because he was in love with Miss Carey but because he liked to listen to me disparage the electress. The electress was taken in by this lie, and though her natural inclination was to prefer me, she forced herself to dote on and befriend Elizabeth. From this moment forward Elizabeth patiently listened to the electress's endless complaints about the elector's jealousy (for the electress really had nothing else to complain of) until Elizabeth herself became jealous. It will hardly be credited that I was the object of her jealousy or that a brother whom I treated with filial respect (and who was old enough to be my father) could be suspected of being my admirer. The electress tried to forbid the elector's visits to my room, but this only made him more determined to come nearly every evening attended by his entire court, which further enraged her. It then came out that in her anger the electress had written to several people telling them that the elector was in love with me and that I was playing along in order to receive gifts from him. All this would not have distressed me had I been in a place where everyone could see and judge my conduct and

74. While at the imperial diet, the electress gave birth prematurely to her third child, a boy given the name Frederick, who died shortly thereafter on May 12, 1653. The elector blamed the child's death on what he considered to be his wife's overly active lifestyle at the diet (among other supposed prepartum excesses: she went hunting).

75. Del Pano (1632–96), a Roman castrato, sang at Ferdinand III's court from 1650 to 1654, after which he returned to Rome, where he was employed mainly at the Sistine Chapel, rising to the post of *maestro di cappella* in 1669.

disposition. But after our return to Heidelberg, where I lived immured in the palace and was seen only by servants, I feared that the rumors might damage my reputation, all of which made me want to escape this awkward situation by getting married.

At about this time Prince Adolphus, the king of Sweden's brother, arrived at our court.[76] He was fairly good-looking and reasonably tall but had an extremely unattractive face with a long pointed chin like a shoehorn. He had only been in Heidelberg for a short while when he asked the elector for my hand in marriage. The electress, wishing to be rid of me, had no small part in bringing this about. She contrived to conceal from the elector and me that Prince Adolphus was ill-tempered and had beaten his first wife.[77] The elector was firmly devoted to the king of Sweden and therefore unwilling to refuse anything to the king's brother. He consented on the condition that the king also approve the match and ratify all the advantageous terms the prince had readily promised. Prince Adolphus sent Colonel Moore to Sweden to ask for the king's consent.[78] Having been given a portrait of me, the prince then went on to Italy, planning his return to Heidelberg to coincide with the colonel's. Meanwhile, the news of my engagement to Prince Adolphus spread everywhere, although the elector's consent had only been conditional.[79]

Duke George William of Brunswick-Lüneburg, then the duke of Hanover, heard the news of my engagement at a time when his estates

76. Palsgrave Adolphus John I of Zweibrücken-Kleeburg (1629–89), younger brother of Charles Gustavus of Zweibrücken (1622–60), who, as the nearest relative, became King Charles X Gustavus of Sweden when Queen Christina (1626–89) abdicated in 1654. In 1649 Charles Gustavus, then serving as a Swedish general, provided strong diplomatic support to Sophia's brother Charles Lewis in the latter's efforts to resolve issues relating to the restitution of the Palatinate (Hauck, *Karl Ludwig*, 90–91).

77. Else Beate (1629–53), daughter of Count Peter von Brahe.

78. Moore left for Sweden in late September 1654 (Bromley, *Collection*, 172).

79. As for Sophia's mother, she was, as a Stuart princess, too proud to welcome—but, as the deposed queen of Bohemia, too realistic to oppose—her daughter's marriage to the younger son of a comparatively minor noble house that through mere chance had acceded to the Swedish throne: "I cannot be against [it], considering the condition wee are all in" (Elizabeth, *Letters*, 218; letter dated October 6, 1654).

were pressuring him to marry. He had replied that he could only do so if they would increase his revenues. During these negotiations the duke came to the conclusion that, if he was going to be forced to drink the bitter cup of matrimony, he could think of no princess he would rather drink it with than me. He therefore sent Mr. von Hammerstein, who was well known at our court, to ascertain the truth of my reported engagement and to inform us about the state of affairs at Hanover.[80] The elector told Hammerstein that Prince Adolphus had made many promises that apparently stood little chance of being kept; that, according to Colonel Moore, the king of Sweden could not agree to allow me to exercise my religion; that the prince had promised me a much larger income than he had the means of providing; and consequently that it was the elector's decision whether to break off or go forward with the marriage.[81]

Armed with this information Hammerstein returned to Hanover. Soon afterward the duke and his brother, Duke Ernest Augustus, arrived in Heidelberg on their way to Italy. Duke George William at once accosted me, inquiring about my reported engagement and paying me countless compliments, to all of which I responded not too clumsily. At last he said the magic words, desiring to know whether he had my permission to ask the elector for my hand. Unlike the heroine of a novel, I did not hesitate to say yes. I infinitely preferred the duke to Prince Adolphus, to whom I had developed an aversion that only an act of willpower could have overcome. I also knew that the elector loved me enough to approve of my sensible choice, as this match was much superior to the other. Like me, the elector did not wait to be asked twice and gave his consent immediately. A marriage contract was drawn up and signed by the elector, the duke, and myself. The duke then continued his journey to Venice to await the conclusion of the negotiations with his estates. He desired that the marriage contract be kept a secret, knowing that his estates would not increase his revenues

80. Georg Christoph von Hammerstein (1625–87), chamberlain and councilor to Duke Ernest Augustus, later privy councilor to Duke George William.

81. Though from a Calvinist noble house like Sophia (one of the reasons for the two families' close ties), Charles X Gustavus had adopted Lutheranism on his accession to the Swedish throne.

if they found out that he was already betrothed. The elector, for his part, preferred to keep the arrangement confidential so that he could more tactfully break off my engagement to Prince Adolphus. Hence, no one else knew about the matter except Duke Ernest Augustus. And he would have preferred to keep his brother, whose full confidence he enjoyed, entirely to himself rather than to share him with a wife who might come between them. We saw the two brothers off after being assured of their speedy return. Meanwhile, Duke George William and I were to exchange letters.

Duke George William wrote to me from Venice that poor Prince Adolphus, who was there also, had shown him a portrait of me and told him that I would soon be his bride.[82] Soon afterward the prince returned to Germany to stay with his sister, the margravine of Baden-Durlach, and sent Mr. Lasalle to tell the elector that he was ready to come to Heidelberg as soon as the elector deemed it appropriate.[83] The elector did everything in his power to forestall the prince's arrival. He informed Lasalle that matters had taken a different turn and that although the king of Sweden, perhaps thinking the affair too far advanced to be stopped, had written in the most gracious terms of his brother's forthcoming marriage, he knew on good authority that His Majesty had kindly expressed a fear that I might not be happy with his brother and that his brother's many promises would not all be kept. The elector broke this to Lasalle as gently as possible, assuring him that even if I was not so fortunate as to become Prince Adolphus's wife, he himself would remain the prince's obedient servant, ready on all occasions to serve him to the utmost of his ability. The quick-witted Lasalle guessed immediately what was up. On passing the duke of Hanover's portrait, which was hanging in a room along with those of other princes, Lasalle bowed low and was heard to say, "I am the

---

82. Sophia gives the impression that it was only in Prince Adolphus's mind that the wedding was a certainty. But her family considered the plans firm enough for the Palatinate's diplomatic agent in France to be tasked with arranging for wedding clothes to be made in Paris. On April 30, 1665, the agent reports that the clothes will be ready the following week (Bromley, *Collection*, 185).

83. Christina Magdalena (1616–62), originally palsgravine of Zweibrücken-Kleeburg, married Margrave Frederick VI of Baden-Durlach (1617–77) in 1642.

very humble and most obedient servant of Your Highness the duke of Hanover." I think, however, that he had too much regard for us to reveal all he knew to Prince Adolphus. The elector sent him on his way laden with fine presents. I do not know how he explained matters to his master, but his powers of persuasion failed to prevent the prince from appearing in Heidelberg accompanied by his sister the margravine. Prince Adolphus tried to insist on the marriage. Possessed by the idea that he must possess me, he did everything he could to gain the object of his desire. At times he wept, at times he flew into a rage and cursed Colonel Moore for having served him so poorly. Finally, seeing that he was not getting anywhere and that the elector firmly insisted on the king's ratification of the marriage contract, he decided to go himself and persuade his brother to take up his cause. But he found the king engrossed in a war with Poland, with neither the time nor the desire to intercede.[84] Besides, His Majesty was very astute and had quickly perceived that the elector did not really want the match.

In Venice, meanwhile, the duke of Hanover had taken up with the first courtesan he had met, a Greek woman whose only charms were her pretty clothes. She infected him with a malady ill suited to marriage. Far away from me, unable to resist Venice's libertine temptations, and unrewarded by his estates with a revenue increase, the duke began to regret his spoken and written promises to me. His letters to me grew colder, and he failed to return to Heidelberg on the appointed date, which made the elector uneasy. For my part, I was too proud to let it bother me.

To avenge myself I lent a willing ear to the duke of Parma's marriage proposal which was conveyed to me by one of the duke's subjects, a monk named Father Manari. He had shown my portrait to his duke and now showed the duke's to the elector. Hoping to make his fortune by this alliance, Father Manari had led the duchess dowager of Parma

84. The First (sometimes referred to as the Second) Northern War (1655–60) between Sweden and a coalition consisting of Poland, Russia, Denmark, Austria, and later Brandenburg (which had initially sided with Sweden). It ended with the Peace of Oliva in which John II of Poland renounced his family's claim to the Swedish crown and confirmed Sweden's sovereignty in North Livonia, part of present-day Estonia.

to believe that I was willing to convert to Roman Catholicism, and the prospect of gaining a soul made her eager for the match.[85]

The duke of Hanover, casting about for an honorable way out of our engagement, hit on the idea of asking his brother Duke Ernest Augustus to marry me in his place. As part of the proposed arrangement, he offered his brother the family domains provided that he himself would receive a large income so that he could pursue his pleasures. He also assured his brother that he would sign a document in which he pledged never to marry and to live the rest of his life the way that suited him best: as a bachelor. Duke Ernest Augustus listened with pleasure to this proposal. He was of the opinion, however, that he could not receive the family domains without the consent of the next heir, their brother Duke John Frederick. They therefore decided to speak to him together and confide to him all that had transpired at Heidelberg.

Duke George William assured Duke John Frederick that a plan advantageous to their younger brother need not be disadvantageous to him. For was George William to die, Ernest Augustus would cede the domains to John Frederick, which the latter could not possess during George William's lifetime anyway. Duke John Frederick did not like this proposal in the least and replied, "Why are you giving the princess to my brother and not to me? I'd be a fool to agree to a plan so favorable to my younger brother." Enraged by this response, George William rudely demanded that John Frederick move out of Hanover palace where he had been staying. Notwithstanding John Frederick's good qualities, which should have earned him better treatment from George William, there was a sort of natural antipathy between the two brothers. George William used to mock John Frederick in the grossest way imaginable. As I shall relate in due course, however, John Frederick was eventually to obtain both revenge and respect.

85. Ranuccio II Farnese, duke of Parma and Plaisance (1630–94). The duchess dowager is his mother, Margherita de' Medici, widow of the previous duke of Parma, who died in 1646.

[Spring 1657]

Duke George William decided to send Duke Ernest Augustus to Hanover to arrange matters. On the way he fell gravely ill in Vienna. A courier was at once dispatched to inform Duke George William. On opening the letter he saw the German word for death and in despair tore it up without reading further. Haxthausen, Duke George William's equerry, put the pieces of the letter back together and proved to him that his brother was still alive.[86] The duke set off immediately by post, not stopping to eat or drink before reaching Vienna, where he was overjoyed to embrace his brother, who was already out of danger.

A few days later the two brothers started for Hanover. On their arrival Duke George William announced to his privy council that he had resolved never to marry and had persuaded his brother Ernest Augustus to bear the burden of matrimony in his place. He therefore demanded that his brother's income be considerably increased so that he could maintain a wife. Although the privy councilors did not like the proposal, they were forced to accept it and obey their master by raising the necessary funds. The dukes confided the business to Hammerstein, entreating him to aid in extricating Duke George William from his predicament by obtaining the elector's consent to the two brothers' plan. Hammerstein accordingly set off, finding the elector at Frankenthal, whither he had gone to escape his domestic discord in Heidelberg.[87]

---

86. Arnold Ludwig von Haxthausen. His son, Christian August von Haxthausen (1653–96), was a page in Duke George William's household and a childhood friend of Sophia's niece Elizabeth Charlotte.

87. Sophia's actual words are "rumor in casa" (Sophia, *Memoiren*, 57), the same used by her mother the queen of Bohemia in a letter to Charles Lewis: "I ame verie sorie to heere of your romor in casa, which is no secret heere, your ennemies laugh at it and your friends are sorie for it, and being the first of them I onlie pray, it may fall out well at the end" (Elizabeth, *Letters*, 205; letter dated August 6, 1654).

PRINCE RUPERT.

OB. 1682.

FROM THE ORIGINAL OF VANDYKE IN THE COLLECTION OF

THE RIGHT HON.ᴮᴸᴱ THE EARL OF CRAVEN.

Nineteenth-century print of Sophia's brother, Prince Rupert,
as a teenager

Finally tiring of his ill-tempered wife, whom he had striven vainly for seven years to placate, the elector had taken as his mistress one of his wife's ladies-in-waiting, baroness von Degenfeld, whom his wife had ordered some time ago to sleep in the same room with her.[88] The elector had been courting the baroness for quite awhile without the electress suspecting anything. Indeed, the electress only perceived my brother Prince Rupert's infatuation with the baroness, for it was in Rupert's eyes that the electress wished to appear as the belle of her court. She discovered Rupert's desire in a love letter the prince had written to the baroness. The letter had no addressee on it, however, and the baroness, thinking that it was intended for the electress, gave it to her. Quite willing to believe the letter was meant for her, the electress said to Prince Rupert, "I don't know how I've given you cause for complaint or what I've done to make you doubt my affection." At her words the prince blushed to his ears, and his distress made her realize that the love letter had not been intended for her after all. Enraged, the electress loudly accused the baroness of coquetry, an allegation that was quite unfounded, since the girl had repelled Rupert's advances. In fact, Rupert had been the first to realize that he had a rival who was enjoying greater success. The electress was forced to come to the same conclusion herself when she awoke one night to find the elector sleeping next to the baroness. The uproar was tremendous. The elector had a difficult time keeping his mistress out of his wife's reach, though the electress did succeed in catching hold of the girl's little finger, which, in her fury, she bit to the bone. As her rage began to subside, her ladies-in-waiting begged her to restrain herself. The elector swore that the baroness had not consented to the liberty he had taken with her and that nothing improper had transpired between them. So the electress and the elector made peace with each other, with the electress promising not to mistreat the baroness.

---

88. Baroness Maria Louisa von Degenfeld (1634–77), daughter of Baron Christoph Martin von Degenfeld, a Swabian noble. In 1658 the elector took the baroness as his morganatic wife, resurrecting for her the ancient title of raugravine. She bore him thirteen children, eight of whom survived childhood and were also created raugraves and raugravines. At this stage, the electress is unaware of the elector's wandering eye and asks the baroness to share her bed chamber in order to deter him from exercising his conjugal rights.

Normalcy returned, with dancing and comedies serving to entertain the electress. Matters doubtless would have continued along this course had the electress not brought a world of trouble on herself by rummaging in the drawers of the baroness's dresser, where she found not only all the love letters but also the jewels the elector had given the baroness. Inclined to fits of anger even in the absence of such provocation, the electress was now furious and raised a frightening racket. She sent for my sister Elizabeth and me, while the baroness alerted the elector. On entering the room we were confronted with an extraordinary scene. The elector stood in front of his mistress to shield her, if necessary, from his wife's blows. The electress paced around the room holding her rival's jewels. Quaking with rage, she strode up to us and said, "So, princesses, here's the strumpet's reward. Shouldn't they belong to me?" Unable to repress my laughter at this question, I let out a guffaw that seemed to infect the electress, who also began to laugh. But her anger returned a moment later when the elector told her that she would have to return the jewels to their rightful owner. Scattering them around the room, she replied, "If they're not to be mine, then take them."[89] The elector escorted his mistress to his room and locked her in so that she would not come to any harm. Later, while the electress was having supper, the elector installed the baroness in a fine apartment directly above his own. He then had a trapdoor cut into the ceiling so that he could ascend a ladder to her chamber. The electress soon discovered this arrangement and would have ascended herself, knife in hand, had her ladies not restrained her.[90]

To avoid all this hubbub, the elector decided to go to Frankenthal for awhile where he could enjoy his mistress's company in peace.[91] It was

89. In a letter to her brother the landgrave of Hesse-Kassel, the electress provides a precise description of the jewels (including estimates of their value) and states that she returned them but kept the letters as evidence of her husband's plan to divorce her and marry the baroness. See Charles Lewis, *Schreiben des Kurfürsten Karl Ludwig von der Pfalz und der Seinen*, ed. Wilhelm Ludwig Holland (Tübingen: Litterarischer Verein, 1884), 16–17; letter dated March 17, 1657.

90. Köcher contends that key elements of the story (particularly: the electress's physical violence) are fabrications or exaggerations (Sophia, *Memoiren*, 19–20).

91. Frankenthal is about eighteen miles northwest of Heidelberg. Charles Lewis's mother did not approve of his arrangement: "I uill deal plainlie uith you as I ame bound by what I

here, as I mentioned, that Hammerstein found him and presented him with the duke's proposal: if the elector would bestow me on Duke Ernest Augustus, Duke George William of Hanover would pledge never to marry, to augment considerably his brother's income, and to settle on me the same dower that I would have received as his own wife. Furthermore, Ernest Augustus would, in accordance with the provisions of the Peace of Westphalia, be appointed the next bishop coadjutor of Osnabrück, where I would be able to live quite comfortably when he acceded to this post.[92] Meanwhile, I would be the chatelaine at Hanover, and my children, should God grant me any, would inherit all the Brunswick-Lüneburg possessions. This was because Duke Christian Lewis of Celle, the eldest brother, had been married for a long time with no heirs in sight, and Duke John Frederick was thought to be too fat to father any.[93] Hence, I would become matriarch to the family and the domains just as if I had married Duke George William.

ame to you to tell you that your open keeping that wench doth you no smale dishonneur to all persons of all conditions. If euerie bodie coulde quitt their husbands and uiues for their ill humours, there woulde be no smale disorder in the worlde" (Elizabeth, *Letters*, 273–74; letter dated July 12, 1658).

92. The Treaty of Westphalia established Catholic-Protestant alternation for the see of Osnabrück, with Protestant bishops to come from the House of Brunswick-Lüneburg. At the time of the negotiations for Sophia's marriage, the bishop was a Catholic (Count Franz Wilhelm von Wartemberg), so it was Brunswick's turn next. Besides Sophia's husband, future Protestant bishops included her youngest son Ernest Augustus (who held the post from 1715 to 1728) and King George III's second son Frederick Augustus (1764–1802). It was papal practice to excommunicate the Osnabrück canons who cast votes for a Protestant bishop even though, under the treaty, they had no choice. The canons would then file petitions and be quietly reinstated. Excommunication followed by reinstatement was how Rome maintained doctrinal consistency (canons cannot be allowed to elect heretics with impunity) while accepting the political order established by the Treaty of Westphalia. See Karl Otmar Freiherr von Aretin, *Das Alte Reich 1648–1806* (Stuttgart: Klett-Cotta, 1993–2000), 1: 47.

93. The oldest of the four brothers, Christian Lewis (1622–65), was married to Dorothea of Holstein-Glücksburg (1636–89). The couple remained childless. In 1668 Duke John Frederick (1625–79) married Benedicta Henrietta (1652–1730), the daughter of Sophia's brother Prince Edward (1625–63) and Anna Gonzaga (1616–84), by whom, his obesity notwithstanding, he had three daughters. Corpulence was his defining characteristic. Sophia's mother referred to him simply as "the fatt Duke of Lunebourg" (Elizabeth, *Letters*, 262).

Somewhat surprised by this proposal, the elector pointed out that there was no guarantee that the demonstrably irresolute Duke George William would keep his promise to remain a bachelor. If the duke was to change his mind again, there was no law to make him keep his word. Hammerstein assured the elector that he need have no apprehensions on this score, for the duke's debaucheries in Venice had rendered him incapable of begetting children, which was the reason he wanted his brother to marry me. The elector said that he would write to me and announce his decision after receiving my response. He then honored me with a letter in which he informed me of all that Hammerstein had told him, adding that for his part he preferred Duke Ernest Augustus and considered him both more amiable and more sensible than Duke George William. I replied that the only love I had felt was for a good establishment and that if I could obtain this I would have no difficulty trading the older brother for the younger. Since I looked on the elector as my father, I told him that I trusted his judgment entirely and would gladly do whatever he thought best.

[June 1658]

On receiving my answer the elector began negotiating the marriage contract with Hammerstein, who was the dukes' plenipotentiary in the matter. The articles were drawn up, and the elector permitted me to accept from Duke Ernest Augustus a present and the kind of letter usually written on such occasions.[94] I replied in the same terms, and nothing now remained but the wedding itself, which the duke, who strongly disliked pomp, wished to celebrate in Hanover. This, however, the elector would not hear of, declaring that the king of Sweden had come all the way to Heidelberg to marry our great-grandaunt.[95] He added that if the duke wanted to avoid ceremony he could come to Heidelberg by post chaise for the wedding and that afterward I could travel to Hanover with a retinue befitting my rank. The duke agreed to the first but not to the second of these proposals, saying that after I became his wife he would be responsible for my journey to Hanover

94. The articles are dated June 5, 1658, in Sophia, *Memoiren*, 59. According to Charles Lewis, they were actually signed on June 6 (Charles Lewis, *Schreiben*, 77).

95. King Charles IX of Sweden married Princess Anna Maria, daughter of Elector Lewis VI, in 1579.

and that he could accept the elector's offer of a retinue only as far as the Palatine frontier.

These arrangements having been completed and the time for my wedding set, the elector went to Frankfurt to attend the imperial diet. During this time poor Father Manari had anxiously been awaiting the arrival of a special courier from Parma bearing a letter empowering him to negotiate my marriage to his sovereign. But as time went on and no messenger appeared, he began to suspect that the duke of Parma had changed his mind. His anxiety grew when he read a story that the duke was going to marry a princess of Savoy. Though the gazette in question frequently printed false information, the report made a deep impression on the good friar. In this dejected state he drowned while bathing in the Neckar River. Whether it was by accident or design I cannot say. Italians have violent emotions, but they are also fondly attached to life. Some days after this misfortune the duke of Parma sent Count Landi to the elector, whom he found at Frankfurt, only to learn that he was too late.[96] Wishing still to see me, he came to Heidelberg to pay me a visit at which we exchanged copious civilities. With Manari drowned, he could not accuse anyone of having misled the poor friar.[97]

96. In a letter to baroness von Degenfeld dated May 20, 1658, Charles Lewis says it was Count Rosa-Scalco (not Count Landi) who represented the duke of Parma. He also admits that he had been unjust toward "that poor devil" Father Manari, whom he had viewed as a fraud. From Count Rosa-Scalco, Charles Lewis learned that one of the court of Parma's conditions was that Sophia and her entire entourage must convert to Catholicism (Charles Lewis, *Schreiben*, 74).

97. The duke of Parma's unbuoyant envoy was not the only person kept out of the matchmaking loop. On June 24, 1658, the queen of Bohemia writes huffily to Charles Lewis: "[A]s for this great secret of Duke Ernest Augustus it was onelie a secret to me, for ... euerie where it was known before I knew it .... I doe not at all dislike the match concerning the person, being no exceptions against him, for whome I haue a great esteeme, which is all I uill answere; since neither my opinion nor consent hath bene asked, I haue no more to say, but uish that it may proue for Sophies content and hapiness" (Elizabeth, *Letters*, 275). Three weeks later Sophia's brother Edward writes to Charles Lewis, expressing his surprise at her groom-swap, his concern that she will be less secure financially with the younger brother, and his disapprobation of the older brother's actions, which he calls those of a dishonorable man ("malhonest homme") (*Briefe der Kinder*, 139; letter dated July 12, 1658).

In Hanover, meanwhile, Duke George William's promises to his brother were being put into effect. The duke accordingly wrote (in his own hand), signed, and gave to Ernest Augustus a document in which he pledged never to marry.

Duke George William's renunciation of marriage

Having perceived the urgent necessity of considering how our house of this line may best be provided with heirs and perpetuated in the future, yet having been and remaining up to the present date both unable and unwilling to marry, I have induced my brother Ernest Augustus to declare that, on condition of receiving from me a renunciation of marriage, written and signed by my own hand in favor of himself and his male heirs, he is prepared forthwith and without delay to enter into holy matrimony and, as may be hoped, soon to bestow the blessing of heirs on our country and its people, as has been agreed and settled between him and myself. And whereas my brother Ernest Augustus, for the reasons mentioned above, has entered into a marriage contract with Her Highness Princess Sophia, which contract he intends shortly to fulfill, so I, for my part, not only on account of my word given and pledged, but also of my own free will and consent, desire to ratify and confirm the aforesaid conditions to my aforementioned brother and promise, so long as the said princess and brother continue in life and in the bonds of matrimony or, after their decease, their male heirs continue in life, that I neither will nor shall on any account enter into, much less carry out, any marriage contract with any person. I wish nothing else than to spend what remains of my life entirely in celibacy, with the intent that the male heirs of the aforementioned princess and my brother, in whose favor this renunciation is made, may attain and succeed to the sovereignty over one or both of our principalities. For the safer and truer assurance of all these conditions, I have,

by my own hand, written and signed this renunciation and sealed it with my seal and thereafter handed it
over with all due care to my brother's own charge and
keeping.

Hanover, April 21, 1658

George William

Duke of Brunswick and Lüneburg

Writing merely for my own enjoyment, I do not wish to go to the
trouble of translating the renunciation.[98] Suffice it to say that the duke
handed it to his brother with pleasure and would, I believe, with equal
pleasure have fulfilled the rest of his promises had he followed the
dictates of his own heart. His councilors, however, soon interfered
and set out to temper his generosity, persuading him to reduce the
yearly income promised to his brother by the not inconsiderable sum
of twenty thousand crowns. This proved to be yet another occasion for
this good prince to demonstrate his weakness and inconstancy. Duke
Ernest Augustus, being already engaged to me, was unable to contest
the matter.

---

98. Sophia left the renunciation in its original German.

Chapter 3
Hanover (1658–62)

Our wedding day arrived.[99] As had been agreed, Duke Ernest Augustus posted to Heidelberg with a small retinue.[100] Resolved to love him, I was delighted to find him lovable. The day of the ceremony I was dressed, in the German style, in white silver brocade, my flowing hair adorned with a large crown of the family diamonds. My train, which was of prodigious length, was borne by my four ladies-in-waiting, not by daughters of imperial counts, as is usually the practice at grand weddings.[101] I was led to the altar by two of my brothers, the elector and Prince Edward.[102] Duke Ernest Augustus was escorted by the little electoral prince and the palsgrave of Zweibrücken.[103] Adorned with ribbons in our armorial colors (blue and white for me, red and yellow for the groom), twenty-four gentlemen marched before us bearing lighted torches.[104] A cannon salvo was fired at the moment the pastor

99. October 17, 1658.

100. Mail carriages also carried paying passengers. Vestiges of this practice were *Postbüsse*, yellow omnibuses operated by the German Federal Postal Service that provided regional passenger and mail transport until the mid-1980s. Austria still has *Postbüsse* (at least in name), which are operated by the Austrian Federal Rail Service.

101. The ceremony was scheduled for six in the evening, although in a letter written that day Charles Lewis predicts that it will start late because Anne Carey, one of Sophia's ladies-in-waiting, is slow at dressing the bride. The next day he reports that the ceremony did not actually begin until nine in the evening and that finally marrying off Sophia greatly relieved not only his mind but also his treasury: the wedding cost him thirty thousand rixdollars (Charles Lewis, *Schreiben*, 91 and 93). He was spared the expense of Sophia's dowry, which, as stipulated by the Treaty of Westphalia, was paid by the emperor: "his Sacred Imperial Majesty (according to the Affection he has for the Palatinate House) has promis'd to ... each of the Sisters of ... Lord Charles Lewis, when they shall marry, ten thousand Rixdollars" (*Treaty of Westphalia*, Article XXIV, avalon.law.yale.edu/17th_century/westphal.asp).

102. Sophia's brother Edward had journeyed from Paris to Heidelberg for her wedding, arriving in mid-August and departing at the end of October 1658 (Charles Lewis, *Schreiben*, 87 and 95).

103. Frederick of Zweibrücken (1616–61). Although Sophia refers to him as a duke, his title is actually palsgrave.

104. In heraldically correct terms, the colors are azure and silver for the House of Palatine, gules and gold for the House of Brunswick (Sophia, *Mémoires*, 73). A teary-eyed Charlotte,

joined us in matrimony. We were then placed across from each other under baldachins, with the elector under his own, for the singing of the *Te Deum*. After the ceremony we were escorted to our rooms, where I renounced all claim to the Palatinate. The elector's daughter would later make the same renunciation when she became duchess of Orleans. Supper was then served at an oval table. The duke and I sat at the center, with the elector on our right and the electoral prince on our left. Then came the elector's daughter Elizabeth Charlotte and the palsgravine of Zweibrücken.[105] After supper we danced in the German fashion, with the princes bearing lighted torches and dancing in front of and behind the bride and groom.

A few days after our wedding the duke posted back to Hanover, returning by the same means by which he had come, except that in the interim his feelings for me had undergone an unexpected change. As for me, my affection for him far exceeded the esteem his good qualities had always commanded, and I now felt for him all that sincere passion can inspire.

My husband swiftly sent a large entourage, with Hammerstein in charge, to convey me to Hanover. When the time came for my departure the elector did me the honor of coming along—with his entire court—as far as Weinheim.[106] On parting from him I shed tears that would have flowed more freely had my heart not been elsewhere. Besides, I hoped to see him again from time to time and, in the interim, to be honored with letters from him.

Charles Lewis's spurned wife, watched the wedding procession from a window (Charles Lewis, *Schreiben*, 93).

105. Anna Juliana, wife of Palsgrave Frederick.

106. Eleven miles north of Heidelberg; Sophia departed on October 25, 1658.

CAROLVS LVDOVICVS DEI GRATIA COMES
PALATINVS RHENI.SACRI ROMANI IMPERY
ARCHIDAPIFER ET ELECTOR.DVXBAVARIÆ etc.
B. Moncornet excu cum Priuilegie

Seventeenth-century print of Sophia's brother, Elector Charles Lewis

On leaving my homeland I entered the domains of the elector of Mainz, by whose orders baron von Hoheneck entertained me.[107] We then traveled to Darmstadt, whose landgrave was my husband's uncle.[108] Accompanied by his wife the landgravine and his large family, the landgrave did me the honor of coming to meet me well outside of town.[109]

Etiquette was strictly observed at the landgrave's court. The young princesses, for instance, did not dare to ride in a carriage with married ladies, which meant that I traveled with the landgravine and her daughter-in-law. Imperial countesses, in turn, did not dare to ride with the princesses and had separate carriages of their own, as did the other noble ladies. The same protocol was observed as we watched a fireworks display said to be the handiwork of the young landgrave, whose hands indeed bore its marks.[110] Each rank of nobility had its own appointed room from which to view the pyrotechnics, and my ladies were not pleased to find themselves so far from me. Still greater was their surprise on seeing the landgravine's ladies-in-waiting observe the etiquette of their court by lining up to form a cordon beside the halberdiers guarding the door to my room. My ladies had no intention of copying them.

The day after my arrival I paid my respects to the landgravine. In her room was a sideboard on which was displayed a collection of bowls and glasses, as one would expect of a daughter of the elector of Saxony.[111] In the evening she danced a ballet with her children, at which I was told not to be surprised, as her mother had done the same in her generation. On the third day I left this court with the same ceremonies that had attended my arrival, feeling highly pleased at all the honors I had received.

107. Johann Philip von Schönborn, archbishop and elector of Mainz (1605–73).

108. George II, landgrave of Hesse-Darmstadt (1605–61), whose sister, Anne Eleanor (1601–59), was Duke Ernest Augustus's mother.

109. Landgravine Sophia Eleanor, daughter of Elector John George I of Saxony.

110. Landgrave George II's son, the future Landgrave Lewis VI of Hesse-Darmstadt.

111. Saxony was, and is, renowned for glass and porcelain, although manufacture of the latter did not begin until the early eighteenth century.

I then went to Frankfurt, where nothing remarkable occurred, the mayor merely doing his customary duty. Leaving Frankfurt I reentered the domains of the landgrave of Hesse-Darmstadt, who saw to it that I was properly received—indeed, he paid the costs of my journey—as I passed through Friedberg, Butschbach, and Giessen and the rest of his magnificent country. Leaving his territory I entered that of the landgrave of Hesse-Kassel who had me received at the frontier and escorted to his capital. He, his wife, and all his court received me outside the town, but nothing out of the ordinary was done for my amusement.[112]

On leaving Kassel I entered Duke George William of Hanover's domains. I spent the night at Minden, where the white bread was so hard and unpalatable that I regretted not having taken along my own baker. To my great relief I discovered a few days later that I had no need for one after all, when, at the duke of Celle's behest, I was entertained sumptuously by Mr. Oeynhausen, the bailiff of Grubenhagen, in a town where the bread was excellent.[113]

As I approached the town of Hanover the four brothers—along with a huge retinue and a magnificent cavalcade—did me the honor of coming out to meet me. I alighted to greet them, after which we all got into my carriage. I entered Hanover to the sound of cannon and was received at the carriage door by my mother-in-law the duchess dowager, the duchess of Celle, and the wife of Duke Anthony Ulric of Brunswick-Wolfenbüttel.[114] My husband took my hand and led me to a very fine room that the duke of Hanover had had decorated for me. All the dukes and duchesses did me the honor of escorting me there.

112. William VI (1629–63) and his wife Hedwig Sophia (1623–83), daughter of Elector George William of Brandenburg. William VI, the brother of Elector Charles Lewis's spurned wife Charlotte, was furious with the elector and had contemplated challenging him to a duel. Van der Cruysse rightly surmises that enmity between the two families was why the landgrave spared all effort to entertain Sophia (Sophia, *Mémoires*, 76).

113. Heinrich Hermann von Oeynhausen (?–1671).

114. Sophia arrived on November 19, 1658. The duchesses in the order mentioned: Dowager Duchess Anne Eleanor (1601–59); Duchess Dorothea of Celle (1636–89), born a princess of Holstein-Glücksburg; and Duchess Elizabeth Juliana of Brunswick-Wolfenbüttel (1634–1704), born a princess of Holstein-Norburg. Anthony Ulric (1633–1714).

The next day we had a wedding party under a canopy of gilded copper, a contrivance I greatly admired, having never seen anything like it. In the evening we danced, and on the following day I was made to do the honors as chatelaine by accompanying the princesses beyond the city gates on their departure.

I take pleasure in remembering how we rejoiced to be left to ourselves after all the princes and princesses had gone and how much passion my husband showed toward me. Having married purely out of self-interest, he had expected to feel indifferent. But now his sentiments made me think that he would love me for as long as he lived. As for myself, I so worshiped him that I felt lost when he was out of my sight. We were never apart, and my good friends saw nothing of me except in the evenings and mornings, an arrangement by no means to their liking. This vexation preyed on Madam Withypoll, now the widow of an excellent husband whose loss she felt deeply. Her sister Miss Carey, now no longer young, thought that she ought to take a husband to avoid being branded an old maid. Because my heart now belonged solely to my husband, and I liked only what he liked, I had no regrets about allowing Madam Withypoll to return to The Hague and Miss Carey to marry baron von Bonstetten.[115]

I could see that my husband and Duke George William of Hanover were close friends. To please the former, I paid much greater attention to the latter than to their two other brothers. He took part in all our amusements (cards, hunting, and walks) and spared no pains to make himself agreeable to me. My husband, who knew his brother better than I did, fell prey to a jealousy of which I was wholly unaware. One day the duke of Hanover felt ill, and my husband took me to see him. I seated myself at the duke of Hanover's bedside to talk to him, while my husband sat down at a table and began leafing through a book. I directed the conversation to the duke's favorite topic—Italy—and said, among other things, that he must wish he were there. Out of politeness

115. Franz Ludwig von Bonstetten (1629–82), a Swiss nobleman who served as an officer in the Hanoverian and Palatine armies, as military governor of Germersheim (a fortress on the left bank of the Rhine fifteen miles southwest of Heidelberg), and as Palatine envoy to the coronation of Charles II in London.

the duke replied that, with me now in Hanover, he did not desire to be anywhere else. Laughing, I quoted the words of a song that went, "If you can't have what you love, love what you have." My husband, who heard these words but who had not been listening to the conversation that had preceded them, thought I was trying to say that I had had to content myself with him because I had not been able to marry the duke of Hanover. This notion distressed him terribly, and when we returned to his rooms he refused to speak to me. I tried to ask him what was wrong, but he would not reply, reducing me to utter despair. I wished I were dead, as life without his love would be unbearable. Finally, touched by my tears, which showed him that my heart really did belong to him alone, he told me the cause of his distress. I proved to him that he had been mistaken, and we made up.

The two brothers, who were always talking of the delights of Italy, persuaded me to accompany them there by post chaise in the middle of winter. We had been gone only one day when I realized that I was unable to go further. I was obliged to return alone to Hanover while the two dukes continued their journey. Surrounded by so many uninteresting people and disconsolate without my husband, I was unable to restrain my tears. Ashamed of such weakness, I avoided appearing in public and only took pleasure in receiving my husband's letters. The duke of Hanover also wrote and surprised me by complaining that on taking leave of him I had withdrawn my hand just as he was about to kiss it, a reproach I considered too ridiculous to merit a response. To my great joy I learned from my husband that my solitude would be of short duration. He proposed to meet me in Herzberg at the residence of his mother, to whom I was to pay my respects while awaiting his arrival.[116] I was received very kindly by this most excellent princess, who was tenderly attached to her children and now counted me among them. Impatient for the dukes' arrival, she sent Mr. Stechinelli to meet them and learn what news they had.[117] As it turned out, the messenger only slightly outpaced the message, and great was the duchess's joy— and even greater was mine—as we heard in the distance Stechinelli

116. Herzberg am Harz is located sixty miles southeast of Hanover.

117. Giovanni Francesco Maria Capellini, known as Stechinelli, an Italian gentleman employed at the court of Hanover.

blowing his post horn to announce the arrival of the dukes, who were right behind him. I ran to meet my husband, quite forgetting to greet his brother the duke of Hanover, and my husband had to remind me that etiquette required me to greet his brother first. My faux pas ought to have shown my husband the sincerity of my affection for him. But jealousy blinds people to the truth and makes them see chimeras, as events would later prove.

[April 1659]

After spending several very pleasant days at Herzberg we returned to Hanover. From there we went to the dukes' hunting retreat at Hümmling where we enjoyed ourselves immensely. The duke of Celle, my husband's oldest brother, and Prince Lewis of East Friesland were also there.[118] The duke of Hanover and my husband saw a great deal of the duke of Celle during our stay in Hümmling, but they were not as close to him as they were to each other. The duke of Celle was a drinker, although this was truly his only fault. As for our two dukes, they were inseparable. I was like the third wheel of this delightful—albeit unstable—conveyance. After the three of us spent all day together enjoying ourselves at cards or on a walk, my duke had a companion for the night, whereas his brother did not. I do not know whether the duke of Hanover had been expecting a more satisfying arrangement. After all, in Italy when one brother marries, the others say, "Siamo maritati" ('We're married'). Be that as it may, one day the duke of Hanover went so far as to tell me that he heartily regretted giving me to his brother. I cut the conversation short by pretending not to hear what he had said.

My husband, who knew his brother better than I did, easily read his thoughts. Moreover, my husband's own amorous conquests had given him a poor opinion of women. He feared that I would not be able to resist his brother, in whom he saw many fine qualities that in my opinion were not as great as his own. Given the choice between the two brothers, I would have picked my husband every time, for I would have been the clear loser in the other match. Nevertheless, my husband convinced himself that I was attracted to his brother, a partiality

118. Prince Enno Lewis of East Friesland (1632–60).

I had never felt. As my husband's mistaken notion could only arise from his ardent affection for me, I loved him all the more for it and believed that my conduct would soon convince him of his error. I found pleasure even in the precautions he took to guard me. For when it was time for his afternoon nap he would seat me in a chair opposite him and place his feet on its armrests so that I could not escape him while he dozed. This would last for hours on end and would surely have bored anyone who loved him less than I did.

I did all in my power to conceal my husband's jealousy from his brother, for fear of causing ill-feeling between them. Despite my efforts, the duke of Hanover plainly saw that my manner toward him was now more distant. One morning he came to my room, as he usually did, before I was dressed. This time, however, I felt very uneasy because my husband had made it clear that these visits had begun to displease him. To get the duke of Hanover out of the room I told him that I was going to get dressed. He left thinking he would be able to come right back in. But when he tried to open the door he found it locked. This drove him to despair, for he believed that I was sacrificing him to his brother. He reproached me for making him lose his best friend in the world. I responded by assuring him that I had not said anything to my husband, yet reminded him of my husband's temperament; that if he did not want to ruin my life, he must rid himself of his supposed infatuation with me; that my manner toward him would never have changed if his own behavior had remained within acceptable bounds; but that the reckless things he persisted in saying to me had made it necessary for me to limit our encounters little by little so that others would not divine the reasons behind my actions. My words calmed him with regard to his brother but upset him with regard to everything else. His ardor was undiminished, and my husband's jealousy grew despite all my efforts to convince him otherwise. I now hardly ever saw the duke of Hanover except during meals. To put it more accurately, I was with him every day without actually seeing him, having schooled myself to avoid looking at him, for at the slightest glance my husband would accuse me of making eyes at his brother. Indeed, I can say truthfully that for years the duke of Hanover escorted me from my chamber to dinner without my seeing anything more than his shadow on the floor.

My husband, at last becoming fed up with the strained atmosphere of our life at the duke of Hanover's residence, proposed to take a tour of Italy with his brother, while I might have the pleasure of visiting my mother at The Hague until their return. He assured me, moreover, that I had completely cured him of his jealousy.

[November 1659]

Because the duke of Hanover planned to go by way of Holland, I remained in Hanover for a fortnight after my husband's departure, something I would not otherwise have done. My hope was that the duke of Hanover would have left Holland before my arrival. But not only had he not yet left, he received me at Leiden and put me in a very difficult situation by overwhelming me with unwelcome attention. Not really knowing what to do, I decided to entreat him, for the love of God, to depart at once unless he wished to make me the most miserable person in the world. He was good enough to put my mind at ease by doing as I had bid him and continuing his journey to Italy, although he acted as if I should be deeply obliged for his complaisance.

After his departure I had a very pleasant time with my mother the queen, who graciously expressed her joy at having me near her again. I had also taken along my niece, the Electoral Princess Elizabeth Charlotte, now duchess of Orleans, on whom the queen doted, perhaps in part because the princess was the only one of her grandchildren she had ever seen.[119]

---

119. In a letter to Charles Lewis dated November 17, 1659, the queen of Bohemia writes of Elizabeth Charlotte, known in the family as Liselotte, "She is verie prettie and you may beleeue it … , for you know I care not much for children, but I neuer saw none I like so well as her, she is so good natured and wittie, all the Hagh is in loue uith her …. I can assure you I loue her extremelie, as well as her Aunt [Sophia] doth but not so fonde, for she is monstrous fonde of her" (Elizabeth, *Letters*, 290). Elizabeth Charlotte stayed with her aunt Sophia from June 1659 to April 1663.

Because I was pregnant I was obliged to return to Hanover in the eighth month of my pregnancy.[120] My husband arrived a few days later, greatly delighting me by his return. The duke of Hanover having chosen to go to Holland until I had given birth, our tranquility was undisturbed. When the child came, my suffering was so great (I was in labor for three days and three nights) that it was feared that I or the child must die. My husband's distress was so keen and his tenderness to me so touching that I took heart for his sake to bear the pain. Great was the joy of my husband and of all the duchy's subjects when our son was born alive. He was baptized without ceremony and named George Lewis after two of his uncles.[121]

The duke of Hanover returned. He believed that his absence had cured my husband and sought to reassure him further by speaking incessantly of a Miss Wattinsvain whom he had met in The Hague and as whose admirer he posed. He was a bad actor, however, and my husband's slumbering jealousy awoke with fresh fury, which so distressed the duke of Hanover that he fell ill. I did not dare either visit him or ask how he was doing. As we seldom dislike those who love us, I must confess that I felt sorry for him, for he had little companionship in his family. His physician advised him to take the Pyrmont waters. My husband, like his brother, had a bad spleen and felt that the waters would do him good too. So in the end we all went to Bad Pyrmont together.[122] Because the brothers stayed in different houses, all went well for me. The dukes decided to spend the winter in Italy and for me to spend it in Heidelberg. This plan was carried out, and on their return they retrieved me from Heidelberg.

---

120. While visiting her mother in The Hague, Sophia was apparently reluctant to jinx her pregnancy by admitting to it. The queen of Bohemia writes to Charles Lewis, "I beleeue some six months hence she [Sophia] uill make you an Oncle, but God for bid it shoulde be beleeued, for her ladieship [Sophia] doth not beleeue it" (Elizabeth, *Letters*, 290–91, letter dated November 17, 1659). Two weeks later, the queen reports that Sophia is starting to show, or, as she puts it, "to be in ernest bigg" (Elizabeth, *Letters*, 293).

121. The son, born on June 7, 1660, is the future King George I of Great Britain and Ireland (d. 1727); his namesakes are his uncles George William and Charles Lewis.

122. A spa since the sixteenth century, Bad Pyrmont is located between Detmold and Hameln on the Emmer River.

But first I ought to explain that immediately after the dukes' departure I went to Heidelberg with my infant son, whom I was very glad to have as an object of my affection during my husband's absence. As I approached Heidelberg the elector honored me with a state reception and permitted all the schools of the university to offer me an oration in expression of their joy at my return to my homeland. I was equally delighted to see again so beloved a brother and to find his affection for me undiminished. He was now entirely separated from his wife and still attached to baroness von Degenfeld. I visited the former, and he pressed me to visit the latter, which put me in an awkward position. I feared it might be taken to mean that I approved of my brother's divorce.

The English people, and the royal family in particular, observe the first day of March by eating in the evening a leek they have worn in their hats throughout the day, in memory of a battle the Prince of Wales won while so attired. On this March 1 the elector arranged to send leeks to all the English residents, baroness von Degenfeld, her children, and me. He invited me to come and eat mine in his rooms, where I met his mistress and the prettiest little son and daughter in the world. I greeted them all and fussed over the children, for they were quite charming little creatures.[123] However, I avoided further contact with them for fear of giving the electress cause for complaint and of possibly eliciting my husband's disapproval. For the baroness had not yet attained the standing that she later would have, and the electress had not yet entirely given up her position, as she afterward did by retiring to Kassel.[124]

[Spring 1661]

As planned, around Easter the dukes arrived in Heidelberg to retrieve me. The elector lent us a pinnace in which to sail down the Rhine. The duke of Hanover slept in another boat. We had chosen this mode of conveyance because I was pregnant with my second child. We reached Rotterdam just as my mother the queen was about to embark for

123. As of this date Charles Lewis had three children by baroness von Degenfeld: Charles Lewis (October 15, 1658), Caroline (December 29, 1659), and Louisa (January 25, 1661).

124. The electress left Heidelberg to return to her family in Kassel in June 1663.

England. This good princess gave me her blessing for the last time, as I had the sorrow of losing her the following year.[125] The duke of Hanover took us to The Hague so that we could go to the theater and admire the town's belles. We then returned to our usual life at Hanover; that is, I returned, for my husband's sake, to watching where I looked, which I did willingly as proof of my affection for him.

The duke of Hanover, however, saw that I conversed easily with everyone but him. He then got it into his head that I was in love with a certain Mr. Villiers whom he considered the most appealing gentleman at his court. In a fit of jealous anger he denounced me to my husband, who laughed at my supposed infatuation and later said to me in private, "I'd never suspect you of falling in love with anyone but my brother." A person with a disposition different from mine would have had a difficult time living with two such jealous men. The one, however, was so dear to me that I looked on his unmerited reproaches as endearments, being convinced that they could be prompted only by the warmth of his passion for me. The other, considering himself slighted, transferred his attentions to Miss von Landas, one of my ladies-in-waiting, a development for which I was truly thankful as long it lasted.[126] But his ardor proved to be fueled by straw and was consequently of short duration.

At this time I gave birth to my second son, whom we named Frederick Augustus after his uncle Duke John Frederick and Duke Augustus of Brunswick-Wolfenbüttel.[127] My husband was by my side throughout my confinement. After a fortnight he had me moved out of my room into his, where he asked me to remain throughout the rest of my lying-in. I was perfectly happy to grant his wish, though I caught a cold

---

125. The queen of Bohemia died on February 13, 1662.

126. The daughter of Johann Friedrich von Landas, Palatine privy councilor and grand steward.

127. Frederick Augustus was born on October 3, 1661. Augustus, duke of Brunswick-Dannenberg and Brunswick-Wolfenbüttel (1579–1666), was also known as Augustus the Younger. His collection of books, which at his death numbered 180,000 volumes, formed the basis of the famous Wolfenbüttel library, of which Enlightenment dramatist and theorist Gotthold Ephraim Lessing (1729–81) was later librarian.

there that so undermined my health that it was a long time before I was able to bear living children.[128]

Meanwhile, the duke of Hanover amused himself with traveling, and during his absence my life was perfectly tranquil. My husband sent for the Hamburg theater troupe, and I still remember their performance of a play about Doctor Faust who was carried off by the Devil.

News reached my husband that the bishop of Osnabrück had, like Faust, gone to another world.[129] I was delighted, since my husband's accession to this dignity would take me away from Hanover and the awkward situation there. The duke of Hanover returned from his journey, and my husband made all the necessary preparations for his grand entry to his bishopric. It was judged unfitting that I attend my husband's investiture, and he judged it unwise to leave me in Hanover with his brother. He consequently arranged to send me to Celle to stay with his sister-in-law for a few days before joining him. I set off from Celle, following his instructions to the letter. On my way I had to pass through a town called Sulingen belonging to the duke of Hanover, who had written me a note asking my permission to come and take leave of me there. I found his note and request equally irritating, as he ought to have known. Replying that if he had the slightest consideration for me he would refrain from coming, I continued my journey without further interruption. My husband did me the honor of coming out to meet me as I approached Iburg, his new residence, which I liked extremely. The palace too was so well furnished that I was quite satisfied with it.[130]

[October 1662]

The first thing we did was to find a husband for Miss Landas, whose reputation had been somewhat tarnished by her liaison with the duke of Hanover. To return her honor to its former luster, my husband set her up with an old attendant of his named von Lenthe, who was a

128. Sophia had miscarriages in 1661 and 1664.

129. See footnote 92; the bishop died on December 1, 1661.

130. Bad Iburg is eight miles south of Osnabrück.

perfect gentleman, though hardly quick-witted.[131] The bride, however, was quite pleased with the groom and through good conduct and cleverness was an excellent wife to him. Their concord served to refute as ill founded the salacious gossip about her and the duke. Invited to the wedding by my husband, the duke of Hanover viewed the proceedings without betraying the slightest sign of regret. The ceremony gave us the opportunity to see the bishopric's beauties, who turned out to be not very alluring.

131. Presumably Kurt Wilhelm von Lenthe, equerry to the dukes of Hanover. His father, Jobst Heimart von Lenthe (1590–1649), had also served the House of Brunswick as equerry.

Chapter 4
Italy (1664–65)

The holy bonds of matrimony had not changed my husband's gallant disposition. He grew bored of possessing the same thing and found a reclusive life irksome. He felt like going to Venice and believed that he would enjoy the trip more was I to accompany him. I would gladly have followed him to the ends of the earth, so I raised no objection. He went on ahead, having left me at Heidelberg where I was to spend the winter and proceed to Venice after Easter.

My husband wanted my court—or more precisely, the beauty of my ladies-in-waiting—to cause a stir in Italy. He therefore desired me, as I passed through Kassel on the way to Heidelberg, to see two ladies-in-waiting who were in the service of the princess of Tarentum.[132] One of the ladies, named d'Olbreuse, had been much praised for her beauty by the duke of Hanover. The other lady, named de La Motte, was recommended by Duke John Frederick, although the princess of Tarentum found her too prim and proper and did not really care for her. If I thought them worth the trouble I was instructed to take them with me to Venice. On reaching Kassel, however, I found that they and the princess of Tarentum were gone. The two ladies soon returned, albeit without their princess, so I was obliged to take Miss de La Motte solely on Duke John Frederick's recommendation. Finding her a most satisfactory person, I never had cause to regret my decision. Miss d'Olbreuse refused to come with me, preferring to follow her mistress to Holland. Duke George William also went to Holland and appeared to be much smitten with Miss d'Olbreuse.

A miscarriage detained me at Heidelberg. As soon as I had recovered we started for Italy. The elector, honoring me with his company as far as Bretten, feared that such a long journey might be bad for my

---

132. Princess Emilia (1626–93), born a princess of Hesse-Kassel. I confess to reordering, for clarity's sake, several sentences in this paragraph.

health.[133] So great, however, was my impatience to see my husband again that I regretted that my large caravan could not go faster.

I passed through the duke of Württemberg's beautiful domains and then the town of Ulm. In Augsburg we had to stop to have the axles of our carriages shortened for the narrow Alpine roads. To while away the time I went to a church to behold a miraculous eucharistic wafer that was said to have been transformed into human flesh. I saw that it was just a piece of red wax and said so to the priest who was displaying it with ostentatious piety. He replied that I was correct but that the flesh was *inside* the wax. This one had to take on faith since it was impossible to see.

[April 1664]

With all now ready to continue the journey, I set off and reached Innsbruck incognito. My lodgings were just beyond the town. From here, my ladies-in-waiting and I walked back to the town to look it over. A lunatic standing at the palace gate pointed out the archduchesses, one of whom has since become empress.[134] As well as one could judge from a distance, the archduchesses seemed quite lovely.

That is all I remember of what took place between Augsburg and Bronzolo, which I reached in nine days, except that on the way the carriage tipped over several times, which so terrified my ladies that Miss von Keppel went nearly the entire distance on foot, while Miss de La Motte rode a horse. Because I traveled in a sedan chair, I ran no risk of mishap. Our journey took us through Trent, where the council made such a stir.[135] At Bronzolo I had the great joy of being reunited with my husband.[136] In addition to his own retinue, he was accompa-

133. Bretten is twenty-five miles south of Heidelberg.

134. Claudia Felicitas (1653–76), daughter of Ferdinand Charles, archduke of Austria and prince of Tyrol (1628–62), became the second wife of Emperor Leopold I (1640–1705) in 1673.

135. The nineteenth ecumenical council was held in Trent between 1545 and 1563. On September 17, 1562, the council reaffirmed transubstantiation along with a number of other doctrines.

136. Sophia has her itinerary wrong: Trent is south of Bronzolo (Sophia, *Mémoires*, 82).

nied by two Venetian noblemen, Giovanni Morosini and Leonardo Loredan, and by Felice Machiavelli and Dr. Tack.[137] My entourage was considerably more numerous. Seldom indeed has so brilliant an incognito been seen. Accompanying me were the grand equerry Mr. von Harling, Mr. von Lenthe, Chevalier von Sandis, and Messrs. Droit and von Nehm; Madam von Lenthe and the Misses von Keppel, de La Motte, and von Ahlefeld; as well as my whole ordinary household, even including Remo and the violin band.[138] My ladies and women occupied four carriages, the gentlemen rode, and everyone else traveled in carts.

With this huge caravan we arrived incognito at Verona. No sooner had the news of my arrival spread through the city than the magistrates sent refreshments, and a large number of ladies came to see me. I was prepossessed by the idea that only angels of beauty populated the country that time and again had proved irresistible to the Brunswick dukes, from whom I had heard so much about the ladies of Italy. Great, therefore, was my surprise to see frightful faces which only magnificent attire rendered tolerable. But as soon as the ladies spoke I was delighted by their wit and charming manners. They took me to see a lovely garden and a very ancient amphitheater. They then took me to a kind of marketplace where, exposed to sun and dust, the ladies promenaded every afternoon, more delighted to converse with gentlemen than distressed about ruining their complexions.[139]

137. Otto Tachenius or Tackenius (early 1600s–ca. 1670), an itinerant apothecary from Westphalia, earned a doctorate in medicine at the University of Padua in the late 1640s. Around 1650 he settled in Venice where he developed a flourishing practice thanks to a universal elixir of his own invention known as viper salts. Tachenius was an early proponent of the chemical origins of all physiological and pathological phenomena and published a number of books in support of his theory (*Allgemeine*, 37: 340).

138. Anna Dorothea von Ahlefeld later married Otto Grote (1636–93), a Hanover privy councilor. Wilhelm, Ritter von Sandis was one of Sophia's chamberlains and later a Hanover councilor and bailiff of Lemförde, a town about sixty miles west of Hanover. Christian Friedrich von Harling was Duke Ernest Augustus's grand equerry and married to Anna Katharina von Offeln, the governess of Sophia's niece Elizabeth Charlotte.

139. In addition to Verona's famous amphitheater, the sights Sophia saw were likely the Giardino Giusti and the Piazza della Erbe (Sophia, *Mémoires*, 88).

From there we went to Vicenza, whose ladies, wishing to surpass the civility of the Veronese, all gathered outside the city gates to welcome me. They were attended by the town's numerous and polite noblemen, with Count Gabriel Pozzo at their head.[140] Among the belles, Countess Auriga bore the palm and would have been something of a marvel in her native Verona. The nobility of Vicenza neglected nothing for my amusement, even permitting masked encounters. I was taken to a lovely garden where Madam Legge, the chief magistrate's wife, was waiting for me disguised by a mask, for she did not dare meet me under normal terms owing to the difference in our ranks. But this did not prevent her from flaunting her charms and giving my husband the pleasure of acting as her admirer in the Italian style. We later saw her in the same costume at a ball where I learned to dance, or rather to march, to the music of violins. Your partner, while leading you around the room by the hand, is obliged to say all the flattering things he can think of. I had the pleasure of hearing myself compared to the stars.

On the next day I was taken to the Campo Marzio, a fine meadow where the ladies sit in carriages lined up single file while the gentlemen walk among them, conversing with the ladies through the carriage windows and displaying their wit by improvising sonnets, at which Giambattista Fracassan was quite marvelous. They then showed me the beautiful amphitheater, where, in my honor, two couples performed dances called the Mustard and the Marionette, for which they received thunderous applause. Everyone cried, "Bene, bene! Viva, viva!" This showed me that Italian ladies have the good fortune of being able to render themselves pleasant with very little effort.[141]

I then traveled by water to Venice, which I reached late in the evening. My husband asked me whether I found the city beautiful. I did not dare say no, though it made a profoundly melancholy impression on

---

140. The manuscript reads Porto; Pozzo is an emendation suggested by Köcher (Sophia, *Memoiren*, 73).

141. The Campo Marzio, outside Vicenza's old city wall, is now opposite its main train station; the amphitheater is the Olympic Theater, begun by Andrea Palladio (1518–80) and completed by Vicenzo Scamozzi in 1584.

me.[142] For all I saw was water and all I heard was "Premi e stae," the cry of the gondoliers as they guide their black, coffin-like craft.[143] For my amusement I was taken to see some nuns (who were only interested in men) and churches (which served primarily as lovers' rendezvous). The Grand Canal pleased me most, for there one can enjoy fresh air without the annoyance of dust. But there was no conversation whatsoever, for the gondolas glided by so swiftly that one could hardly distinguish the beauty of the ladies who occupied them. Every now and then I therefore had a gondola stopped beside my own.

About all that I did in their city the Venetians remarked, "È la moda Francese" ('It's French fashion'). This emboldened me to dance in the streets in the evenings with my husband and my ladies, a French liberty that was loudly applauded by some Venetian nobles who watched us. Still more extravagantly, we tilted at the ring on the Lido before a crowd of over one hundred thousand people.[144] We dressed like actresses in gold and silver brocade and were adorned with many feathers, and each lady was attended by a knight-errant. The calashes were decorated with gilded copper in lightweight embossing instead of heavy carvings.

My husband had brought along a Sicilian cavalier named d'Artale who was also an accomplished poet.[145] Dressed in a diamond-encrusted coat on loan from the opera house, he entered the field of play and is-

142. In a letter to Charles Lewis dated May 9, 1664, Sophia describes Venice as "one of the most beautiful cities in the world" (Sophia, *Briefwechsel*, 67, my translation).

143. The manuscript reads "Premi e stali." The emendation, a shortened version of "Premi il remo sulla forcola e stae," a call for other gondoliers to make way, is suggested by Van der Cruysse (Sophia, *Mémoires*, 90).

144. In a letter to Charles Lewis dated July 4, 1664, Sophia estimates that there were only about two thousand people in the crowd (Sophia, *Briefwechsel*, 72).

145. Giuseppe d'Artale (1628–79), soldier of fortune and poet. He wrote the lyrics to a number of the pieces in *Arie*, the eighth volume of vocal music by the Italian composer Barbara Strozzi (1619–77). Published in Venice in 1664, *Arie* is dedicated to "Altezza Serenissima di Madama Sofia, Dvchessa di Bransvich e Lvnebvrg, nata Principessa Elettorale Palatina." The first piece in the collection, "Ciele, Stelle, Deitàdi ['Heavens, Stars, Deities']," is an encomium to Sophia's beauty, grace, and wit. Barbara Strozzi, *Opera Ottava: Arie & cantate*, La Risonanza. Fabio Bonizzoni (Glossa 921503, 2001), CD booklet. It may be the

sued a challenge (in verse form) to the other cavaliers. Though he tilted too badly ever to touch the ring, he was enthusiastically applauded by the onlookers, who, accustomed only to their gondolas, regarded this novel competition as something miraculous. Our ladies also made a sensation that day and gained many admirers, both of their persons and their skill. I would have been mortified to remain the only lady unattended by a cicisbeo in a place where it is the fashion to have one, so my husband chose for me a procurator named Soranzo, a very harmless person.[146] Madam von Lenthe had Count Durini; Miss von Keppel, who flirted with everyone who looked at her, had several cavaliers; Giovanni Morosini was Miss de La Motte's admirer; and blond, fair-skinned Miss von Ahlefeld charmed all. In the evenings we laughed over the follies of the day, and it was only my husband who profited from this gallantry and whose attachments were real. Duke John Frederick was also an assiduous amorist. He and his suite were lodged in our palazzo at my husband's expense, although this did not prevent him from having a little house outside the city for his assignations.[147]

Italy's customs disagreed with me as much as its air. I sank into melancholy and suffered from an ailment not uncommon to travelers: everything I ate passed straight through me. This so weakened me that I frequently fainted. I also suffered from a low-grade fever which sometimes confined me to my bed. Duke John Frederick had arranged a concert to entertain the ladies, but they refused to attend without me. For his sake I made a great effort and went, accompanied by Countess Serini and her daughter, since pursuant to a senate decree the Venetian ladies were not allowed to visit me.[147a]

text of this aria that Sophia remembers when she writes that during the dance in Vicenza she was "compared to the stars."

146. Cicisbeo: a cavalier servant who chaperones ladies. "This supernumerary slave, who stays/Close to the lady as a part of dress/His is no sinecure, as you may guess;/Coach, servant, gondola, he goes to call,/And carries fan and tippet, gloves and shawl" (George Gordon Byron, *Beppo, a Venetian Story*. Boston: Monroe & Francis, 1818, 15).

147. The Brunswick palazzo for this visit was the Casa Fascari. See Maria Kroll, *Sophie, Electress of Hanover: A Personal Portrait* (London: Gollancz, 1973), 100.

147a. Van der Cruysse attributes the decree to the senate's wariness about Venetians developing relationships with high-ranking foreign visitors that could have undesirable political consquences (Sophia, *Mémoires*, 91).

This did not prevent the wife of a procurator named Dolfine from defying the senate by coming aboard my gondola as it plied the Grand Canal (an act for which her husband had to make copious excuses to the Venetian authorities). Madam Dolfine was smitten with the French ambassador, a man named Bonzi who was later made cardinal, and wanted me to help her get things started with him.[148] Her plan was to let the ambassador know that I wanted him to ask on behalf of the king of France that the Republic of Venice permit ladies to continue to visit me. To allow me to meet the ambassador in all innocence, she informed him that I desired to speak to him at a wedding I was going to attend wearing a mask. He swallowed the bait and, having donned a mask himself, approached to ask whether, as Madam Dolfine had given him hope to believe, he could be of some service to me, saying it would give him great pleasure to do so. I thanked him for his complaisance and told him that was I ever to ask him to use his influence with his king it would be for something more important than being allowed to meet with the ladies of Venice. I think he easily divined that Madam Dolfine was more interested in meeting him than I was.

We had been so taken with the courtesy of Vicenza's nobility (and my husband with the lovely Madam Legge) that we returned for a second visit. The Vicenzans had heard so much about our Venetian tournament that my husband desired us to repeat the entertainment on Vicenza's Campo Marzio. The local nobility begged permission to have the honor of tilting at the ring and accompanying the ladies' calashes.

When all was ready a terrible mishap occurred. We were staying in a hilltop villa called Casa di Brunsvic because it was built by a man named Volpe with money he had won at cards from the dukes of Brunswick.[149] As we descended the hill from the villa, the horses pulling Miss de La Motte's carriage became skittish. She got out and

148. Piero de Bonzi (1631–1703), a Florentine in the French diplomatic service. He was France's ambassador to Venice from 1662 to 1665, to Poland from 1665 to 1669, and to Spain in 1670. Named archbishop of Toulouse in 1671, he was made cardinal by Pope Clement X in 1672.
149. Volpe (or Wolpe) was a Venetian count serving as governor of Vicenza.

climbed into the next carriage, in which Miss von Keppel sat with her admirer, an Englishman named Hels. The horses of the now empty carriage charged ahead with such fury that they rammed and overturned Miss von Keppel's carriage, reducing its three occupants to a piteous state. The first to emerge was Mr. Hels, with no more serious damage than torn clothes. Instead of rushing to his lady's rescue, however, he berated a servant for neglecting to bring his horse along. If it had been there, he said, the mishap would not have befallen him. Count Quinto, who was also on Miss von Keppel's team for the tournament, stood staring at her as if in a trance. Only Chevalier von Sandis, who later married Miss von Keppel, gave any proof of sincere affection by dragging first her and then her companion from under the horses' hooves. The poor girls had been so severely knocked about that they were hardly recognizable. It took more than a fortnight for them to recover from their injuries.

This mishap spoiled the day's festivities. The rest of our days in Vicenza passed in all sorts of amusements. My husband often arranged musical performances for the beautiful Madam Legge. In the evening there were gatherings, and in the amphitheater we held a rhetoric contest whose question was, "If one must go mad, what form of madness would one choose?" Chevalier d'Artale excelled at this, maintaining that the best form of madness would be to laugh all the time. He had good reasons for his opinion, seeing that the chief magistrate's sexagenarian wife had become infatuated with him. He even felt compelled to appear at the rendezvous she had arranged for them, hoping to experience the pleasure of her purse if not of her person. But since she wanted to pay him in the coin of love (and not of the realm) and he would only offer a token of his esteem, they parted mutually dissatisfied.

It may be imagined how out of place a German like me felt in a country where love is all they think about and where a lady without admirers would consider herself disgraced. I had always learned to view coquetry as a crime, which is contrary to Italian manners. I was surprised to hear a Venetian lady of quality named Bragadin ask Miss de La Motte, "Miss, how do they make love in France?" "I don't know anything about that," replied Miss de La Motte. "Oh, really," said Madam Bragadin, "did you leave France at such a young age?"—as if a girl was supposed to know such things. This same person always followed my gondola. The purpose of this attention, she said, was to repay me for the honor that my husband had paid her by courting her in earlier days, for he had once been smitten with her. She had some vestiges of her former beauty, though not enough to rekindle his flame.

As I had seen everything there was to see in Venice, my husband decided to travel with me to Rome by way of Milan. It was late in the evening when we reached this fine city, where St. Charles Borromeo has left so many beautiful monuments.[150] Count Durini lodged us in one of his palazzi and showered us with polite attention. He informed us that a great ball was being held and that we could go there wearing masks and see Milan's ladies. Our curiosity proving stronger than our weariness from the journey, we went and found that the ladies were indeed worth the exertion. Several had very good figures and danced very well, their half-Spanish dress lending them a pleasing dignity. Countess Bianca, daughter of Countess Hippolita Visconti, shone among the dancers, and her beauty charmed me as much as all the polite attention her mother showed me. Countess Hippolita entreated me to unmask myself. I hesitated for a moment between the discomfort of the heat and that of displaying myself in traveling costume and hat. But since comfort always carries the day with me, I gratified her by acceding to her wish.

The next day she came to visit me accompanied by nearly a hundred ladies who stayed until nightfall. Dancing was one of their favorite diversions, so they were anxious that I, too, continually experience its pleasures. So we danced every evening, which completely wore me out. Milan's entire nobility was extremely gracious and obliging, neglecting nothing to please me. They showed me all the city's beautiful

---

150. St. Charles Borromeo (1538–84), archbishop of Milan and papal secretary of state under Pius IV.

sights. The church and hospital built by St. Charles Borromeo are admirable edifices.[151]

Just as we were about to continue on to Rome, Madam von Lenthe, who was pregnant, injured herself and had to give birth in a makeshift bed in one of the carriages. Miss von Ahlefeld also fell ill. Her beauty, which had caused such a sensation in Rome and Venice, was assailed by smallpox, and I had to leave her behind in Bologna.[152] It would take an entire volume to describe all the particulars of this great journey. I only remember the main events and that I did not find it in the least bit tedious because I had had a table installed in my carriage on which I played brelan with Morosini and Loredan all the way to Rome.[153]

Our two Venetian nobles had very different dispositions. As we approached the Holy House of Loreto, Loredan, who had often heard what an emotionally powerful place it is, was moved by the power of his own imagination, whereas Morosini had trouble restraining his laughter.[154] We stopped there for a day to have a good look at the miracle, which is indeed noteworthy, since it renders people foolish enough to travel long distances to seek their salvation in worshipping a truly awful Madonna statue with a broken nose. We saw pilgrims from all parts of Christendom, but none with better sense than a German who became a fixture in our kitchen. "I believe the Blessed Virgin is very good," he said, "but she doesn't give you anything to eat."

When I went with my husband into the supposed Holy House of Our Lady of the Broken Nose, I felt quite ill from the smoke and heat of

151. The church is the Milan cathedral on the Piazza del Duomo, begun in 1386, consecrated by St. Charles Borromeo in 1577, and completed in the nineteenth century. The hospital is the *Ospedale Maggiore*, commissioned in 1456 by Francesco Sforza, duke of Milan. It now houses the University of Milan and was not, in fact, commissioned by St. Charles Borromeo (Sophia, *Mémoires*, 94).

152. An error by Sophia: she and her entourage have not been to Rome yet, so Miss von Ahlefeld's beauty could only have caused a sensation in Venice (Sophia, *Mémoires*, 94).

153. Brelan, similar to bouillotte, is an antecedent of poker. See Walter Brown Gibson, *Hoyle's Encyclopedia of Card Games* (New York: Doubleday, 1974), 38–40.

154. The Holy House inside the Loreto basilica is venerated as the Virgin Mary's actual birthplace.

so many oil lamps and had to retreat to the outer church to sit down and recover. One of the Virgin's officiants approached and informed me that it was a small matter for the Virgin to reattach a severed head and that she had instantly cured a disemboweled man who was carrying his intestines in his arms. When I felt restored, curiosity induced me to reenter the Holy House. I was shown a portrait said to be by St. Luke, who, if this claim was true, was a very poor painter.[155] I then saw the bowls from which Our Savior had eaten as a child. I looked fixedly at the priest who displayed them, letting him know that I did not believe a word of his story. This caused him to relax his gravity. After all, he had good cause for merriment, since he earned an easy living. In the Holy House stands a silver, man-sized angel holding in his arms the dauphin of France. The angel, a gift from the dauphin's mother, Anne of Austria, was inscribed with large letters that read, "From you I received him; to you I return him."[156] I also saw a heart-shaped jewel encrusted with diamonds given by Queen Henrietta Maria of England, bearing the words, "Because it is dear to me I give it to you."

The Virgin's treasure was not, it seemed to me, as valuable as that of St. Denis.[157] The reason is that the pope often sells the best items. That year, we were informed, he had sold over one hundred thousand crowns' worth of the Virgin's jewels and bought her land so that she might better maintain her court. For she keeps a complete household, including a carriage led by six horses. She does not, however, use this conveyance to travel about. According to the legend, she ordered angels to fly her and her household from Jerusalem to Loreto, where she desired to settle forever.

Loredan roused his companion Morosini in the middle of the night to tell him the joyful news that I had been deeply affected by the Virgin

---

155. It was a statue, not a painting, of the Madonna that was at one time attributed to St. Luke. The statue was destroyed by fire in 1921.

156. Anne of Austria (1601–66) sponsored several shrines to give thanks for the seemingly miraculous birth of her first child, the future Louis XIV, in the twenty-third year of her marriage to Louis XIII. The statue in Loreto, the work of Jacques Sarazin (1590–1660), was commissioned by Cardinal Richelieu (1585–1642).

157. Sophia visited the royal abbey of St. Denis in 1679.

and would doubtless soon become a Roman Catholic. But he was a poor physiognomist. Had such a thought ever crossed my mind, Loreto would have dispelled it.

From Loreto we passed through the duchy of Parma.[158] The duke of Parma had sent orders that we should be well received and that on our arrival in Piancenza Count Palpauri should welcome us on his behalf. The count fulfilled this commission assiduously, spoke very eloquently, and insisted on lodging us in the duke's palace, declaring that was he to neglect his duty in serving us he would incur his master's wrath. Though supper was waiting for us at an inn, my husband allowed himself to be persuaded. The count indeed provided us with fine lodgings but left us to die of hunger. After we had waited for a long time a small table was laid in a pretty little boudoir where my husband desired to sup privately, attended by our ladies and our two Venetian noblemen. No sooner was the table laid than we all took our places, not wishing to waste any more time, since it was already very late. At last a small broccoli-and-currant salad appeared and was devoured in an instant. This feast was followed by six hard-boiled eggs. We laughed as we each vied to be the first to snatch one from the bowl. The last course consisted of an eel pie. Never, I believe, was such a bad supper eaten in such good spirits.

The next day Count Palpauri was doubly complaisant and entreated me to praise his excellent arrangements to his master. That it was undoubtedly the duke's intention that we should be entertained with the best regardless of cost we could judge by his splendid hospitality at Parma, where the next day we feasted magnificently in one of his palaces, notwithstanding our wish to remain incognito.

The duchess dowager of Parma expressed a great desire to see me.[159] Since I wished to see one of her daughters who had taken the veil out

158. Sophia recounts her experiences at Loreto first, although from Milan she actually passed through Piacenza, Parma, and Modena before arriving at Loreto (Sophia, *Memoiren,* 79). This is the same Ranuccio II Farnese, duke of Parma and Plaisance (1630–96), who in 1656 made an offer of marriage to Sophia.

159. Margherita de' Medici (1612–78).

of despair at the failure of a plan to marry her to the king of England, it was arranged that we would all meet at the convent. The duchess dowager appeared, attended by her son the reigning duke and by one of her brothers, who was extremely fat. She said many obliging things to me, reminding me of her former wish to have me as her daughter-in-law. That same evening my husband went to see the young duchess of Parma. She asked him to be seated, but his unwillingness to doff his hat in her presence, we later heard, was ill received. For his part, my husband was taken aback that the duchess's ladies remained seated throughout the encounter.

We passed through Modena but did not stay overnight. My husband, growing tired of our slow rate of progress, took a post chaise to Rome. My ladies, Miss von Keppel especially, went nearly the whole way on foot, fearing that their carriage might tumble down one of the frightful precipices along our route. I was not so prescient, and my carriage would certainly have been overturned had not Dr. Tack and a page, who by good fortune were on foot at that moment, rushed to rescue me from a danger that an absorbing game of brelan had prevented me from perceiving. With considerable difficulty I was extricated from the carriage, which I exchanged for the safety of my sedan chair. During this journey Dr. Tack called my attention to a quite large comet, which did not make much of an impression on me.[160]

It was already evening when I entered Rome incognito with a suite of nearly two hundred people. We had excellent lodgings in a palace lent to us by the grand duke of Tuscany.[161] Prior to our arrival, Abbot Tassis had taken care to fill it with enough furniture. My husband had gone to see Madam Colonna, so I was received by Felice Machiavelli, who relayed my husband's instructions that I receive no visitors so as to avoid questions of protocol. That evening Cardinal d'Este sent his compliments.[162] Ignorant of local customs, I did not ask the cardinal's messenger to replace the hat he had doffed on being introduced to

160. There was a widely publicized comet-sighting in Europe in December 1680, at the time Sophia was writing her memoirs (Sophia, *Mémoires*, 98).

161. Ferdinand II de' Medici, grand duke of Tuscany (1610–70).

162. Rinaldo d'Este (1618–72), created cardinal deacon of Modena in 1641.

me. As he left he astonished me by announcing that he would tell His Eminence about the treatment he had suffered at my hands. I replied that he was welcome to do so, as I did not understand the intricacies of the subject. His master, who had traveled to France and learned the customs of other countries, did not seem to have taken offence, for later in my stay he twice waited on me in a garden. He was a most well-mannered, kind-hearted, and estimable prince, who talked volubly and very badly, with a disagreeable Italian accent.[163]

Since my husband spent his evenings playing basset with Madam Colonna, I would have been very bored if I had not had the pleasure of taking walks in Rome's exquisite gardens and the diversion of gambling.[164] Yet I was so curious to see Madam Colonna—a lady who had won the king of France's heart and who even now captured my husband's attention—that I could not wait for her recovery from a recent childbirth to enable her to come to see me. Moreover, I was assured that my intended visit would not establish a precedent (our ranks were too unequal for that) and that she would address me as Your Highness.[165] Consequently, it was deemed acceptable for me to pay her a surprise visit one evening while my husband and she played cards. On the night of our carefully orchestrated impromptu meeting I found her lying in bed. She was clothed in a blue and silver silk

163. Presumably, Sophia means he spoke French very badly.

164. Basset was an "early form of faro popular in Venice" (Gibson, *Card Games*, 23).

165. Madam Colonna, born Marie Mancini (1640–1715), was Cardinal Mazarin's niece, Louis XIV's former girlfriend, and the wife of Prince Lorenzo Onofrio Colonna, duke of Tagliacozzi, prince of Pagliagno, and constable of Naples (1639–89). Because of Sophia's vastly superior rank, protocol dictated that Madam Colonna first wait on Sophia. Doscot states that Sophia's husband was nothing more than a platonic admirer and faithful confident of Madam Colonna. See *Mémoires d'Hortense et de Marie Mancini*, ed. Gérard Doscot (Paris: Mercure de France, 1965), 216. Sophia, who likely suspected that her husband played (or desired to play) more than cards with Madam Colonna, may have been irked that Brémond, the original publisher of the edition of Mancini's memoirs that Sophia seems to have read, dedicated them to Sophia's husband, the "most gallant and magnanimous of princes, into whose protection the fair sex has always been most excellently received" (Mancini and Mancini, *Mémoires*, 91, my translation). For more on Madam Colonna, see Nelson's fine introduction to Hortense Mancini and Marie Mancini, *Memoirs*, ed. and trans. Sarah Nelson (Chicago: University of Chicago Press, 2008), 1–25.

dressing gown with ties in the front made of flame-colored ribbons that clashed with the rest of the garment. On her head was a lace cap that covered her forehead but not her ears. From her general manner and the movement of her lips I divined that she was trying to greet me, but "Highness" was the only word I could distinguish. The duke of Créqui rose from his couch and approached her with devoted eyes and pursed lips, to which her whispered response was to suggest a game of basset, her favorite pastime.[166] So we sat down to play, and the evening passed without giving me any clue as to how this person had made such a stir in the world, although I guessed by her sparkling eyes that she was livelier and wittier with men than with women.[167] After she had fully recovered from childbirth we met quite often, although when she visited me she tried to assert precedence by walking on my right side, which I always contrived to avoid letting her do. Once, when she came to take me to a convent where she had an aunt, I could not resist taking precedence over her, despite being incognito, as we descended and ascended the stairs of our residence in Rome. Caring nothing about ceremony, she did not raise a fuss. Indeed, my husband, who was anxious to please her, was more vexed about it than she was.

One day she got the idea that she should try to save my soul. For this purpose she took me to the Gesù, the Jesuit church, where she had arranged an appointment with the preacher apostolic who was tasked with converting me. His only argument went like this: there are a great many Jesuits in the world, all of them learned; ergo Roman Catholicism must be the best religion because otherwise so many intelligent men would not choose to belong to it. Madam Colonna, astonished that he had nothing more profound to say, whispered to me, "I'd expected better things from him. I don't think he can count himself among the Church's many savants whose knowledge he praised." By contrast, his vicar general, Father Oliva, might certainly rank among them.[168]

166. Charles III, marquis and later duke of Créqui (1624–87), was the French ambassador in Rome at the time.

167. In a letter to Charles Lewis dated November 7, 1664, Sophia is more direct, asserting that Madam Colonna is neither particularly beautiful nor witty. She adds the piquant detail that the duke of Créqui cheated at cards (Sophia, *Briefwechsel*, 80).

168. John Paul Oliva was the vicar general of the Society of Jesus from 1664 to 1681.

He visited me often and was extremely polite. On the feast day of the
Jesuits' patron saint, he received me at the door of his church, to which
he had invited me to listen to the music.[169]

Queen Christina of Sweden came to the church on the following day
expecting to meet me there.[170] Unfortunately, on that day I had come
down with a fever. I never saw her during my entire stay in Rome,
for Her Majesty refused the honor due to my rank in her own house,
and Cardinal Azzolino prevented the meeting in her garden that she
had proposed, although I would have been delighted to pay her my
respects there.[171]

Duke John Frederick, although a Catholic, had had the same dispute
with Pope Alexander, who refused to grant him the same honors he
had shown to Duke Charles IV of Lorraine, excusing himself by saying
that he had done too much for Duke Charles.[172] Duke John Frederick
replied that the pope could just as easily do too much for him as well.
But the dull-witted pope, better versed in poetry than in politics,
preferred to let a Catholic convert prince leave Rome disgruntled. I
was told that the pope would be pleased to see me incognito, but I
sought no opportunity to meet with him, since my brother-in-law felt
snubbed by him.

My society in Rome consisted chiefly of my domestics and the people
who had accompanied me, for I did not meet any ladies. The beautiful Falernière, who had visited me in Venice, did not do so in Rome.
Statues and paintings, therefore, were a greater source of entertainment to me than people, and every day I went to look at them in the

169. The feast day of St. Ignatius of Loyola is celebrated on July 31, the date of his death in
1556.

170. Queen Christina of Sweden (1626–89) was received into the Catholic Church by Pope
Alexander VII (1599–1667) on Christmas Day 1655 after having abdicated the Swedish
throne in 1654.

171. Decio Azzolino, cardinal of Fermo (1623–89), was appointed by Pope Alexander VII
as Christina's liaison to the papal court. Sophia finally met Queen Christina three years later
at a masked ball in Hamburg.

172. Charles IV, duke of Lorraine and Bar (1604–75).

world's most splendid palaces and gardens. I also went to see the beautiful fountains at Frascati. What I most admired, and never tired of, was the Church of St. Peter. The structure and its ornaments are equally superb. Having been there to look at the building, I returned one day incognito to see the pope. The captain of the Swiss Guards guided me to where I could get a close look at him. He entered walking hurriedly and awkwardly. I think his movements were intended as evidence that he was in fine health and not, I hope, as a show to please the ladies. His manner lacked the dignity befitting the head of the Church. He gave us his blessing while passing rapidly from one altar to another, kneeling before each and saying a prayer from his breviary.

I also went to the Church of All Saints (once the Pantheon) and to Blessed Mary of Victory (once the Temple of Jupiter Victor).[173] Here were Emperor Ferdinand's crown and scepter, sent by him to be displayed next to a little portrait of the Virgin that he believed had won him the Battle of Prague against my father the king. The monk who exhibited these fine gifts remarked that so great a princess as I ought also to donate something to the church, which was decorated with captured flags and standards. I replied, "I would if the Virgin had sided with us in the battle."

Having seen everything of interest in Rome, I was delighted to hear my husband talk of our return to Germany, for I longed to see my two sons again. Since he planned to go to the country with Madam Colonna, he thought that I should leave first. Madam Colonna mentions this outing in her book, but having a more fertile imagination but a less accurate memory than I, she dates it incorrectly, saying that it took place on my arrival in Rome, whereas it was actually at the time of my departure. She was kind enough to accompany me to the

---

173. The Pantheon was actually given the name Santa Maria dei Martiri when it was consecrated in 1609 (Sophia, *Mémoires*, 101). The Santa Maria della Vittoria (Blessed Mary of Victory), originally named after St. Paul and not Jupiter, was built by Carlo Maderno (1556–1629).

gates of the city, returning alone in the carriage with the duke, which is quite contrary to the customs of her country.[174]

While passing through the Papal States I was surprised to hear the subjects' poor opinion of their sovereign. When I asked our hostess whether the last pope had been any better than the current one, she replied, "Giusto un ladro come questo" ('A thief just like this one').

Leaving the Papal States I entered those of the duke of Florence, who had issued orders that I be well received throughout his dominions and lodged in his palaces, though I desired to maintain my incognito.[175] On reaching Sienna I alighted from my sedan chair at a very fine palace. Holding candles to light the way, twelve of the grand duke's Rosicrucian knights ushered me into a ballroom filled with magnificently dressed ladies. I was much surprised by—and distressed that we were not better dressed for—this brilliant reception. Having no choice but to go in, we were entertained by tightrope walkers and marionettes that danced to the same music and executed nearly the same steps. Among the guests was a Neapolitan in a black silk suit with breeches so tight that they looked as if they had been sewn to his thighs. We had a good laugh at his expense later in the evening when we had retired and were free to do so without offending anyone. Some of the ladies were very pretty, the hostess especially so. One of Countess Hippolita Visconti's sisters was also there, and she took the same charge of me in Sienna that her sister had in Milan.

Continuing our journey by terrible roads we met with too many adventures to be recounted here. The carriage containing my maids of honor having tipped over nine times in one day, they no longer trusted it and tried riding—cross-saddle, like men—instead. But at this, poor

174. In the edition Sophia seems to have read, Madam Colonna does indeed state that she and her husband spent three days in Cisterne with Duke Ernest Augustus shortly after he and Sophia had arrived in Rome. This is followed by seventeenth-century boilerplate praise of Ernest Augustus's virtues (munificence, valor, courtliness, and grandeur) and of Sophia's manners, character, mind, and fashion sense as a "distillation of all the consummate charm and courtesy of France" (Mancini, *Mémoires*, 129, my translation).

175. The duke is Ferdinand II de' Medici (1610–70), grand duke of Tuscany.

Miss von Ahlefeld fared no better, for her horse threw her into a ditch from which Chevalier von Sandis dragged her out by the head. Next, the exhausted mules pulling my waiting-women's cart were unable to take another step. Baron von Platen, foreseeing my inconvenience if the women were left behind, put them both on post horses, one riding pillion behind himself and the other behind Secretary Beser. So arranged, with a postilion sounding his horn before them, they made their arrival.[176]

At last, late in the evening, we reached Florence. In accordance with the grand duke's instructions we were lodged in one of his palaces. Since he and his court were not there, his brother Prince Leopold, who was later made a cardinal, came at once to wait on me.[177] I advanced a step beyond the door to receive him. The Marquis Vitelli, fearing that Prince Leopold's insignificant appearance might prevent me from recognizing him among his courtiers, whispered to me, "The prince is the one dressed like a priest." I, however, had already identified him by his very noble manner. He possessed both wit and merit in abundance and was untiring in his efforts to please me. I found his manner neither too haughty nor too familiar, and indeed he was on excellent terms with the local nobility. He took me to a ball in the town, and I in return gave one to him or rather to the numerous ladies of Florence, whose good looks, fine clothes, and graceful dancing we much admired. The gentlemen were also very good dancers. In short, Florentines were the epitome of good society. Unlike in the other Italian towns we had visited, here I was not overwhelmed with polite attention, and amusement and comfort were combined in equal measure.

Prince Leopold also took me to a party given by a lady who was effectively his wife. The whole house was lit up, and in every room stood several tables, at each of which four men and four women played a

176. Franz Ernst, Freiherrr von Platen (1632–1709), subsequently count of Platen-Hallermund, Duke Ernest Augustus's prime minister; his wife, Clara Elizabeth, was later the duke's official mistress. A postilion rides one of the horses drawing a carriage to serve as a guide for the coachman or, in the absence of coachman, to steer the team himself.
177. Leopold de' Medici (1617–75), Ferdinand II's younger brother, was made cardinal in 1667.

card game called coconut. The party was very crowded, and the prince referred to the most beautiful ladies as his daughters.

I also went to see the grand duke's residence, Pitti Palace, and greatly admired both the palace and the garden.[178] The last set of rooms shown was Prince Leopold's, and his collection of fine paintings excited the admiration of all connoisseurs. The prince had the most exquisite confectionery laid out as a treat for me. But as I preferred admiring his fine paintings and lovely statue of Venus, he had all the sweets sent to the palace we were staying in. Prince Leopold complimented our Venetian noblemen on the confectionery, for it had been presented to him by the Venetian republic when he was there.

Curiosity induced me to go see the children of the ducal family. One of them, the current grand duke's little brother, was very handsome; the other, his son, was just an infant in swaddling clothes and could be admired only for his plumpness and fair skin.[179]

The grand duke sent me fresh game nearly every day and also presented me with a large quantity of medicine, an ill-chosen gift, for I never take any. A gentleman of his court surprised me by remarking in English, "Doubtless you would've preferred perfumes." I learned later that his name was Gasconi and that he had been the grand duke's envoy to England. The court of Florence's abundant grace and charm left me very satisfied, and I departed the city thinking it the most agreeable place I had visited in Italy.

My next stop was Bologna, where I asked Mr. Marescotti to put me up, since the nobility of each town I had visited had always kindly lodged me in their palaces.[180] He declared that he was most willing to grant my request, and I was received by his wife Madam Laura, the

178. Designed by the Florentine architect Filippo Brunelleschi around 1440, Pitti Palace was completed in the second half of the sixteenth century, with additions made until the 1760s. The garden is now called Boboli Garden.
179. The current duke was Cosimo III (1642–1723); the very handsome boy, Francesco Maria (1660–1711); and the infant, Ferdinand III (1663–1713).
180. Possibly Ercole, the brother or nephew of Cardinal Galeazzo Marescotti.

Countess Capraro (formerly Marchioness Angelotti), and other ladies
of his family.

I was led through a gallery that to hungry travelers seemed like an
enchanted spot, for it was lined from end to end with sideboards on
which a buffet of confectionery was artistically laid out, the whole
scene lit with many candles. Through this gallery I was taken to a fine
room hung with gold brocade, and here I expected Mr. Marescotti's
politeness to end. But when my servants tried to enter the kitchen,
he informed them that he intended to entertain me and my numerous retinue, and, since everything had been prepared in advance,
he hoped I would not insult him by refusing his hospitality. Greatly
embarrassed by his offer, in the end I decided to accept it for myself and to send my attendants to an inn. Undeterred, he replied with
true Bolognese hyperbole that he would murder any innkeeper who
dared give them food. And, indeed, he fed us all most sumptuously.
He seated me alone at a little table set up on a platform next to a very
long table at which all the people of quality ate with me. There was
not enough room at the long table for all the nobility in my entourage,
so he set up another table for them and my ladies-in-waiting and a
number of other tables for my other attendants.

I found the society and lifestyle of Bologna quite agreeable, but
Marescotti's excessive generosity prevented me from staying there as
long as I otherwise would have. A ball was held to show me Bologna's
beauties, among whom Countess Paleotti was the most lovely.[181] I took
much greater pleasure in her conversation than in the mummy of St.
Catherine, a local miracle I was shown.[182] I was also taken to a convent
where I was greeted with a quite extraordinary sight: all the old nuns

181. Duke Ernest Augustus met Countess Paleotti again in 1671 and told Sophia that he
would propose sending the countess to their court as one of Sophia's attendants if Sophia did
not have a "somewhat jealous temperament." See "Briefe des Kurfürsten Ernst August von
Hannover an seine Gemahlin, die Kurfürstin Sophie," ed. Anna Wendland, *Niedersächsisches
Jahrbuch* 7 (1930): 233; my translation.

182. St. Catherine of Vigri (1413–63), superioress of the Poor Clare convent in Bologna. She
was not canonized, however, until 1712, more than thirty years after Sophia had written her
memoirs. Van der Cruysse suggests that Sophia is mistakenly referring to St. Catherine of
Sienna (1347–80) (Sophia, *Mémoires*, 106).

had full beards which made them look like the husbands of the young ones. I was sorry to leave Bologna, having been quite charmed by the politeness of my reception.

At Chioggia I embarked for Venice. My husband, having posted from Rome, arrived there a few days later. Carnival, with its operas and masques, was very enjoyable, as was the freedom with which I was able to walk around the city during the day without being recognized and to play cards in the gaming rooms in the evenings. I found the cold more penetrating than in Germany, which is why my carnival costume was always that of a Venetian noble so that I could wear a fur-lined coat.

Before carnival ended, my husband wished to enjoy it in Milan, where he also expected to find Madam Colonna, though she failed to appear. So that we might travel to Milan more quickly, the nobility of Vicenza and Verona lent us relays of horses. Reaching Vicenza incognito we decided to walk through the town and visit the nuns. The local nobility obliged us by arranging for the convent gate to be opened, enabling us to see all the nuns at once. Overjoyed at the sight of so many men, the poor creatures grasped at the gentlemen's fingers through the grille (our Chevalier d'Artale obliged them by spending the whole night there). Never in my life have I seen pious women in such a state of excitement.[183]

We had already sent half of my ladies on to Milan, and my husband said to me, "We can let the others follow when they like. Why don't you and I travel by post?" I was charmed by the idea. Dressed in a long tight coat and a wig, I rode in the post chaise, while my husband, Count Montalbano, and a valet named Michael went on horseback.[184]

---

183. For a brief discussion of the popularity of convents as early modern tourist attractions, their parlors' role as "salonlike gathering places," and the range of amorous activity that went on there (everything from lusty gazes to trans-grille heavy petting), see Jutta Gisela Sperling, *Convents and the Body Politic in Late Renaissance Venice* (Chicago: University of Chicago Press, 1999), 158–69.

184. Van der Cruysse identifies the valet as Michael Raison (Sophia, *Mémoires*, 107). A post chaise is a carriage that conveys both the mail and paying passengers.

At the sight of me the postillion broke into laughter, thinking that I was the duke's doxy. By good fortune I reached Milan unobserved, for I was terrified of being seen in this outfit by the city's ladies and nobility, who had arranged to give me a big reception.

My arrival having been made known, the Milanese ladies came to see me the next day. I received them with a fainting fit brought on by my pregnancy, a display that distressed them terribly. They undressed me and put me to bed with many expressions of tenderness and exclamations such as *cara gioia, cara cosa, angela*, and all the other pet names their language can command. Countess Hippolita Visconti headed a detachment of ladies that never left my side while I was in Milan. They kept me dancing the galliard without respite day and night for two weeks till I was too exhausted to move. My obliging docility in the matter deserves much praise. Countess St. George delighted me by leaping in the most graceful manner when she danced. What would have been awkward in another woman was charming in her. She arranged a little ballet in my honor, and her agility far surpassed that of her brother-in-law. Dancing was so in vogue in Milan that even the clergy joined in, and I was pleased to see Abbot Grivelli, cassock and all, perform a Spanish pavane with Madam Helena Figarolla.

On leaving Milan I was escorted to the gates by all the nobility and attended by a tremendous concourse of followers. My husband and I began a most fatiguing journey, returning to Germany through the Swiss cantons and the St. Gotthard pass. I traveled with Madam von Lenthe in a sedan chair, but the towering mountains on one side and the frightful precipices on the other were so terrifying that we often got out and walked. There were places where we had to travel on primitive sledges pulled by bullocks, and we crossed a bridge that the peasants believe was built by the Devil.[185]

At last we reached Basel, where, thinking I was alone in my room, I perceived to my great astonishment a swarm of children under the stove, which was surrounded by a balustrade. From Basel we sailed down the Rhine to Selz in the Palatinate and then on to Germersheim, where

185. A bridge across the Reuss River about one mile from Andermatt.

baron von Bonstetten, who had married my good friend Miss Carey, was commander of the fortress. It gave me great joy to see her and talk to her again. From Germersheim we proceeded to Heidelberg, where news reached us of the death of Duke Christian Lewis, my husband's oldest brother.[186] This report, which made us hasten our journey, was confirmed when we arrived in Frankfurt. My husband consequently hurried on by post to Hanover, while I proceeded by easy stages to Iburg.

186. Christian Lewis died on March 15, 1665.

Chapter 5
Iburg, Osnabrück (1665–79)

On reaching Paderborn I was informed that Duke John Frederick, taking advantage of his brothers' absence, had seized control of Duke Christian Lewis's domains. John Frederick's shabby treatment at the hands of the pope in Rome had caused him to leave our travel party and return before us. Moreover, the duke of Hanover had demonstrated severe negligence by remaining in Holland with his beautiful Miss d'Olbreuse despite receiving many letters informing him of his older brother's desire to see him before his death.[187] The only excuse he had to offer for his error was in my opinion both cruel and impertinent: the duke of Hanover feared that his brother would, on his deathbed, ask him to take care of some servants whom the duke of Hanover disliked. His ill-considered caution cost him dear, for the world severely censured his conduct. Duke John Frederick, meanwhile, acquired a reputation for craftiness. Although he had simply opened the door when opportunity knocked, he was praised as if he had been planning this coup for some time.

As my husband approached Hanover he was met by Hammerstein, who gave him an exact account of all that had taken place and tried hard to persuade him to return to Iburg and remain neutral in the dispute between his brothers. Such advice was little suited to my husband's noble sentiments. He informed Hammerstein that he would risk everything rather than abandon, in his hour of need, a brother whom he owed so much. Moreover, my husband believed that his brother had justice on his side, for their father's will, which they all considered to be a fundamental law, stipulated that the oldest brother could choose between the Celle and the Hanover domains. The Celle domains were better, so the choice was easy.[188]

---

187. Eleanor Desmier d'Olbreuse (1639–1722) came from a minor noble family in Poitou in western France. Her parents were Jacobine Poussard and Alexandre II Desmier, sieur de Lolbroire and Olbreuse.

188. Sophia estimated that the duke of Celle's revenues were at least three times the duke of Hanover's (Sophia, *Briefwechsel*, 40; letter dated January 12, 1661).

My husband went on to Hanover where he found his brother in a state of utter, tearful consternation. My husband not only offered counsel to his brother but also raised troops in support of his cause. Duke John Frederick, haughty from his early good fortune in the affair but aware that a civil war would ruin the country and that the intervention of foreign states would be just as bad, began to talk of compromise. He declared himself willing to abide by the terms of their father's will, which gave the choice of domains to the oldest, but also stated that the partition must be equal. If the partition was so adjusted, Duke John Frederick would agree to let his elder brother have first choice. With Count Waldeck's assistance, a compromise was reached and the partition adjusted.[189] The duke of Hanover chose Celle, and John Frederick became duke of Hanover. George William, now duke of Celle, awarded my husband the county of Diepholz to compensate him for the expenses he had incurred during the protracted negotiations.

[August 1665]

My husband sent for me to visit him at Ohsen where he was laid up with a fever.[190] Duke George William of Celle was there too, for the two brothers' friendship seemed stronger than ever. He doted on my two sons, declaring that everything he had would go to them and to their father. Meanwhile, he frequently called on Miss de La Motte, who was a close friend of Miss d'Olbreuse, to whom he had been so devoted in Holland. He informed me that the princess of Tarentum had gone to France, leaving the young Miss d'Olbreuse and her companion, Miss de La Manselière, all alone at 's-Hertogenbosch, where, he claimed, they desired nothing more than to come to see me.[191] He

189. The compromise, which followed five months of negotiations, was reached on September 2, 1665. See Ludwig Timotheus, Freiherr von Spittler, *Geschichte des Fürstenthums Hannover seit den Zeiten der Reformation bis zu Ende des siebenzehnten Jahrhunderts* (Göttingen: Vandenhoeck, 1786), 2: 281–84. George Frederick, prince of Waldeck and count of Pyrmont and Culemborg (1620–92), had served the elector of Brandenburg, the king of Sweden, and the Holy Roman emperor as a councilor and general before becoming a general in the service of Duke George William; he was later a Dutch field marshal.

190. Ohsen is now called Kirchohsen and is located about thirty miles southwest of Hanover. My thanks to Susanne Lademann, a Hanoverian herself, for this information.

191. Susanne de La Chevalerie-Manselière; 's-Hertogenbosch, the capital of the province of North Brabant, is thirty miles south of Utrecht.

told the same story to my husband, persuading him to instruct me to send Miss de La Motte in a carriage and six to 's-Hertogenbosch to fetch them. My husband, knowing that his brother was attracted to one of them, was eager to do his utmost to please him. For my part, I was only too happy to provide him with an amusing companion to divert his thoughts from me. Accordingly, as soon as I was back at Iburg, Miss de La Motte set off for 's-Hertogenbosch.

Miss d'Olbreuse had been described to me as lively and playful. Poking and pinching were said to be the charms she used to ingratiate herself. In Kassel she had succeeded to the point where the landgrave became besotted with her and estranged from his wife.[192] Miss d'Olbreuse delighted in recounting the details of this story, which she saw as a testament both to her beauty (for having attracted so great a prince) and her chastity (for having resisted his advances). Moreover, she believed that the story's virtuous ending would stifle the malicious gossip about her and Schwerin as well as the remark made by the count of Guiche when he learned that her fortunes had changed: "When we're tired of her at the French court, she's still good enough for a German prince."[193]

But I found her to be very different from what I had heard. She affected a grave and dignified manner. She spoke little but expressed herself well. Her face was beautiful, her figure tall and slender. All in all, she pleased me extremely. My husband, who was with his brother at Hanover when she arrived in Iburg, wrote me a letter entreating me, for reasons he would explain later, to give her a most cordial welcome. I found no difficulty in obeying his instructions, for the young lady was a most amenable guest. So, in accordance with my husband's wishes, I believed her to be what she appeared, treating as idle gossip all that I had heard against her, even the ill turns she had done her companions, of which Miss de La Manselière, having suffered firsthand, had a lengthy list.

192. Landgrave William VI (1629–63) and his wife Hedwig Sophia (1623–83).

193. Antoine III de Gramont, duke of Gramont and Count of Guiche (1604–78), or perhaps more likely his son Armand, count of Guiche (1638–73).

When my husband and the duke of Celle arrived at Iburg, the glances the latter exchanged with Miss d'Olbreuse told me of the understanding that existed between them and of her determination to take things much further. She proceeded carefully, causing him to feel both the warmth of her ardor and the coolness of her reserve. The duke of Celle spoke to my husband in glowing terms of her modesty and his desire to possess her. My husband responded that everything has its price and that, judging from what Miss de La Motte had said, Miss d'Olbreuse's price was marriage. The duke of Celle replied, "If that's what she wants, then she can go right back to where she came from. I'd never do anything so foolish. If, on the other hand, she'd agree to live with me, I'd take good care of her and pay her a decent income as long as I live and after my death." He then asked my husband to help him obtain her consent to this agreement (which may already have been concluded between them).

We all were obliged to go to Celle to attend the funeral of the late Duke Christian Lewis.[194] Miss d'Olbreuse went also, traveling with my ladies-in-waiting. The duke of Celle's feelings for her seemed to grow warmer by the day. His suit was successful, and in order to speed matters along, he concluded a prenuptial agreement with her with roughly the following terms:

> Out of affection for my brother and for the benefit of him and his children I am resolved never to marry. Being determined never to waver from this resolution, and Miss d'Olbreuse having agreed to live with me, I hereby promise never to leave her and to settle on her an income of two thousand crowns per annum during my life and six thousand crowns per annum after my death. For her part, she hereby promises to be content with this arrangement and with these sums. This agreement meets with the approval of my above-named brother, who pledges to sign it with me.

---

194. The funeral was on November 11, 1665.

This agreement was drawn up by Miss de La Motte in lieu of a notary, and signed by the duke of Celle, Miss d'Olbreuse, my husband, and myself.

With no further ceremony, the two lovers went to bed together that evening. Hoping to tug at the duke of Celle's heart strings, Miss d'Olbreuse began to weep. Had she married a simple gentleman, she sobbed, she would at least have borne a title. She wished to be called Lady Celle. My husband and I strongly objected. The dowager duchess of Celle was insulted at the idea of her title being bestowed on a private gentlewoman. The duke of Celle, who said he did not want to offend us in order to please his mistress, settled the matter to our great satisfaction by giving the lady the choice between two names: Hoya and Harburg. She chose the latter and was called Lady Harburg for more than ten years entirely to her satisfaction, if one may judge by the letters she wrote to her friends, such as the following to Mr. de Genebat:[195]

Celle, March 14, 1666

As I am better able now than in the past to be of use to you, I regret, Sir, that you have given me no opportunity to do you some considerable service in order to prove that I am as good a friend to you as you have been to me. For I know that out of affection for me you have endured a hundred battles and have stood up for me on every occasion. I assure you that I feel all due gratitude and only desire an opportunity to show it. Regarding the interior decorator whom you so highly recommended and who is now in the duke's service, you need not thank me, as his fine work recommends itself. But even if he were incompetent, for your sake I would declare that he did wonders, for rest assured that I would neglect no opportunity to serve you. Many thanks for

195. Köcher speculates that Genebat is the author of the biography of d'Olbreuse printed in 1679 that Sophia read prior to writing her own memoirs (Köcher, "Denkwürdigkeiten," 39). Genebat later became a courtier in Celle.

having taken up my cause as you have done, and I am convinced that I can win any dispute that you plead for me. I was confident that you would approve of my marriage, and that was enough for me. For in such a matter the approbation of a person like yourself is all that is required. It will be said that I have dispensed with a church wedding and a priest. Yet I can feel no regret, because I am the happiest of women and because it is fidelity that makes a marriage. His Highness has pledged his fidelity to me before his closest relatives, who also signed the contract in which he promises to take no wife but me, to give me the same entourage a princess would have, to pay me an allowance of two thousand crowns a year, and to settle on me, on his death, an estate worth five thousand to six thousand crowns a year or to have his brother pay me the same annual amount in cash so that I can enjoy it where I please. For I would not stay in Germany if he was to pass away before me. The duke has not stopped there and has put me in a position to resist my enemies if it comes to that. I, however, think only of pleasing my duke. You would enjoy seeing us together, for ours is the happiest marriage in the world. Not even your own comes close. Come visit us soon so that you can see for yourself. Lose no time in sending off the letter you have written to me, because I prefer yours to Voiture's.[196] Tell me also what you said on hearing that Miss de La Manselière was no longer with the princess of Tarentum. No one was more surprised than she on hearing from 's-Hertogenbosch that she was no longer wanted, for she fully intended to return. Farewell, Sir. I look forward to hearing from you and remain your very humble servant,

d'Olbreuse, Lady Harburg.

---

196. Vincent Voiture (1597–1648), a French poet celebrated for his letter-writing skills.

This letter shows that she was quite content with her situation and quite capable of presenting it in a favorable light, and it was indeed very respectable for a person of her birth. To please his brother, my husband treated her with the greatest respect, and she, to remain in her duke's good graces, behaved with all due deference toward us, for at this period her influence was not yet boundless.

A year later she gave birth to a daughter.[197] Three months after that I had twin sons, of whom the first was stillborn. My suffering was so great that it was thought that I would soon follow him to the grave. We named the surviving boy Maximilian William after the electors of Cologne and Brandenburg.[198] I gave birth not in Iburg but in Osnabrück, where we were residing (and where my husband, contrary to episcopal custom, had placed a garrison), because Iburg was no longer considered safe after our neighbor, the bishop of Münster, had taken up arms against Holland, with which the dukes were allied.[199]

At that time the two brothers' unity was so complete that they were essentially inseparable; neither would do anything without the other. To enjoy his brother's company, my husband would take his entire court to spend the winter in Lüneburg, where we were diverted by a succession of comedies, card games, balls, and parties. We began to notice, however, that Lady Harburg's influence had increased considerably and that the duke of Celle believed everything she said, even though truthfulness had never been her strong suit. We felt sorry for him, but there was nothing we could do. She led him to believe that she came from a highly respected and very wealthy family and had been the princess of Tarentum's companion, not her attendant. One of her brothers came to Celle to persuade the duke to marry her properly, but the duke directed Colonel du Villiers to explain to the brother all

197. Sophia Dorothea, born on November 15, 1666 (d. 1726); she is the future wife of Sophia's oldest son George Lewis.

198. Known in the family as Max (1666–1726). His namesakes were Maximilian Henry of Wittelsbach, elector and archbishop of Cologne and duke of Bavaria (1621–88), and Frederick William of Hohenzollern, elector of Brandenburg (1620–88).

199. Christoph Bernhard von Galen, bishop of Münster from 1650 to 1678.

the reasons why he was firmly resolved never to take such a step. And we believed him incapable of changing his decision.

[October 1667]

At this time the king of Denmark and his queen, the dukes' sister, came to Glückstadt.[200] Their Majesties desired us to visit them there, and so my husband and I set off. We were welcomed most graciously by the queen, who did us the honor of coming out to meet us as we alighted from our carriage, showed me to my room, and then conducted me to her own antechamber, where I paid my respects to the king. He was tall, good-looking, and rather taciturn, expressing himself more with glances than words. He did not mind it if someone spoke to him without being spoken to, but he preferred cards to long-winded conversations.

On the first evening the queen instructed us to have supper privately in our own rooms because the electoral prince of Saxony would not hear of coming to an agreement about rank with my husband.[201] After supper we met the electoral prince in the queen's room together with his wife the electoral princess and her two sisters, Princess Emilia and Princess Wilhelmina Ernestine.[202] The sisters were quite beautiful, especially Princess Wilhelmina Ernestine, who I thought would be a fine match for my nephew the electoral prince Palatine, who was of a marrying age, was he fortunate enough to win her hand. It can therefore be fairly said that I was the first to plan this alliance.[203]

The queen was so gracious to us that Her Majesty insisted on drawing lots with us to determine the seating order at the king's dinner table. The company enjoying this honor consisted of the prince and princess royal, the two lovely princesses, Duke Ernest Günther of Holstein

---

200. Sophia Amalia (1628–85) married King Frederick III of Denmark (1609–70) on October 18, 1643. Situated on the Elbe thirty miles northwest of Hamburg, Glückstadt was part of the duchy of Holstein; the king of Denmark was simultaneously the duke of Holstein.

201. John George III (1647–91) became elector of Saxony in 1680.

202. The electoral princess of Saxony is Anna Sophia, the queen of Denmark's daughter.

203. Electoral Prince Charles II (1651–85), the son of Sophia's brother Charles Lewis, married Wilhelmina Ernestine on November 20, 1671.

and his wife, and ourselves.[204] Often Her Majesty drew the last lot and found herself sitting far from the king, who always sat at the head of the table. The duke of Celle, who arrived a few days after us, could not refrain from reproaching the queen his sister, who he believed had sided with Duke John Frederick against him. She received his reproaches most graciously, taking them as proof of his affection for her, and did her utmost to win him over. We left the Danish court as content as could be, though much grieved at having to part from the queen, whose goodness and excellent character won every heart.

My husband, who was unable to remain idle and whose gallant disposition would not allow him to be without an amorous liaison, amused himself by telling Miss de La Manselière about his predicament. She was pretty and also very intelligent and virtuous. Her virtue, however, was the source of her unhappiness, for it was paired with a profound piety quite out of tune with her general temperament. This discord caused her intense suffering, and in her agony she would often faint or scream frightfully. The poor girl gave her heart to my husband, whose charms she could not resist. Though smart enough not to do anything criminal, she no longer had the self-possession to control her behavior and convinced herself that their frequent tête-à-têtes were inconsequential as long as she met him in public. She believed that it was acceptable for the two of them to stroll on the terrace every evening because their actions were plainly visible from the palace windows. But the world is not very benevolent, and Lady Harburg, who despised Miss de La Manselière, spread the most vicious rumors about her. Miss de La Manselière heard about these and thought that her departure from the court would silence the gossips. As a pretext she used a lawsuit she supposedly had in France and asked for my permission to attend the proceedings. I did not try to stop her, having always pretended not to notice anything. She could not help but feel affection for me, both for my good treatment of her and for the sympathy that we felt in loving the same person. It weighed on her mind that her conduct had caused me distress, and so she tried to

204. The prince royal is the future King Christian V (1646–99), who ascended the Danish throne in 1670. Ernest Günther, duke of Schleswig-Holstein-Sonderburg-Augustenburg (1609–89).

explain things to me before her departure. I staved off this discussion for as long as I could by acting as if I did not understand what she was talking about. Finally, she broke the ice and frankly conceded that her conduct must have given me cause to think poorly of her but avowed that her heart had been firm enough to resist and that she was going to leave in order to show the world that she had no desire to taint her reputation by doing something despicable. I replied that my affection for her made me wish that she had conducted herself more discreetly in public but that I had never mentioned this to her because she had always maintained, contrary to my own opinion, that it was enough for a woman to remain innocent of actual wrongdoing. I told her that a woman's good conduct was a component of the virtue necessary to maintain her honor, adding that it was just as much a sign of weakness to show a lack of restraint in public as it was to do something indecent in private. Tears were her only answer as she sat on the floor beside my bed. I kissed her several times to show that I held nothing against her and gave her two armbands as tokens of my affection. But the more kindness I showed the more she believed she had wronged me. Her tears made this apparent, and her sobs became frightful screams. Suddenly, she seemed to lose consciousness, though she continued to shriek. I had never seen her like this before, and it gave me a terrible fright. I got out of bed in my nightgown to call for help. She was taken from my bedroom and brought to her own where she was revived.

She left the next day, believing that this would save her honor. But it had precisely the opposite effect, giving rise to the rumor that she was pregnant, which was a complete lie. I was quite happy to see her go, since I feared that a woman who could earn my husband's esteem would gain too much sway over his heart and lessen his affection for me. Nevertheless, I did all that I could to defend her reputation. I sent her my portrait in miniature and began exchanging letters with her, which I enjoyed, for she wrote very well. My husband entered into a clandestine correspondence with her, which I pretended not to know about, since he wished it to be kept a secret from me. A few years later my husband suggested that she become one of my ladies-in-waiting, since I was already familiar with her virtuousness. I explained to him that this was impossible, for a young princess's attendant must be a person with an untainted reputation. I told him I was of one mind with Caesar, who said that it was not enough for his wife to be chaste; she must also have a reputation for chastity.[205] The poor girl later died of a poison that a mountebank had passed off to her as medicine. I shall always remember her as an extraordinary person whose soul was very beautiful and whose body was a great inconvenience to her.[206] Before her departure I gave birth to a girl whose pale skin was similar to Miss de La Manselière's.[207] Having three sons already I was delighted to have a daughter.

My husband, who was much attached to his sister the queen, wished to please her by arranging a marriage between my nephew the electoral prince Palatine and her daughter Wilhelmina Ernestine. For this purpose he and I journeyed to the Palatinate, although I was at that time very pregnant with Prince Charles. As we approached Heidelberg, the elector, lively and cheerful as ever, came out to meet us with his son, daughter, and entire court. My niece kissed me repeatedly, expressing her delight at seeing me again and remembering the happy times she had had while living with me.[208] My nephew was much obliged to us for planning to marry him to a king's daughter, especially when he saw her portrait, which pleased him enormously. The elector, however, was too prudent to make an immediate decision, so we merely laid the matter before him and then departed, sailing down the Rhine to return home via Holland. The journey was very pleasant. My vigilant midwife, fearing an accident, followed me everywhere. She was dressed in the Heidelberg style, which drew derisive hoots from the Amsterdam riffraff, which harassed us too.

205. Plutarch, *Lives*, Caesar, Section 11: "I wished my wife to be not so much as suspected." The traditional saying is "Caesar's wife must be above suspicion."

206. The de La Manselière episode is one of the longest sections Forester expunged from his 1888 edition of Sophia's memoirs.

207. Sophia Charlotte (1668–1705), known in the family as Figuelotte, was born on October 20, 1668. On October 8, 1684, she married Frederick, electoral prince of Brandenburg (1656–1713), who became elector in 1688 and king of Prussia in 1701.

208. Elizabeth Charlotte lived with Sophia from June 1659 to April 1663.

On our return my husband sent Hammerstein to Denmark to negotiate the marriage contract and promised his sister that he and I would conduct the princess to Heidelberg. In the meantime I gave birth to my son Charles.[209] I never expected the wedding arrangements to take so long that I would be pregnant again by the time I was required to accompany the princess, but that is precisely what happened.

The electoral prince wanted to see his future bride before marrying her. He passed through Osnabrück while my husband was at the siege of Brunswick and about the time that a chancellor named Schütz entered the duke of Celle's service. The many troubles this man later caused give me ample reason to remember well when he first came on the scene.[210] He was a tireless administrator but also dishonest, venal, and imperious to such a degree that he desired to have undisputed sway over his master, whom he immediately perceived to be incapable of acting without guidance. He realized that my husband's influence diminished his own and that to gain his end he must sow dissension between the two brothers.

A suitable opportunity for beginning this game soon presented itself. Duke Anthony Ulric of Wolfenbüttel, an impoverished and indebted younger son, asked for Lady Harburg's daughter in marriage for his eldest son, a fine young prince, hoping to use her money to ameliorate his financial situation.[211] The duke of Celle, fearing that his daughter might be snubbed was she to enter this family without an honorable rank, spoke of asking the emperor to legitimize her. The chancellor secretly hinted that the matter would be solved if the duke married the girl's mother. The duke, however, stood firm and contented himself with arranging with my husband that the emperor should legitimize

209. Charles Philip, born on October 13, 1669, died in combat in Albania on January 2, 1690.

210. Brunswick was besieged June 6–12, 1671. Johann Helwig Sinold, Baron Schütz, had actually been named chancellor of Celle a year earlier, on June 22, 1670.

211. Anthony Ulric (1633–1714) was the younger brother of Rudolf Augustus (1627–1704), the reigning duke of Brunswick-Wolfenbüttel. Anthony Ulric succeeded his brother as reigning duke in 1704 and converted to Catholicism in 1710. The son in question is Augustus Frederick (1657–76).

her to the degree that she could bear, without the bar sinister, the arms of any great house she might enter.[212] For the time being, the chancellor was also content with this solution, having pocketed half of the sixteen thousand crowns he persuaded his master the legitimation had cost. My husband, as next heir, contractually assured her of the same great estate that his brother had bestowed on her and believed that he had made her position advantageous enough that she had every prospect of happiness.[213] The duke of Celle also seemed very satisfied with these arrangements and, we believed, would always remain so.

At this time Lady Harburg became pregnant, and my husband and I went to Altona, where the queen of Denmark desired to hand over the princess royal to my charge for the journey to Heidelberg.[214] The duke of Celle was anxious to present his mistress to the queen. Her Majesty prevaricated, but my husband, wishing to please his brother, was so persuasive that she consented to the interview. Lady Harburg accordingly came to Altona. She greeted the queen, who did not kiss her, although she did invite her to dinner. Piqued by this reception, Lady Harburg avenged herself by making sarcastic remarks about the poor fare served at the queen's table. Her mind was too base to comprehend that the gods of this earth nourish themselves with higher things than ragouts and that to them food is merely a source of sustenance.

She and the duke of Celle returned to Harburg before us, for my husband wished to escort Princess Wilhelmina Ernestine through his domains. He gave her an excellent reception at Harburg and then took us through Lüneburg and Ebsdorf to Celle, where we rested for a day. The duke of Celle, my husband, and I traveled with the princess in one carriage, while Lady Harburg followed in another with the French envoy Mr. Verjus and some ladies.[215] Lady Harburg confided to the princess (and to many others) that the duke of Celle would marry her

---

212. A diagonal black bar on a coat of arms indicates bastardy. Sophia Dorothea's imperial patent giving her the right not to bear the bar sinister is dated July 22, 1674.

213. The estate of Wilhelmsburg on the lower Elbe. The document is dated September 5, 1672.

214. Altona is now part of greater Hamburg. The visit was in August 1671.

215. Louis Verjus, count of Crécy (1626–1709).

if she bore him a son. During this journey the chancellor dared to propose to my husband that his brother marry this lady in order to make
their daughter truly legitimate. My husband succeeded in parrying
the blow for the present but was distressed by his brother's vacillation.

We continued our journey to Hanover. It was late when we arrived,
so Duke John Frederick had illuminated all the town's streets, which
was a delightful sight. His duchess was pregnant, as was I. She hoped
for a son, whereas I wanted to have another daughter. The good Lord,
however, had other plans for the duke of Hanover's domains.[216]

Passing through Kassel we saw neither the landgravine, who was regent at the time, nor her eldest son, who was in Berlin suffering from
smallpox.[217] Two younger sons, however, did the honors, meeting us
outside the town with their entire court.[218] On entering the courtyard of the palace we saw the electress Palatine, her sister Princess
Elizabeth of Hesse-Kassel, and her niece standing at the foot of the
staircase to receive us.[219] The electress overwhelmed me with her displays of affection, but I felt so ill that day that I feared that I would give
birth in Kassel. Meanwhile, the electress was offended that Princess
Wilhelmina Ernestine, her future daughter-in-law, spoke so little to
her. Being suspicious by nature she believed that I was the cause of the
princess's reserve, when in fact the Danish royal family is characteris-
tically taciturn. The princess, however, was very bright and could be

216. Duke John Frederick's wife gave birth to a daughter, Charlotte Felicitas (1671–1710),
who later became duchess of Modena, and subsequently to two other daughters. Because
John Frederick had no male heirs on his death in 1679, his domains passed to Sophia's
husband.

217. Landgravine Hedwig Sophia's husband, Landgrave William VI, died in 1663, leaving her
regent during the minority of their sons, William VII (1651–70) and Charles (1654–1730).

218. Prince Philip (1655–1721), the future landgrave of Hesse-Philippsthal, and Prince
George (1658–75).

219. Charlotte of Hesse-Kassel, the repudiated wife of Sophia's brother Charles Lewis, had
retired to Kassel in 1663. Charlotte's sister, Princess Elizabeth (1634–88), became abbess
of the Protestant convent in Herford on the death of Sophia's sister Elizabeth in 1680.
Charlotte's niece, Princess Elizabeth Henrietta (1661–83), was to become the first wife of
Frederick I (1657–1713), elector of Brandenburg and later king of Prussia. Sophia's daughter
Sophia Charlotte would become Frederick I's second wife.

quite affable with people she knew well. She shone in private, though was apt to appear rather dull in public because she had never been taught how to entertain company.

As we left Kassel I decided to travel by sedan chair. To avoid the uneven surface of the cobblestones and the throng accompanying the princess, my bearers took a detour.[220] Not expecting anyone on this path, the landgrave's artillery had aimed their cannon in its direction to fire a salute at the princess's departure. Round shot fell thick and fast around my sedan chair, terrifying our Italian musicians and causing them to quicken their pace considerably. But not destined to be killed by a cannonball like Marshal Turenne, I escaped unhurt.[221] The landgravine of Hesse-Kassel paid our expenses throughout her territory, and the landgrave of Hesse-Darmstadt did the same, although with even greater ceremony and magnificence. In Frankfurt my husband insisted on paying for everything, entertaining the princess and her retinue sumptuously for three days.

Leaving Frankfurt on our way to Darmstadt we passed through the territory of the elector of Mainz, who also welcomed and entertained us.[222] The landgrave of Hesse-Darmstadt was the son of the landgrave I mentioned earlier in these memoirs.[223] He, his second wife (a princess of Saxe-Gotha), and his rather large family met us outside the city.[224] We saw a great change for the better in his court, in terms of both cleanliness and orderliness. Still, we dined for five hours, which

220. The throng was considerable: the Danish princess's entourage numbered 463 people mounted on, or drawn by, a total of 548 horses (Sophia, *Mémoires*, 122).

221. The anecdote is almost certainly a fabrication, since cannon are not loaded with shot to fire a salute. It also reveals that being a court musician meant having a second, more physically demanding job: serving as Sophia's sedan-chair bearer. Henri de la Tour d'Auvergne, viscount of Turenne and marshal of France (1611–75), was killed by a cannonball on July 27, 1675, while reconnoitering an enemy artillery position near the town of Sasbach, fifteen miles southwest of Baden-Baden. Marshal Turenne was distantly related to Sophia, being the son of her grandaunt Elizabeth of Orange-Nassau (1577–1652).

222. Johann Philip von Schönborn (1605–73).

223. Lewis VI (1630–78), son of George II (1605–61), whose sister Anna Eleanor (1601–59) was Sophia's mother-in-law.

224. Elizabeth Dorothea of Saxe-Gotha (1640–1709).

was considered a brief meal at this court, for the landgravine's ladies said to ours, "Surely your duchess must have been ill, since dinner was over so soon." The music during our repast seemed to us most extraordinary, consisting of bells like the ones in Holland that mark the hours by playing various airs. We were told that this was the landgrave's favorite music. The next day we again dined for a very long time, and on the third day we set out for the Palatinate.

The electoral prince Palatine, anxious to demonstrate his impatience, came out to meet us incognito and joined us in our carriage. Count Löwenstein welcomed the princess in the elector's name. We spent the night in Weinheim, which is only eleven miles from Heidelberg. Because all was not ready for our grand entrance, the elector begged the princess to rest in Weinheim for three days.

Three days were too much for me, since I needed to be ready for my next child to enter the world and not just for the princess to enter Heidelberg. Feeling extremely ill, I decided to travel with Madam von Harling in a sedan chair with my midwife in another and to make my way to Heidelberg with all possible speed.[225] The fair princess was sad to see me go. Not knowing anyone else, she felt lost without me. I reached Heidelberg in one piece, and since the warm weather had put color in my cheeks, the elector did not suspect that I was unwell. He consequently talked to me for an entire hour without inviting me to sit down. He assumed that I would be joining him for supper, but I excused myself and got into bed. After supper the elector seated himself next to my bed and spoke to me for another two hours. When he left I was never so glad to be rid of his company, since it was my midwife's that I needed more. I was sick all night and until ten the next morning, when I gave birth to a son whom we named Christian after the king of Denmark.[226] The elector, who still thought I was feeling fine, sent to ask when I would be ready to go with him to receive the princess royal.

---

225. Anna Katharina von Harling, née von Offeln, wife of Duke Ernest Augustus's grand equerry, Christian Friedrich von Harling.

226. Christian Henry, born on September 29, 1671, drowned in the Danube on July 31, 1703, while in imperial military service. Sophia was two weeks from her forty-first birthday when she gave birth to Christian Henry.

I replied that I was otherwise engaged, and he came at once to offer his congratulations now that I was over the worst.

He then went to receive the princess royal, and the wedding was celebrated with a magnificence that neither gave me any pleasure nor caused me any inconvenience.[227] The electoral prince, who had been raised in an atmosphere of great modesty, asked for my husband's advice on a subject wholly unfamiliar to him. It appears that he was a poor pupil, as his wife has yet to become pregnant.[228] After the wedding was over, my husband went to Venice, and the electoral princess and the elector both begged me to stay with them at Mannheim until his return.

Before his departure the elector confided to us that a marriage was being negotiated between his daughter and the duke of Orleans.[229] My husband did his utmost to induce the princess to consent to the marriage despite her religious scruples. Loving and esteeming her as he did, he was most anxious that she not pass up an opportunity to secure her future happiness. After my husband had left for Venice the elector received a letter from the princess Palatine, our sister-in-law, in which she fixed the time for her visit to Strasbourg, where the elector, his daughter the electoral princess, and I were to meet her.[230] I accompanied them to Strasbourg even though it had been just four weeks since I had given birth. The princess Palatine duly arrived for the rendezvous, and so adroitly did she manage matters that the marriage was settled during our stay. The marquis of Béthune, who signed

227. The wedding took place on September 30, 1671.

228. The electoral prince and his wife were to remain childless and later became estranged. By helping to arrange this failed marriage Sophia inadvertently helped secure her place in the Protestant succession in Britain. Had the couple had children, they, as the grandchildren of Sophia's older brother Charles Lewis, would have been ahead of her and her children in the line of succession.

229. Philippe I, duke of Orleans (1640–1701). His first wife, Henrietta of England, died on June 30, 1670.

230. In 1645 Sophia's brother Prince Edward (1625–63) converted to Catholicism and married Anna Gonzaga (1616–84), the second daughter of Charles Gonzaga, duke of Nevers, Montferrat, and Mantua; Anna was subsequently known at the French court as the princess Palatine.

the marriage contract on behalf of the king of France and the duke of Orleans, solemnly declared to the elector in front of us all that no pressure would be put on his daughter's conscience.[231] The elector therefore had every reason to be pleased with the match, though, as time would prove, he gained nothing by it. Being tenderly attached to his children, he felt keenly the parting from his daughter, while her tears proved the warmth of her affection for him. Never was there so touching a farewell.

When the young princess had left with the princess Palatine, we returned to Mannheim, where for me the winter passed as tolerably as was possible in my husband's absence. Besides the elector's lively and clever conversation, I had the company of the electoral princess, whom I loved so tenderly that we were inseparable during my stay in Mannheim. As spring approached, my husband returned to Heidelberg. We put on a *Wirtschaft* in which the King of Contentment was represented by a straw figure that was half man and half woman to signify that there can be no perfect contentment where there is sensibility. The king was paraded in a procession followed by his court consisting of various nationalities and the gods and goddesses of mythology. We had drawn lots to see who would play each character. The electoral princess was Minerva, and I was Night. After the performance was over, my husband and I returned to Osnabrück.[232]

As winter approached, the duke of Celle invited us to spend it with him, telling us that we would be joined by the delightful princess of East Friesland.[233] In her agreeable company we passed the time very pleasantly. I saw that the duke of Celle's love for me had been replaced by a sincere friendship. I took the occasion of our visit to complain to

231. François Gaston, marquis of Béthune, Louis XIV's envoy.

232. Ernest Augustus and Sophia moved their residence from Iburg to Osnabrück in 1672 after the completion of their palace, built between 1667 and 1672 and modeled after the Palazzo Madama in Rome. Under Sophia's direction, the palace garden was laid out by Martin Charbonnier, a pupil of André Le Nôtre (1613–1700), who designed Versailles park and gardens.

233. Christina Charlotte (1645–99), regent in East Friesland from 1665 to 1690 during the minority of her son, Christian Eberhard (1665–1708).

him that Lady Harburg had told the electoral princess Palatine that he would marry her was she to bear him a son. He became extremely angry, saying that he could hardly believe that she would say anything so foolish. Declaring that he would do nothing of the kind, particularly if she had a son, he offered to reprove her severely in my presence. I, however, earnestly entreated him to keep the matter quiet and told him that I was quite satisfied with his assurances.

Wolfenbüttel, meanwhile, was shaken by the news that Duke Anthony Ulric wanted to marry his son to Lady Harburg's daughter. The reigning duke was indignant, for he had conferred many benefits on Duke Anthony Ulric with the idea that the son would marry one of his own daughters. He considered it disgraceful that Lady Harburg's bastard daughter should be preferred to a princess of his own house. Duke Anthony Ulric found himself in an awkward situation, but his desire for a rich daughter-in-law prevailed over his regard for family honor, even though his brother had pointed out the disgrace their house would incur by admitting an illegitimate girl. Seeking a remedy, Duke Anthony Ulric thought it best to ask Chancellor Schütz to intercede for him. The chancellor, who desired nothing more than the opportunity to create discord between my husband and the duke of Celle, advised the latter to marry Lady Harburg. This would fully legitimize their daughter without, the chancellor assured him, threatening his brother's succession. The duke of Celle lent a willing ear to this proposal and, allowing himself to be persuaded that it could be carried out without injury to my husband and his progeny, yielded to it with little difficulty. The chancellor's delight was unbounded. He was well aware that any opposition on my husband's part would arouse the anger of his brother and Lady Harburg. If my husband yielded, on the other hand, the chancellor would have it in his power to do him even greater harm.

At the chancellor's instigation the duke of Celle sent Hammerstein to present this proposal to my husband. Hammerstein duly employed all his eloquence in trying to obtain my husband's consent to the duke of Celle's morganatic marriage, from which the children would not be in the line of succession or be styled princes. He further assured my husband that Lady Harburg was only to be made a countess and that the duke of Celle was willing to give him all the guarantees he wished to assure his own succession. My husband did not relish this proposal at all, either for himself or for his brother, whom he loved too much to look on unmoved as he made such a big mistake. But he saw that his brother had been blinded to the point of really desiring this fine marriage. He believed that his brother was irresponsible enough to go through with it on his own and so thought it better to give his consent and to obtain guarantees for his succession than to allow his brother to commit this act of folly without us gaining any advantage. He therefore told Hammerstein to tell his brother that he would consent to the marriage if it could be done without any disadvantage to him.

Hammerstein also spoke to me, on the duke of Celle's behalf, about the same subject. Having been informed in advance about everything, I made the same reply. Hammerstein assured me that my husband's succession would be better secured by a morganatic marriage, which would remove all fear of the duke of Celle marrying Lady Harburg in another fashion. I yielded to his arguments, which so gratified the duke of Celle that he obliged Lady Harburg to thank me for deciding in her favor. I could tell that his intentions had been good but that she had obeyed his orders reluctantly and ungraciously. With tears in her eyes she assured my husband that she had too much regard for him to wish for any change in her own condition and only desired the marriage to legitimize her daughter, who would otherwise be snubbed. Duke Anthony Ulric, who said the same thing to me on Lady Harburg's behalf, also begged me to tell everyone that she and the duke of Celle had been married from the beginning. Not being in the habit of telling lies, I declined to do so.

[January 1675]

Meanwhile, my husband had those of his councilors who understand legal matters draw up provisions for securing his succession, most of which were to be executed before the marriage. The chief points were that Lady Harburg should be created countess of Wilhelmsburg only; that her issue would be no more than counts and countesses of Wilhelmsburg; that the estates, ministers, and army should declare in

writing that after the duke of Celle's death they would acknowledge
no other successor than my husband and his descendents; that if Lady
Harburg became pregnant, all the subjects would take an oath of allegiance to my husband; that all princes of his house would promise
to maintain his rights; and finally that the emperor would confirm all
these articles and issue an order forbidding the Chamber of Speyer
ever to admit a lawsuit on the subject.[234]

While these articles were being sent to the emperor, the dukes proceeded with their troops to the Mosel, where, thanks to my husband's
generalship and conduct, they won a famous battle against Marshal
Créqui.[235] This battle having made such a stir, I do not need to go into
details and will merely insert the letter my husband wrote to me on
the occasion:

> From the battlefield, August 11, 1675
>
> This is to inform you that today we achieved the most
> complete victory imaginable. We entirely defeated
> Marshal Créqui, fording a river before his eyes and
> attacking him in his camp, though the marshal sal-
> lied and counterattacked with considerable vigor. All
> my men performed marvelously, and I dare say that
> Offeln's regiment carried the day for us. Old Lt.-Col.
> Hulsen and Hammerstein did wonders. Hacke also did
> very well with his regiment, but his brother was killed.
> Vogt has three or four sword cuts, and Ranzo is also
> badly wounded. Even worse, Hinderson is so severely
> wounded that he can hardly hope to recover. Weihe has
> a thigh wound. Bragelonne is well, and my guards, who
> formed a squadron with those of my brother, did won-
> ders. My company of dragoon guards suffered severely,
> and poor Brandstein is missing. We know that he was

234. The two brothers' agreement is dated May 15, 1675; the Chamber of Speyer was an
imperial court of justice.

235. On August 11, 1675, troops led by the two dukes defeated French forces commanded
by François de Blanchefort de Bonne, Marshal Créqui, at Conz, five miles southwest of Trier
near the confluence of the Saar and the Mosel.

badly wounded, but his body has not been found, so we cannot tell whether he was killed or taken prisoner. Molte is mortally wounded, and Colonel Offen, who only had two cavalry squadrons under his command, distinguished himself and is unhurt. Ferquen's little regiment, which was much despised according to the duke of Holstein, did very well, though I could not see for myself because it was too far away. Beauregard did very well, as did Malortie and Melleville, though the latter's squadron was routed. Haxthausen, who is badly wounded in the leg, was deserted by his men. Your Benjamin [this was my husband's nickname for our eldest son] never left my side, and I may say that he's a son worthy of his mother. We had to face some sharp musketry, but in the end our victory was quite complete. We captured their baggage train, numerous flags, standards, cannon, all their generals with the exception of Marshal Créqui, and their camp, which we now occupy. I lost but one of my servants (a groom) and one horse. The two were blown up by a barrel of the enemy's powder that had caught fire. Borg was guarding our baggage train with his regiment and a squadron each of Offen's and Hitzfeld's cavalry, an assignment that prevented them from taking an active part in the fight. It has been a glorious day, and I am certain that in the future Osnabrück troops will be treated with a little more respect. My son Johannes (that is, Bouche) is well but had his best horse shot from under him.[236] In a word, I could not be more satisfied with my men and have seen that all warriors are not heroes, etc.

I so rejoiced at this news that I immediately sent it to Lady Harburg, pointing out to her that all the Osnabrück troops had fought well, but not the Celle troops, by whose misconduct Melleville and Haxthausen

236. Geerds speculates that this is Johann von dem Bussche (1642–93). See *Die Mutter der Könige von Preußen und England. Memoiren und Briefe der Kurfürstin Sophie von Hannover*, trans. and ed. Robert Geerds (Munich and Leipzig: Langewiesche-Brandt, 1913), 126.

had been wounded. I added that I hoped my husband would be content with this victory and that he would have better luck in battle than at basset, where he invariably won at the beginning of the game only to lose in the end.

Unable to conceal her venom on this occasion, this malicious woman misconstrued my letter to mean that I attributed all the martial glory to my duke (whose good fortune she envied) just because I failed to mention her duke (although it was her responsibility to send me news of him). She tried to start a quarrel between me and the duke of Celle and wrote some very irritating things in her reply. To preempt the mischief she was trying to cause, I sent her letter to him. He ordered her to beg my pardon and to express her regret if she had been so unfortunate as to have written anything that displeased me. Since she had misinterpreted my letters, I stopped writing to her in order to avoid future complications.

The dukes and their allies also captured the town of Trier and took Marshal Créqui prisoner.[237] Meanwhile, the bishop of Münster, whom they mistrusted, made some conquests in the bishopric of Bremen, which brought the dukes home to look after their own interests. They both came to Osnabrück, and I truly rejoiced to see them again. The duke of Celle left us the night after his arrival, and my husband followed him a few days afterward to Harburg. The duke of Celle, anxious to please his mistress, astounded my husband by remarking, "I think now is a good time for me to get married." Fearing to bring on himself one of the duke of Celle's frequent insulting outbursts, my husband initially raised no objection. Afterward, however, he sent his brother a letter expressing his hope that their agreement still stood and that all the promised provisions would be carried out before the wedding was celebrated. This, to Lady Harburg's great indignation, delayed the wedding. Duke Anthony Ulric also greatly annoyed my husband by requesting, at the chancellor's instigation, that Lady Harburg bear the title of princess. This my husband flatly refused, returning to Osnabrück in a very bad mood. He then left to travel in Holland, partly on business and partly for pleasure.

237. The French garrison at Trier surrendered on September 4, 1675.

Meanwhile, the rumor was circulating that Lady Harburg was soon to be given the title of princess, which caused me to write the following letter to the duke of Celle:

Osnabrück, February 1, 1676

I have learned, Sir, that you are preparing to execute the proposal made to me on your behalf by Grand Bailiff Hammerstein at Bruchhausen, despite the fact that this proposal is quite contrary to the assurances you have given to me both in writing and on countless occasions in person. I was most desirous to gratify you in this matter, since Hammerstein assured me on your behalf that your marriage would not prevent my children from succeeding to your domains, that you would provide guarantees to this effect, that Lady Harburg would never claim any title or rank other than countess, and that your sole wish in marrying her was to enable you to arrange an advantageous match for your daughter. All these considerations persuaded me to agree to your requests, and you were gracious enough to show your satisfaction and even to ask Lady Harburg to thank me, which she troubled herself to do before I departed from Bruchhausen.

To my surprise I now learn that she wishes to go much further, contrary to her promise to my husband. Nevertheless, I am convinced that, when you take a moment to reflect on the dishonor this would bring on the House of Brunswick, you will choose to dissuade her from this notion rather than encourage her to pursue it. She is said to be pregnant. Even with all your good intentions, you cannot control how your children will behave toward mine if they are the issue of a legitimate marriage between a prince and a princess. Moreover, there is no precedent for a prince's consort to bear the title of princess if her children are excluded from the line of succession. You know from your own fateful experience just what a prince is capable of once he appears on the scene.[238] It seems to me, therefore, that one should take as many precautions as possible, for I would be deeply saddened if a dispute or distrust ever arose between your children and mine. But this is precisely what could happen if your children are born of a princess.

So grand and so noble are your intentions to secure your house's advantages that you even assured me that you would go to war before you would allow your nephews ever to become slaves of France. All the more reason, it seems to me, for you to wish to avoid anything that could disturb the future peace of their realm. The duke of Lorraine and the prince of Vaudémont get along splendidly because their positions are indisputable: the one is legitimate, the other is not.[239] Here, however, the children of our two families would be equally legitimate. If, in addition, your son was born of a princess, it could lead to situations to which I would be reluctant to subject my children. I therefore hope, Sir, that you will not think it strange that I am completely opposed to this new title. I would be most sorry if, through my opposition, I should have the misfortune to displease you. However, you have only yourself to blame, since you were the cause of your brother's marriage to me. I have always felt that I owe you a debt of gratitude for your choice, since it has conferred on me countless pleasures. But now it is a source of concern, since it has placed me in a position that renders me incapable of fully satisfying the wishes of a person

238. Van der Cruysse proposes that this is an allusion to Duke John Frederick's seizure of the domains that should rightly have fallen to Duke George William on the death of their older brother Duke Christian Lewis in 1665 (Sophia, *Mémoires*, 131).

239. Charles Henry of Lorraine, prince of Vaudémont (1649–1723), the son of Charles IV, duke of Lorraine and Bar (1604–75), and Béatrice de Cusance (1614–63), was excluded from the succession because Pope Urban VII declared the parents' union illegitimate (Sophia, *Memoiren*, 107).

you love. Nevertheless, I tell myself that you have too much consideration for me to wish me ill and to deny me the continuation of your friendship, which I shall seek to retain at every encounter and to demonstrate that I am your most humble and obedient servant,

Sophia.

The duke of Celle sent me the following reply:

Celle, February 9, 1676

I have received two letters from you in the past eight days, Madam, but I think you will be content with one in response. It is your second letter, therefore, to which I must respond and tell you that it is true that I am on the verge of finishing the business that was discussed at Bruchhausen. But it will be done in such a way that you will certainly suffer no injustice and that will provide you and your children with the most complete assurances. Considering all that I have done in this matter, it seems to me, Madam, that you have nothing more to fear. Even if Lady Harburg should desire to bear the title of princess, this would be done under terms that would prevent your children from suffering any disadvantage. The title of princess would not in any way alter the line of succession. The prince of Vaudement is a case in point, since his mother received the honors due a duchess of Lorraine, as I believe you well know. Moreover, I think you are also aware that questions of succession are decided according to existing agreements and that the marriage contract I concluded with Lady Harburg stipulates that her offspring shall bear the title of count and shall not inherit the duchy as long as the House of Brunswick exists. The emperor has ratified this arrangement, and Lady Harburg cannot alter it in any way even if she wanted to. Of my own volition I promised my brother to make him heir to my dominions. If I intended to change my mind, you can be sure, Madam, that I would not go to such great lengths to reassure him and blindly grant, as I have done until now, his every request for guarantees. In view of this it seems to me that you can put your mind at ease and be convinced that I as long as I live I shall take care of your interests, as I am truly, more than any other person on earth, your very humble and obedient servant,

G.W.

The duke of Celle's answer proved that he had the best of intentions and that Duke Anthony Ulric and Chancellor Schütz would never have succeeded in inducing him to act against his brother's interests had they not made him believe that he was not doing so. He ordered his estates, his officer corps, and his councilors to sign written declarations that on his death they would recognize no other successor than my husband and his descendents. The emperor ratified the other articles as well, although the duke of Celle, under the chancellor's influence, was less than compliant.[240] For no sooner had the marriage been privately celebrated with only Duke Anthony Ulric, his wife, and the chancellor in attendance, than Anthony Ulric went about hinting that the duke of Celle would be pleased to see his wife receive the honors due a duchess.[241] He also arranged it so that she and her daughter should be publicly prayed for in the realm's churches, as is customary for a duchess and a princess. Gersdorf, the imperial envoy, was the first to address the new duchess as Your Highness. My husband, hearing of what was going on at Celle, wrote to complain to his brother and express his surprise that promises of such great importance could be forgotten so soon. The duke of Celle replied that it was not he who had addressed his wife as duchess nor was it in his power to prevent others from doing so. I considered this a very poor excuse.

240. The articles are dated November 2, 1675.

241. The marriage took place in April 1676.

We also learned that Lady Harburg was pregnant, which she had concealed in order to facilitate her daughter's engagement to the prince of Wolfenbüttel.[242] When my husband heard of this he immediately demanded that his brother's subjects take an oath of fidelity to him in accordance with the two brothers' agreement. Under frivolous pretexts, however, the chancellor evaded this demand. He also played another of his cunning tricks by stealing from the imperial chancery the emperor's order forbidding the Chamber of Speyer to receive any lawsuit disputing my husband's right to the succession. My husband plainly saw what this man's game was should Lady Harburg have a son. And although the Almighty scotched his plans by sending Lady Harburg a stillborn daughter, the chancellor still succeeded in estranging the brothers.

The chancellor persuaded his master that my husband was merely being stubborn in refusing to grant Lady Harburg the title of duchess and that such obstinacy about a mere title showed my husband's want of affection and consideration for his brother. It was, however, a vital point, and one on which my husband could not yield without himself annulling the entire agreement ratified by the emperor. For had he yielded this point in direct contradiction to the agreement, the outcome would have been extremely uncertain. However, the duke of Celle would no longer listen to reason. He was completely under the sway of his wife and the chancellor, who increasingly poisoned him against us.

When this fine marriage between the duke of Celle and Lady Harburg became known, those who had formerly esteemed the duke refused to believe it. The duchess of Orleans wrote that she could not refrain from telling me that Lady Harburg had written to inform her friends in France that she was married to the duke of Celle and hoped soon to present him with an heir. The duchess of Orleans added that, although she knew this to be untrue, she thought it only right to inform me so that I might stop this creature from spreading rumors so damaging to the duke of Celle. For if this prince had ever meditated committing such an act of folly, she was sure he would give up the idea when he

242. The document arranging the marriage between Prince Augustus Frederick of Wolfenbüttel and Sophia Dorothea is dated April 2, 1676.

heard of the derision it excited at the French court, a derison so general that it encompassed the servants, since one of the duke of Orleans's
valets, named Colin, had once been engaged to Lady Harburg.

I replied to the duchess of Orleans that I was unable to deny that the
duke of Celle had indeed married Lady Harburg but assured her that
he was too devoted to my husband and to the glory of the House
of Brunswick to act in a manner prejudicial to either. I added that
he had given my husband ample guarantees for the succession and
that Lady Harburg was to be merely countess, and her male children
merely counts, of Wilhelmsburg. I thought I was telling the truth, but
time proved that I had unintentionally told a falsehood. For the duke
of Celle, through his own weakness, dispelled the favorable light in
which I had presented his marriage. The duchess of Orleans expressed
great joy on hearing that the marriage had caused my husband no disadvantage. When someone told her that Lady Harburg was a duchess,
she grew angry and quoted the contents of my letter. This reached the
ears of Lady Harburg, who, to put me on utterly bad terms with the
duke of Celle, persuaded him that I had repeatedly ridiculed him in
my letters to the duchess of Orleans. The poor duke was deeply hurt,
for it never occurred to him that his wife seldom told the truth.

[Summer 1679]
Meanwhile, some genuinely or supposedly well-meaning people in-
tervened to reconcile the two brothers. But there was no way to undo
what had been done, nor could my husband yield without gravely
compromising his interests. A marriage was proposed between the
duke of Celle's daughter and our eldest son, but my husband considered the match so beneath our son that he resolved to consent only if
it seemed to defend our rights against any future machinations should
Lady Harburg have a son. He therefore demanded two fortresses and
one hundred thousand crowns a year and let the negotiations drag
on without coming to a conclusion. The duchess of Mecklenburg also
became involved in the matter.[243] But Lady Harburg, who had become

243. After the death of her first husband, Gaspard de Coligny, duke of Châtillon (1620–49),
Elizabeth Angelica de Montmorency-Bouteville (1627–95) married Christian Lewis I, duke
of Mecklenburg-Schwerin (1623–92), in 1664.

very haughty, insulted her by remarking that it was the duchess's amorous sentiments for my husband that made her take such a warm interest in his affairs.

Chapter 6
France (1679)

The beautiful duchess of Mecklenburg, who was passing through Osnabrück on her return to France, inspired me with a powerful desire to accompany her and visit the duchess of Orleans, my sister the abbess of Maubuisson (whom I had not seen for thirty years), and my sister-in-law the princess Palatine (who had written several times to express her wish to discuss a marriage between my oldest son and her granddaughter the princess of Hanover).[244] To induce my husband to consent to the journey, the duchess of Mecklenburg proposed that we take along my daughter in the hope that her beauty might bring about a marital alliance between us and France, for the dauphin was unmarried. All these reasons were required to obtain my husband's permission for the journey. For my part, I was very eager to go and required no such persuasion.

My husband kindly accompanied us as far as Amsterdam, where he came down with a fever. I refused to leave him in this state, and the duchess of Mecklenburg, though accustomed to leisure, tended him without interruption. As soon as he had recovered we set out.[245]

I was attended only by Madam von Harling and my ladies-in-waiting, for Madam Sacetot, who was supposed to have come with us, fell ill and stayed in Amsterdam.[246] The gentlemen accompanying me were Mr. von Harling, Chevalier von Sandis, and Mr. von Rosen.[247] I had

---

244. One of the princess Palatine's daughters, Benedicta Henrietta (1652–1730), was married to Sophia's brother-in-law Duke John Frederick of Hanover. Their oldest daughter Charlotte Felicitas (1671–1710) is presumably the princess of Hanover under discussion here; she ultimately married Rinaldo d'Este, duke of Modena (1655–1737).

245. July 20, 1679.

246. Catherine de Sacetot, née de la Chevallerie, was Sophia's chief lady-in-waiting. About two months before the Paris trip, she married a courtier named Sacetot, a former page of Sophia's oldest son George Lewis (Sophia, *Briefwechsel*, 359).

247. Presumably this is the Lt. Col. von Rosen who accompanied Sophia's son Frederick Augustus on a cavalier's tour of Italy in 1680 (Schnath, *Geschichte*, 1: 284).

quite a few servants with me and three carriages. All this was considered a rather large entourage in France.

It could be said that departing Amsterdam we sailed with a steady breeze from astern, for old Madam Withypoll, who insisted on coming part of the way, broke wind frequently.[248] The duchess of Mecklenburg could not endure my friendliness toward this good woman, whom age had made unappealing in the duchess's eyes, though not in mine. In spite of her flatulence, I had the greatest esteem for her for having taken such good care of me in my youth.

We left Madam Withypoll at Leiden and were joined on board by the French ambassador, the count of Avaux, whose dapper and fragrant person perfumed the entire ship with jasmine and a thousand other sweet scents.[249] Our new guest cheered up the duchess of Mecklenburg, who found his company as delightful as I did, and we conversed as long as daylight permitted. Soon after midnight, however, all the ladies went to bed, with the exception of the countess of Chavagnac, the duchess's niece, who remained awake, endeavoring to rekindle the flame that had once burned for her in the ambassador's heart.[250] But time was short, and he had to leave us when we boarded a large sailboat lent to us by the prince of Orange to take us to Trois Fontaines, near Brussels, where carriages awaited us.[251] We had a delightful time aboard the sailboat until the duchess and her niece became alarmed about one of the captain's children who was said to have smallpox. Although the little boy was immediately transferred to the luggage boat and we were assured that he only had scabies, he remained a source of grave concern to the two ladies, for whom beauty was the highest good. After many anxious exclamations we reached Antwerp,

---

248. Mary Withypoll, née Carey, is one of two sisters who accompanied Sophia to Heidelberg in 1650 as her ladies-in-waiting.

249. Jean Antoine de Mesmes, count of Avaux (1640–1709).

250. Possibly the wife of the count of Chavagnac, a noble from the Auvergne region who was standard-bearer in the duke of Orleans's light horse regiment and, from January 1699, the duchess of Orleans's equerry (Sophia, *Mémoires*, 138).

251. William III (1650–1702), stadtholder of the Netherlands and subsequently king of Great Britain and Ireland from 1689 to 1702.

where the pleasure of seeing so lovely a city caused this disagreeable adventure to be forgotten.

From Antwerp we went to Trois Fontaines, where we spent the night. The next day we proceeded to Hal, where the duchess of Mecklenburg paid her devotions to the Virgin, presumably to preserve her beauty.[252] I contented myself with buying medals and rosaries for our Osnabrück nuns. The following day we dined in Soignies, which was noteworthy because of the demise of the duchess's she-monkey. The duchess was convinced her pet had died of unrequited love for my daughter's little dog, which was also female, a fact that inspired her to make many clever remarks about her monkey's fatal attraction. That night we spent in Mons. Having heard so much about the beautiful canonesses of Mons, I went to the church to see them but did not find them worthy of their reputation. They asked me for money, at which I laughed and said they did not need any.

The next day we reached Valenciennes. Although Count Magalotti, the town's governor, was absent, I was put up in his rooms, which were extremely well kept and had a pretty garden outside.[253] The following day we reached Cambrai. Hearing of my arrival, the governor, Mr. de Susane, came to look for me at the inn and found me in a church not far from his house.[254] He asked for the honor of my company at dinner in so frank and friendly a manner that I could not refuse. He was quartered in a fine but very dirty house. The dinner, however, was excellent, and I noted that the French are as particular about good food as the Italians are about clean rooms. After dinner the magistrates presented me with some delicious preserves, and the bishop, who was

252. "Hal ... is celebrated throughout Belgium as a resort of pilgrims ... [T]he church of Notre Dame (formerly St. Martin), a pure Gothic edifice, [was] begun in 1341 and consecrated in 1409 ... The miracle-working image of the Virgin has been in Hal since 1267" (*Belgium and Holland including the Grand-Duchy of Luxembourg. Handbook for Travellers*, 15th ed. Leipzig: Karl Baedeker, 1910, 8).

253. Bardo de Bardi, Count Magalotti, the first French governor of Valenciennes after its surrender on March 17, 1677. Sophia is traveling through an area of the former Spanish Netherlands that had come under French control the previous year in accordance with the Treaty of Nijmegen of August 10, 1678, which ended the Dutch War.

254. The Church of Notre Dame (Sophia, *Mémoires*, 139).

a most agreeable person, paid me a visit and provided me with fresh horses to take us to Péronne that same day.[255]

As I approached this town in the evening, its governor, Mr. de Hottincourt, came out to meet me. Dismounting his horse at my carriage door, he said, "Mr. de Hottincourt begs you to do him the honor of taking a light supper with him." After this debut he remounted and rode on before us. His words left us in doubt as to whether it was indeed the governor himself who had said them, for the duchess of Mecklenburg had been unable to recognize him in the twilight. He had cannon fired as we entered the town and had me alight at his own house, where I thought he meant to lodge me, though it turned out we were staying at the inn. Madam de Hottincourt and her daughter gave me a most polite reception, but supper was long in coming. Although I felt more inclined to sleep than eat, I put on a brave face. After supper I was most politely escorted to the inn by Mr. de Hottincourt, who was indeed a charming little man. It was quite evident that his wife was in charge and ordered him about as she pleased. She came the next day to the inn to bring me to their house for dinner. In the evening we went on to Roye.

The next day we dined in Estrées-St.-Denis. The inn was very dirty, so we ate our meal in a house lent to us by a certain Mr. de La Letterie and his wife. The entire dwelling, which turned out to be little better than the inn, consisted of a kitchen and three rooms hung with Bergamo wallpaper whose colors were concealed by a thick layer of dust. A small vegetable garden was the couple's only source of comestibles. Their sole consolation, as far as I could see, was a huge volume of Seneca, from which they had doubtless learned to despise riches. They had not made their way to Germany, where their countrymen have found that the courts of princes are the best refuge from poverty at home. Good Mr. de La Letterie was too old to go seek his fortune. Otherwise, he too might have come to our courts to pass himself off as a great nobleman and nourish himself with good food instead of Seneca's teachings.

255. Jacques Théodore de Bryas, archbishop of Cambrai between 1675 and 1694.

In the evening we reached Liancourt-en-Beauvaisis, one of the most delightful places I have ever seen. The duchess of Mecklenburg put me up in the beautiful palace, with its enchanting garden.[256] She insisted on doing the honors and entertaining me, which she did in the most charming manner. It seemed that she preferred for me to stay at Liancourt rather than at Marlon, which was perhaps in disorder because of her absence, although in Germany she had always expressed her desire to lodge me at the latter. I had heard so much about Father Desmares, who had been exiled to Liancourt as a Jansenist, that the duchess, who held him in high esteem, sent for him. He was a decrepit little old man, firmly convinced of the inevitable damnation of all who did not share his opinions and incapable of listening to reason on the subject.[257] He seemed very pleased with himself and therefore quite happy. He would have been miserable, in my opinion, if he had sought his happiness in pleasing others, for there was nothing appealing about him either to God or man. The day after this meeting I left Liancourt, wishing that it were my husband's estate, for it truly was a most beautiful retreat, perfect for mental relaxation. I arrived in Beaumont, where I dined in high spirits in anticipation of seeing my sister at Maubuisson later that day.[258]

I had traveled for twenty-two days since leaving Amsterdam, reaching Antwerp on August 11, 1679, Trois Fontaines on the 13th, Hal on the 14th, Mons on the 15th, Valenciennes on the 16th, Péronne on the 17th, Roye on the 18th, Liancourt, where I rested, on the 19th, and Maubuisson on the 22nd.

256. The impressive chateau and gardens at Liancourt, which became the property of the La Rochefoucauld family in 1659, were largely destroyed during the French Revolution (Sophia, *Mémoires*, 140).

257. Joseph Desmares (1603–87), also known as Toussaint-Guy-Joseph Desmares, was a renowned Jansenist orator; the manuscript refers to him as La Mare (Sophia, *Mémoires*, 140).

258. The Abbey of Notre-Dame-la-Royale de Maubuisson, located across the Oise River from Pontoise, was founded in 1241 by Blanche de Castille for Cistercian nuns. Sophia's sister Louisa Hollandina became its abbess in 1664 (Sophia, *Mémoires*, 141).

Intending to enter the convent unseen, we all were dressed in simple clothes and therefore greatly surprised to learn that Monsieur, Madame, and Mademoiselle were there with their entire court.[259] We had no means of freshening up, at which the duchess of Mecklenburg and the countess of Chavagnac were more distressed than Madam von Harling and I. As we drove into the courtyard I saw Madame running as fast as she could to meet us, with Mademoiselle right behind her. I hardly had time to alight from the carriage to pay her the honors due her rank. Weeping for joy at seeing me again, Madame kissed me and held me tightly, releasing me from her embrace only long enough for me to greet Mademoiselle, while she affectionately kissed Madam von Harling, who had been her governess. She then put her arm around me again to introduce Monsieur, who was standing at the convent door with my sister the abbess. Monsieur welcomed me most civilly, treating me as if he had known me all his life. While I embraced my sister, he went upstairs with Mademoiselle to the convent parlor. I followed soon after with Madame, who still clasped me tightly. We sat without ceremony on taborets, and Monsieur tried at once to awaken in me a desire to go to the Palais Royal and see the beauty and splendor of his preparations for Mademoiselle's marriage to the king of Spain.[260] I prevaricated, expressing my reluctance to leave the convent, but he answered all my objections, declaring simply, "You must claim the same honors claimed by the duchesses of Savoy and Lorraine." I was anxious, however, to avoid all that by remaining incognito, with which he seemed quite pleased, saying that if I wished to come to the Palais Royal I had only to put on a black sash, and to these terms I agreed.[261]

259. Monsieur is the court title for the king of France's younger brother (in this case, Philippe I of Orleans), Madame the title for Monsieur's wife (in this case, Sophia's niece Elizabeth Charlotte), and Mademoiselle the title for their oldest daughter (in this case, Marie Louise, 1662–89, from Philippe's first marriage).

260. King Charles II of Spain (1661–1700).

261. Titles granted by foreign sovereigns (say, an English earl or, in Sophia's case, a duchess of the Holy Roman Empire) did not give their holders an official rank at the French court. See Henri Brocher, *À la cour de Louis XIV. Le rang et l'étiquette sous l'Ancien Régime* (Paris: Félix Alcan, 1934), 18. The black sash indicates to other nobles that Sophia is incognito, meaning that the usual rules of protocol can be ignored and that honors denied or granted set no precedent.

Monsieur and Mademoiselle returned that evening to Paris, and Madame stayed for the night at Maubuisson, where she also dined the next day with my sister, me, and some other ladies. After dinner we took a carriage to Paris. To avoid all questions of precedence it was agreed that Madame should go first to her children's room and I to Monsieur's, where she would come to fetch me, and we would then get into his carriage without ceremony. Madame sat beside the duchess of Mecklenburg to allow my daughter, who could not travel facing backwards without feeling sick, to sit next to me. I was surprised that Madame's horses went so slowly. She shouted, "Faster!" but it made no difference. She told me that Monsieur's equerry received a fixed sum to furnish horses for the carriage and therefore took great care not to overwork them.[262]

When we reached the Palais Royal the marchioness of Foy, formerly Miss Hinderson, came to greet me as I climbed out of the carriage.[263] Madame went to the nursery while I talked to the marchioness, who accompanied me to Monsieur's rooms. He was waiting to take me to dinner with his favorite, the chevalier of Lorraine, who was lodged in a pavilion on the palace grounds.[264] Monsieur was annoyed to hear that I had already dined with Madame and so could not partake of the excellent dinner that had been prepared especially for me. He went to eat it himself, with Mademoiselle, the duchess of Mecklenburg, and Madam de Fiennes, while Madame and I chatted with a number of

262. There may be another explanation for the horses' slow pace. In 1644 John Evelyn states that most of the roads in France are "paved with a small square freestone" that is "somewhat hard to the poor horses' feet, which causes them to ride more temperately, seldom going out of the trot, or *grand pas*, as they call it" (*The Diary of John Evelyn*. London: J.M. Dent, 1950, 1: 68).

263. One of Madame's ladies-in-waiting. Sophia, in her correspondence with Charles Lewis, periodically refers to reports she receives from "Mlle de Hinderson" at the French court. It is therefore likely that Miss Hinderson (later the marchioness of Foy) is the daughter of Lt. Col. Hinderson of the Osnabrück Guards, who is mentioned as a casualty of the Battle of Conz Bridge in 1675, and that she received her position as Madame's lady-in-waiting through Sophia's intercession.

264. Philippe de Lorraine-Armagnac (1643–1702), known as the chevalier of Lorraine, was the most prominent (and well rewarded) of Monsieur's male lovers.

persons of quality.[265] I took great pleasure in admiring the chevalier's beautiful collection of paintings.

After dinner we went upstairs to a large gallery where Monsieur had ordered all of Mademoiselle's wedding clothes to be laid out for display, as well as the items of her dresser set, which were so well gilded that I took them for solid gold, particularly as I was asked to admire them. Monsieur, however, had no desire to deceive me and told me the truth. He then took me into another room to show me all his own jewels and those he intended to give to Mademoiselle. Among his own were some very fine diamonds. The emeralds, rubies, and sapphires were of no great value, but the pearl set was very beautiful. The jewels meant for Mademoiselle, topazes set with small diamonds, were pretty but not particularly valuable. He supplemented them with a very fine set of matching pearl earrings. Having excellent taste in such matters, he took it upon himself to have all my jewels reset according to the current fashion, a project he oversaw with great care.

As for me, I was quite stupefied from seeing so many unfamiliar faces and such a bewildering array of objects. I had been apprehensive about showing myself in a French court. But on seeing the wife of Marshal Plessis, Madam de Fiennes, Madam Gordon, and the governess of Madame's maids of honor, who were the only ladies present that day, I took heart, perceiving that this court boasted as many different species as Noah's Ark.[266] Madame's ladies did not appear because all their finery was packed away for the trip to Fontainebleau, where Mademoiselle's betrothal was to be held.

---

265. This spelling is Van der Cruysse's emendation; the manuscript reads "du Fresne" (Sophia, *Mémoires*, 143).

266. In the order mentioned: Colombe de Charron (1603–81), one of Madame's ladies-in-waiting and the widow of César, count of Plessis-Praslin and duke of Choiseul, marshal of France and Monsieur's former tutor (1598–1675); Henriette Gordon-Huntley, one of Madame's ladies-in-waiting, whose habits (among which: frequent expectoration) are described by Madame in *Elisabeth Charlottens Briefe an Karoline von Wales und Anton Ulrich von Braunschweig-Wolfenbüttel*, ed. Hans F. Helmolt (1789; repr., Annaberg: Grasers, 1909), 5–6. The governess of Madame's four maids of honor was the marchioness of La d'Aubiaye (Sophia, *Mémoires*, 144).

Monsieur told me that his brother the king would be quite pleased if I came to Fontainebleau incognito and that His Majesty would see to it that I was lodged in a room from which I could watch the marriage ceremony, which was expected to be quite beautiful. I was dying to see the king and his court and so accepted this invitation with great delight. As Monsieur did not wish to be ashamed of anyone he was to introduce at court, he insisted on helping select the fabrics of the dresses we were to wear on this great occasion. The discussions on this subject detained us so long that it was late in the evening before I returned to Maubuisson, where I thoroughly enjoyed being with my sister, free to laugh with her at the folly of the world and at the attention devoted, for its sake, to the most insignificant matters.

After spending three enjoyable days with my sister I went to the house of Madam de Gonelle in Paris, who was kind enough to put me up. There, tailors and seamstresses fitted us out with dresses and beauty marks so that our appearance would be according to the latest fashion.

Thus attired, my daughter and I went to Fontainebleau on August 30, accompanied by the duchess of Mecklenburg, Madam von Harling, and the marchioness of Foy. On arriving I went to Madame's rooms, where I found Monsieur and a great crowd of people. Monsieur took me straight into a little boudoir to show me the justacorps he was having embroidered with diamonds to wear at Mademoiselle's wedding. He then took me to my own rooms and expressed regret that they were not better, explaining that the marchioness of Montespan had the best rooms and that these suited my incognito.[267] They really were quite wretched, consisting only of two small rooms for my daughter and myself, the two ladies, and all our attendants.

After I had rested for a short time Monsieur sent to ask whether I would like to see the ceremony of Mademoiselle's betrothal by proxy to the king of Spain, which was to take place in the king's presence chamber. I refused nothing that could satisfy my curiosity, so at the hour appointed for the ceremony the marquis of Effiat led me by one

267. Françoise Athénaïs de Rochechouart, marchioness of Montespan (1640–1707), Louis XIV's mistress.

hand, Chevalier von Sandis by the other, into the king's chamber.[268] I saw His Majesty sitting at a table with the queen and all the princes and princesses of the blood, except the House of Condé, which was not represented. As soon as the Grande Mademoiselle saw me she got up from the seat she occupied according to her rank and came over to embrace me, saying that I was her relative, after which she returned to her seat.[269] The marriage contract was read aloud and then signed by the king and queen, by all the princes and princesses of the blood who were present, and even by the king's children by La Vallière and Montespan.[270] The duke of Los Balbases signed for the king of Spain, and the whole ceremony was conducted with many low bows, in which its beauty chiefly consisted.[271]

Having taking it all in I wished to return to my rooms, but Monsieur said that I must wait to see the conclusion, at which a handsome stranger turned to me and said, "Monsieur thinks that everyone likes ceremony as much as he does." The conclusion I stayed to witness consisted of all the princesses filing out one after the other, bowing low to the king and queen as they went. Last of all the queen bowed to the king and also retired. When she was gone the king turned to me and greeted me in a most gracious manner. He expressed the high esteem in which he held the House of Brunswick in general and my husband in particular, declaring that he would be happy to demonstrate it on any occasion. He also said that he could bear witness to Madame's tender devotion to me and that he was happy to do her the service of telling me so. He added that although this was not the proper place to welcome me, he hoped I would not take it ill, as the flurry of the

268. Antoine Coiffier-Ruzé, marquis of Effiat (1638–1719), another of Monsieur's lovers.

269. Anne Marie Louise d'Orléans, duchess of Montpensier (1627–93), the daughter of Gaston of Orleans, known as the Grande Mademoiselle. She is Louis XIV's first cousin and, indeed, a distant relative of Sophia: Sophia's great-grandmother and the Grande Mademoiselle's mother were both of the House of Bourbon-Montpensier (Sophia, *Mémoires*, 145).

270. Louise Françoise Le Blanc de La Baume (1644–1710), created duchess of La Vallière in 1664, was another of Louis XIV's mistresses. She retired to a Carmelite convent in 1674.

271. Pablo Vincenzo Spínola y Doria, third marquis of Los Balbases and second duke of San Severino and Sesto (1630–99), was the grandson of Ambrogio Spínola y Doria (1569–1630), the Spanish general who invaded and occupied the Rhenish Palatinate in the early 1620s.

marriage had prevented him from coming to see me. After saying these words he bowed and left me, exiting through one side of the chamber, while I retired through the other to return to my rooms.

Next I was taken to the *Comédie Française*, where my incognito did not prevent people from barking out, "Make way for Lady Osnabrück!"[272] The seat assigned to me, however, suggested that it was understood that I wished to remain incognito, for it was on a well-appointed platform far from the king and the royal family, who were seated below, opposite the stage. I was too busy looking at the audience to pay any attention to the actors. I saw the duchess of Fontanges, the king's current favorite, sitting far from him and near the door so that she could step out if her pregnancy made her feel ill.[273] The crowd was so large and the heat so stifling that I discovered that the pleasures of the French court are accompanied by great discomfort. Lemonade was served as a refreshment, and when I asked for some, they called out, "A drink for Lady Osnabrück," which I considered a most impertinent thing to do in the king's presence.

When the play was over I returned to my little room, where the king's servants brought me supper and handed me my napkin, not permitting my own servants to interfere. No one supped with me but my daughter, the duchess of Mecklenburg, Madam von Harling, and the marchioness of Foy. Though it was very late, after supper I felt like seeing Madame again before going to bed. I found her and Monsieur attired in dressing gowns, with Monsieur in a nightcap tied under his chin with a flame-colored ribbon. He was busy arranging some jewels for Madame, himself, and his two daughters. Ashamed of being seen in this guise he repeatedly turned his head away from me. But I put him at his ease by helping him with the jewels and arranging a band of them for his hat, with which he seemed much pleased. After completing such an important task I could sleep in peace and so retired to bed.

272. Lady Osnabrück ("Madame d'Osnabrück") is Sophia's pseudonym in Paris while incognito.
273. Marie Angélique de Scorailles de Roussille, duchess of Fontanges (1661–81), formerly one of Madame's ladies-in-waiting. The child she was carrying would die in infancy.

The next day I was led through a huge crowd to the chapel where the wedding ceremony was to take place, the king having ordered a seat to be reserved for me. The duke of Luxemburg, who was on guard duty, led me with great care through the crush.[274] I will leave it to the *Mercure Galant* to describe the details of the ceremony, in which the cardinal of Bouillon played a principal role, and will only mention the cardinal's tendency to laugh and his difficulty in repressing it.[275] As for the king, he looked with far greater devotion at the duchess of Fontanges than at the altar. Since she was seated on a raised platform by his side, he was obliged to look up frequently in order to see her. The marchioness of Montespan, whose star was in the descendant, sat in the same row as, but at some distance from, her rival. In dishabille with an embroidered bonnet, she was sullen at the triumph of a younger woman, who was in full dress and apparently in high spirits. The duchess of Mecklenburg, who sat next to me, made every effort to ingratiate herself with anyone she thought might be of use, principally the marchioness of Montespan and the marquis of Pomponne.[276] I secretly blessed my own good fortune, which had so happily placed me above such maneuvers. The queen appeared to be much incommoded by her attire, for, despite the extreme heat, her skirt was more heavily embroidered than a caparison. Monsieur seemed delighted, having the happy faculty of being able to enjoy royal pomp without possessing royal power. Madame seemed very pleased to see her stepdaughter become a queen, and the little Mademoiselle appeared to hope for a similar lot.[277] The Grande Mademoiselle looked most imposing, the

---

274. François Henri de Montmorency-Bouteville, duke of Luxembourg (1628–95), was made captain of the Life Guards in 1673 and marshal of France in 1675.

275. Emmanuel Théodose de La Tour d'Auvergne, duke of Albret and cardinal of Bouillon (1643–1715), Marshal Turenne's nephew, was made a cardinal in 1669 and made chief almoner to Louis XIV in 1671. The cardinal is the grandson of Sophia's grandaunt Elizabeth of Orange-Nassau (1577–1652). The *Mercure Galant* was a Parisian monthly magazine.

276. Simon Arnauld, marquis of Pomponne (1618–99), French secretary of state for foreign affairs, was replaced in November 1679—only two months after Sophia's visit—by Charles Colbert, count of Croissy (1625–96) (Sophia, *Mémoires*, 147).

277. Anne Marie de Bourbon (1669–1728), Monsieur's younger daughter by his first marriage, became duchess of Savoy in 1684.

duchess of Guise just the reverse.[278] The latter's sister, the grand duchess of Tuscany, seemed to me amiable, and Mademoiselle de Blois, daughter of La Vallière, very beautiful.[279] I noticed that when the king grew weary of the ceremony he opened his mouth and shut his eyes. As for the dauphin, he looked quite vapid, and the prince of Conti rather ordinary, even though his cloak was covered with diamonds that his niece, the duchess of Enghien, had inherited from her aunt, the queen of Poland.[280] The prince of La Roche-sur-Yon was no better-looking than his brother, but the count of Vermandois, son of La Vallière, was adorable.[281] I also admired the duke of Verneuil, son of Henri IV, who was an amazingly well-preserved octogenarian.[282] His wife was equally impressive and had her train carried like, although it was not as long as, a princess's.[283] All the princes and princesses spared no effort in bowing to the altar, the king, and the queen. In conclusion the king went through the ceremony of swearing to a peace with the king of Spain. The beautiful young queen was the victim sacrificed on the altar of this supposed reconciliation. The duke of Los Balbases kissed the king's hand. After both had sworn on the Bible to an inviolable peace, we all went to dinner.

278. Elisabeth d'Orléans (1646–96), duchess of Guise and of Alençon, widow of Louis Joseph de Lorraine, duke of Guise (1650–71). She is the Grande Mademoiselle's half-sister.

279. Marguerite Louise d'Orléans (1645–1721), the duchess of Guise's older sister, the Grande Mademoiselle's half-sister, married Cosimo III de Medici, grand duke of Tuscany (1642–1723), in 1661. Marie Anne de Bourbon (1666–1736), the first Mademoiselle de Blois, legitimized daughter of Louis XIV and La Vallière, married the prince of Conti four months after Sophia's visit. She became a widow five years later.

280. Louis, the grand dauphin (1661–1711), Louis XIV's only surviving legitimate son. Louis Armond I de Bourbon, prince of Conti (1661–85). Anne Henriette Jolie, the daughter of Sophia's brother Edward and Anna Gonzaga, married to the duke of Enghien, whose title at court was Monsieur le Duc. She inherited the diamonds from her aunt, Louisa Maria Gonzaga, who had been the wife of two Polish kings, Ladislas Sigismond IV and his half-brother, John Casimir.

281. François Louis de Bourbon (1664–1709), prince of La Roche-sur-Yon, succeeded to the title prince of Conti on his elder brother's death in 1685. Louis, count of Vermandois (1667–83).

282. Henri de Bourbon-Verneuil (1601–82), natural son of Henri IV and Henriette de Balzac, marchioness of Verneuil.

283. Charlotte Séguier (1623–1704), duchess of Sully and afterward duchess of Verneuil, was a daughter of the famous Chancellor Séguier.

When dinner was over, Madame came to see me. She told me that the king wished to pay me a visit and desired to know where I would like to meet him. As I received no visitors in my own room I asked for the interview to take place in His Majesty's, where I accordingly went early that evening. The Grande Mademoiselle also came there to meet me and said that she would have visited me in my own room had she not been told that I did not receive there. After paying me many friendly compliments she informed me that her sister the grand duchess of Tuscany had asked her to mention when I was in Madame's room so that she also might come to see me. But the Grande Mademoiselle said she would do nothing of the kind. She blamed her sister for not getting along with her husband the duke, for whom she herself felt a sincere friendship. Madame sat down on a taboret, and we did the same. Shortly afterward the dauphin came in. I rose and went up to him, but he did not say a word. I tried to start a conversation, but he only answered "Yes" or "No," despite my repeated sallies. To my intense relief the king was announced. Madame hurried to meet His Majesty, as did I. He said, so that everyone could hear, "It's not you I've come to see, Madame, but Lady Osnabrück." He asked at once whether the queen had come, so that I might know that he had wished her to do so. Her Spanish notions of grandeur, however, had prevented her. Everything in the king's manner and conversation demonstrated that he was one of the world's most polite princes. Monsieur tried to whisper to him, but His Majesty said aloud, "It's rude to whisper in front of Lady Osnabrück." Monsieur repeated these words with emphasis so that I would take note of how anxious the king was to please me. And indeed, His Majesty omitted nothing that could prove his wish to do so. He said all manner of agreeable things and even reminded me of the battle that my husband and brother-in-law had won against him, saying that he had known he was facing them. I replied that since they had not enjoyed the happiness of possessing his favor they had at least striven to earn his esteem. The king responded that there had been a time when he would not have dared to seek their friendship. I replied that I was delighted that such a time was past, since I had seen him swear to a peace. He said that the agreement contained a proviso that peace would last only for as long as it was in France's best interests. I said I hoped that this would be for a long time. He replied, drawing himself up, "I don't think the princes of Germany will wage war on me again." He then spoke of his many troops, of the number he had discharged from service, and of the large contingent he still retained. All this Monsieur did his best to exaggerate. The king also praised my daughter's good looks, adding that he had heard she was clever as well. He asked whether she should be called Madam or Mademoiselle, saying that he believed the former to be the German fashion. After some indifferent conversation he took leave of me. Madame and I wished to accompany His Majesty, but he absolutely would not allow us.

That evening we went to the *Comédie Italienne*, which was so burlesque that it held my attention better than the *Comédie Française* had. Sitting at my feet were the duke of Saxe-Eisenach, the duke of Wolfenbüttel, and Prince William of Fürstenberg.[284] After the play Monsieur led me into a vast gallery, where the windows had been thrown open for the king, the queen, and the entire court, who were already assembled there, to watch fireworks. I remarked to Monsieur that it seemed a breech of etiquette for me to be in the same room with the queen without ever having paid my respects to her. He said it did not matter, adding that if I liked, he would take me to her dressing room the next day, where she would be quite alone. I gladly accepted this offer, anxious to see from close up all that I had already seen from afar.

The next day I watched from my window as the king went out hunting with the dauphin and Madame. The king drove the calash himself, in which his only passengers were Madame and Miss Poitiers.[285] Monsieur, meanwhile, was kind enough to show me the splendid palace and gardens. What surprised me most was to discover, judging from the dauphin's room, that he was still treated like a little boy, for

284. Possibly Frederick Augustus, hereditary prince of Saxe-Eisenach. Duke Augustus William of Brunswick-Wolfenbüttel (1662–1731), second son of Duke Anthony Ulric of Brunswick-Wolfenbüttel (1633–1714). Probably Francis Egon, prince of Fürstenberg (1626–82), or his brother William Egon, prince of Fürstenberg (1629–1704).

285. One of Madame's four maids of honor (Sophia, *Mémoires*, 151). A calash is a light, four-wheeled, four-passenger carriage with a folding top in which the two double seats are arranged vis-à-vis.

next to his bed was another just like it for his governor, the duke of Montausier.[286]

Having seen all this, I went to visit the lovely queen of Spain, who was not yet dressed. Monsieur showed me her wedding present from the king of Spain: a large, diamond-encrusted box containing His Majesty's portrait, which was far from handsome. I sought to console the queen by remarking that it was obviously a bad likeness. "Yes," she replied, "but do you know that he's said to resemble that ugly baboon, the duke of Wolfenbüttel," which I refused to concede. When it was time to have her hair done, her attendants brought her usual armchair, which she pushed aside and took a taboret like the one I had been given to sit on. Meanwhile, a great number of ladies had assembled around the dressing table, while Madam Martin dressed her hair and she rouged herself in the Spanish style. Among these ladies was the grand duchess of Tuscany, who was most friendly to me. We sat down together in the recess of a window. She severely condemned her sister's conduct with regard to the marquis of Pynguilhem and justified her own, explaining that Tuscan notions of regimentation and constraint had forced her to flee Florence.[287] She was, she said, much happier at the Montmartre convent, where she could go to bed and get up just when she pleased without being reproached by anyone.[288]

Our conversation was interrupted by Monsieur, who summoned me to pay my respects to the queen of France. Monsieur, who awaited me in the antechamber, seized me by the hand and dragged me so hurriedly into Her Majesty's presence chamber that I hardly had time to stop and make my curtsy. I bowed particularly low in lieu of kissing her dress, as she had wanted me to do. I paid my respects, to which the

286. Charles de Sainte-Maure, duke of Montausier (1610–90), whose handling of the dauphin's upbringing was much criticized (Sophia, *Mémoires*, 151).

287. Antonin Nompar de Caumont, marquis of Pynguilhem, later duke of Lauzun (1633–1723). Louis XIV initially approved the Grande Mademoiselle's marriage to the marquis of Pynguilhem but later changed his mind and had the marquis exiled to Pignerol from 1671 to 1680.

288. The grand duchess fled Florence in 1675 to escape the constraints placed on her by her husband. Her aunt was the abbess of the Montmartre convent.

good queen replied, "I'm glad to see you." Monsieur picked up a candle and brought it near the queen's jewels, saying, "Lady Osnabrück is very fond of jewels. Look, aren't these beautiful?" I took the candle from him, saying to the queen that I was prevented from admiring her jewels by the greater pleasure of admiring her person. She put one little white hand over her jewels and pointed with the other to her face, saying, "You must look here, not there." I was struck by the dazzling whiteness of her skin and found her much better looking seen from up close. For her figure was not attractive, her back too broad and her neck too short, which made her look thickset. Her lips were a brilliant scarlet, but her teeth were discolored and decayed. The labor of keeping up the conversation continued to fall on me. I praised the court of France and said that she clearly had found no difficulty in accustoming herself to its manners. She replied that she had indeed found the task easy because she was so happy, twice telling me, "The king loves me so much. I'm very much obliged to him." I gave the expected reply, saying that this was hardly surprising. I also asked her to tell me how many children she had had.[289] She had no one with her but the Grande Mademoiselle and the marchioness of Béthune.[290] The queen sat down in an armchair, Mademoiselle threw herself on a chaise longue, and Monsieur took a taboret, desiring me to do the same. I, however, did nothing of the kind. Explaining to the queen that Madame was expecting me, I bowed low and retired. Monsieur took me by the hand and asked why I had not sat down, saying that, although I might be able to claim a different seat in Madame's presence, I could not do so in the queen's. I answered that it was impossible for me to accept a taboret from the queen of France after having been honored with an armchair by the Holy Roman empress. Monsieur replied that every country has its customs and that the king must not hear that I had refused to accept a taboret. I said I did not care whether he found out or not.

In the evening I was led through a huge crowd to see the grand ball. Being incognito I was placed behind the king and queen and beside

289. The answer is six, only one of whom, the dauphin, lived past the age of five.
290. Marie Louise de La Grange d'Arquien, marchioness of Béthune, the queen of Poland's sister and one of the queen of France's ladies-in-waiting (1641–1716).

the marchioness of Pomponne.[291] It was like the Golden Age, husbands dancing with wives and brothers with sisters, although with greater stateliness than spontaneity, for each maintained his or her rank, and the dancing was characterized more by etiquette than enjoyment. The count of Armagnac and his son were, I thought, the best dancers.[292] It must be conceded, however, that the king danced with greater bearing, in which he was poorly seconded by his partner the queen, for she had none. He almost looked ashamed of her when they danced together. The dauphin's performance on the dance floor was hardly dazzling, and the prince of Conti expended no effort to outdo him. The German princes had refused to join in the round dance called *branle* in order to avoid disputes about precedence, but Madame made them take part in the rest. The prince of Wolfenbüttel, after having danced with Madame, next chose the queen of Spain as his partner. An ignorant ass expressed amazement at this audacity, but Mr. von Rosen rebuked him so sharply that he afterward held his peace.[293]

When the ball was over I begged Monsieur to ask the king whether His Majesty had any commands for me, since I was to leave the next day. Monsieur gave the king my message, and His Majesty came up to me and spoke very gracious words, first greeting me and then my daughter. The queen also turned to me, and as there was a chair between us, held out her dress for me to kiss. I, however, ignored the proffered garment and contented myself with making a very low curtsy. Monsieur, who had seen the queen's gesture, laughed heartily at it, telling me that she did the same thing with his children and that the little duke of Chartres said, "Do you think I'm going to kiss her dress?

291. Catherine Ladvocat, marchioness of Pomponne, wife of the secretary of state for foreign affairs.

292. Louis de Lorraine, count of Armagnac (1641–1718), governor of Anjou and grand equerry of France, known at court as Monsieur le Grand. He was the brother of Monsieur's favorite, the chevalier of Lorraine. His son, Henri de Lorraine, count of Brionne (1661–1712), was eighteen at the time of Sophia's visit.

293. In line to be the sovereign duke of Brunswick-Wolfenbüttel, Prince Augustus William thought himself at least the equal of the queen of Spain, whose father, the duke of Orleans, was not a sovereign.

She can kiss that idea goodbye."[294] And when Madame asked whether the queen had any commands for her, Her Majesty answered, "I have no commands to give you." There was nothing subtle about the queen. She cared only for eating and dressing up; in these activities she was able to find contentment.

I set out the next day quite content at having satisfied my curiosity and being received with such courtesy at Fontainebleau. I was glad to be heading for Maubuisson, where my daughter and I could enjoy a relaxing time with my sister, for we were extremely tired. I saw plainly that I was better suited to a convent than to a court that went to such great lengths to amuse itself. Even my daughter was feeling slightly feverish, and Madam von Harling was so ill that I was unable to visit Madame in Paris as she had desired. After spending four delightful days with my sister, on September 8 I set out for St. Cloud with the duchess of Mecklenburg. The coachman managed to tip the carriage right in front of the palace door, sending us tumbling to the ground. Monsieur, Madame, the queen of Spain, and the little Mademoiselle all rushed out to help us to our feet. Monsieur took my hand and led me to his own room, shouting "Chamber pots for the ladies," for he was convinced that relieving ourselves would also relieve us of the shock of our mishap. He then showed me his palace, holding my hand the entire time so that I could walk ahead of even the queen of Spain, as the occasion established no precedent. I greatly admired his beautiful gallery and fine drawing room as well as the house's impeccable cleanliness. For Monsieur had mastered the art of managing a household. My room opened on to the garden, which was perfectly beautiful on account of its landscaping and fountains. I never tired of walking in it with Monsieur and Madame, whose extreme kindness I shall forever remember with gratitude. Monsieur always dined with the queen of Spain, and Madame honored me with her company at dinner in my antechamber, where we were served by the officers of her household guard. The duchess of Foix-Randan and the marchioness of Foy dined with us several times, as did Miss de Grancey and Miss Poitiers, one

---

294. Philippe II of Orleans (1674–1723), Madame's second son (her first died in 1676), titled the duke of Chartres during his father's lifetime. He became duke of Orleans on his father's death in 1701 and was Regent of France during Louis XV's minority (1715–23).

of the first Madame's maids of honor.[295] Monsieur introduced her as someone he had formerly loved and for whom he still felt a strong friendship. He also made me kiss the chevalier of Lorraine, who was the only person, besides the king and Monsieur himself, whom I kissed in France, although according to French custom I should have kissed all the dukes and peers and the officers of the crown whom Madame kisses. They, however, had the civility to absent themselves, thereby sparing me a great deal of awkwardness.

On the morning after my arrival at St. Cloud, Monsieur and Madame came to my room by a hidden staircase to ask whether I felt like going for a walk. Since I was not yet dressed, Monsieur set off alone for the palace farm, from which he brought me butter and delicious fruit. In the afternoon we drove through the beautiful gardens. The carriage in which I sat held ten people. At Monsieur's behest the queen of Spain got in first, I followed, and then came Madame, so that I sat between the two. Mademoiselle sat at one door, and my daughter at the other. Opposite us were the marchioness of Foy and Miss de Grancey; behind us, the duchess of Mecklenburg, the marchioness of Clérembault, and Madam de Fiennes.[296] Thus arranged, we had a delightful drive through Monsieur's fairyland of plashing waterfalls and cool glades. Monsieur drove in a calash with the duke of Los Balbases and another of the Spanish ambassadors.

The king had issued orders that I was to be shown Versailles the next day. Such visits had to be arranged in advance so that the fountains could be turned on. The necessary preparations having already been made, we were obliged to go. Untiring in her thoughtfulness toward me, Madame feared that I might not receive the honors due my rank at the dinner that was to be held at Versailles. Monsieur insisted that if he dispensed with an armchair I might do the same. When, by Madame's orders, one was brought to him, he pushed it aside and took

295. Marie Charlotte de Roquelaure (1654–1710), married to Henri François de Foix de Candalle, duke of Foix-Randan (1640–1714). The "first Madame" refers to Monsieur's first wife, Henrietta of England.

296. Louise Françoise Bouthilllier de Chavigny, the widow of the marquis of Clérambault, was one of Madame's ladies-in-waiting (Sophia, *Mémoires*, 56).

a taboret. The queen of Spain, following his example, did the same, so that all passed off to my honor and credit. At dinner the queen of Spain sat at the middle of the table, with Madame on her left and Monsieur on her right. I sat beside Monsieur, and Mademoiselle next to Madame. On rising from table, Monsieur gave me half of his own napkin with which to dry my hands. After dinner we drove through the gardens in the same seating order as at St. Cloud. Wherever we stopped, Monsieur took me by the hand and made me walk with him in front of everyone so that I might see to full advantage the beauties of Versailles, where the marvels of money outdid those of nature. Given the choice, I would take St. Cloud over Versailles. When we had seen everything, some excellent refreshments were served, which were, I thought, worth all the fountains whose functioning had required so much preparation.

In the evening we went to stay in Paris at the Palais Royal, where Monsieur gave me a room close to Mademoiselle's that had been occupied by the queen of Spain before her marriage. Madame, who was kind enough to hold my hand the entire time, took me to the queen of Spain's apartments where the crowd was suffocatingly large. An overcrowded room is a discomfort highly esteemed in France. As for me, I stole away to my own room as quickly and quietly as I could, followed by Madame as soon as she had noticed my absence. There we chatted at our ease, much preferring our tête-à-tête to the idle conversation of antechambers. Madame dined with the queen, and I in my room with the duchess of Mecklenburg and the marchioness of Foy, since Madam von Harling was still very ill.

Madame, who wished me to see the king's wardrobe, took me to the Louvre, where I was shown some very ancient beds and fine tapestries.[297] We then went to the opera, which I thought was inferior to the Hanover opera when my brother-in-law John Frederick had been duke. I sat with my daughter in the same box as the queen of Spain. Monsieur sat beside me until Madame came in near the end of the performance.

297. The Louvre served as the warehouse for the crown's collection of furniture (Sophia, *Mémoires*, 157).

Monsieur told me that he had a favor to ask of me that he hoped I would not refuse. I was delighted, thinking that he was going to give me an opportunity to show my regard for him. It was, however, to ask whether I would permit him to give my daughter a present. He added that the king alone had the right to give me one. Although much surprised, I gratefully accepted this token of friendship he so graciously desired to bestow on my daughter. His present consisted of twelve diamond-encrusted buttons and buttonholes to adorn the cuffs of a dress, as was then the fashion. The little Mademoiselle wore a similar set. A few days before, Madame had told me that she knew from Monsieur that the king intended to give me a parting gift. I replied curtly, "Why does he want to do that? People will say that I came here in order to get one." This she repeated to Monsieur, who relieved my anxiety by assuring me that it was the king's custom to demonstrate his munificence by giving presents to all visitors of my rank.

On leaving the opera the queen of Spain said goodbye to everyone, for the next day she was to depart Paris forever. At this prospect her grief was so intense that she could not restrain her whimpers and tears, which infected everyone, me most of all. For this amiable princess had won my heart with her charming appearance and her countless acts of kindness to me and to my daughter, to whom she had taken so strong a fancy that she said she wished she were a prince so that she could marry her. Perhaps another motive for this wish was that she might not be forced to leave the country she loved so much. Notwithstanding her tears, she did me the honor of taking supper with me in my room on the evening before her departure. The company, which consisted of Madame, Mademoiselle, and the duchess of Mecklenburg, was too sad to eat. After supper Her Majesty refused to allow me to accompany her to her room.[298] But I went there the next day, the sad day of parting. This charming queen held me in her arms for more than an hour, shedding floods of tears and exclaiming, "I shall never see you

298. By waiving the protocol of being escorted back to her room by a lower-ranking noble (Sophia), the queen is demonstrating her affection and esteem for her. Louis XIV did the same thing earlier in Sophia's visit.

again, my dear aunt," for we are indeed related in the Breton fashion.[299] The whole court resounded with sobs and moans, and because it was the fashion to weep, many wept that day who had never even met the young queen.

Monsieur came up to me to give me the king's present, which was a large box set with cheap diamonds and another box set with some lusterless pearls for my daughter—hardly the royal largesse His Majesty had sought to demonstrate. Monsieur was ashamed of the gifts, but I was proud of them, considering them a mark of His Majesty's esteem, which I had earned without having been of service to him. Meanwhile all was ready for the departure of the young queen, who, bathed in tears, embraced me repeatedly. I wished to accompany her to the carriage, but Monsieur stopped me halfway down the staircase, desiring me to go no further because of the huge crowd. There I took leave of him, only wishing that he could look into my heart and see how deep an impression he had made on it by his many acts of kindness, which I shall never forget.

I stayed in Paris that day to do some shopping, while my daughter played with the little Mademoiselle (who was only a year younger than herself), the little duke of Chartres, and his younger sister. The next day I returned to Maubuisson, my haven of happiness in France. I also went to see the English nuns at Pontoise, who served me luncheon to encourage my charity, for they were very poor. I spent eight delightful days with my sister, whose conversation holds an untiring charm for me. Prince William of Fürstenberg and the bishop of Condom visited me at the convent grille.[300] I enjoyed their conversation but thought little of their arguments for my conversion. I have neglected to mention that the duke of Enghien came to see me a few days after my arrival at Maubuisson. His wife, who is my niece, did not accompany him because she had smallpox. The princess Palatine also sent me a

299. By "Breton" Sophia may mean that she is the aunt of the queen of Spain's stepmother (Madame). However, Sophia is also a direct relation (a first cousin, in fact) of the queen's late mother, Henrietta of England.

300. Jacques Bénigne Bossuet (1627–1704) was appointed bishop of Condom in 1669 and bishop of Meaux in 1681.

message nearly every day to express her regrets that she was too ill to see anyone.

Her illness notwithstanding, my niece the duchess of Enghien desired to strike up a friendship with me. She sent Mother Fagon, a nun who had been her governess, to me with the message that she would have herself conveyed to La Raincy, where the air is not infected, if I would honor her with my presence there.[301] The duke of Enghien would come to fetch me in his carriage and bring me back the next day. I accepted this offer, and the duke of Enghien appeared at Maubuisson, where I dined with him outside the grille. After dinner I got into his carriage accompanied by my daughter, the marchioness of Foy (for Madam von Harling was still ill), and Miss de Guénani, the duke's natural daughter.[302] We stopped in St. Denis so that the duke could feed us cheese tarts, for he said that it is the only place where they are well made.[303] It was still quite early when we reached La Raincy, where I found my niece in bed. Embracing me she said, "It gives me the greatest pleasure to see you, dear aunt." I replied, "No one could be more delighted than I, dear niece." Such was the beginning of our conversation, which grew more and more pleasant. She struck me as being very gentle, whereas her husband the duke was all fire and vivacity and had the most polished manners. After talking for a considerable time, during which the duke of Enghien made Mr. de Gourville sit down in our presence, we were told that the evening's performance was ready to start.[304] The duchess left her bed and put on a gold brocade robe fastened all the way down the front with a gaudy, flame-colored ribbon. A black hood over her crumpled white bonnet completed her costume, and so attired she was carried in a sedan chair to a nearby room

---

301. Mother Fagon is an aunt of Guy Crescent Fagon (1638–1718), Louis XIV's chief physician.

302. Julie de Bourbon, Miss de Guénani (1668–1710), legitimized daughter of the duke of Enghien and Françoise Charlotte de Montalais, countess of Marans. Raised at Maubuisson by Mother Fagon, she married the marquis of Lassay in 1696.

303. St. Denis's renown for cheese tarts (*talmouses*) is mentioned in Furetières's dictionary (Sophia, *Mémoires*, 160).

304. Jean Hérauld de Gourville (1625–1703), a *Frondeur*, financier, and memoirist.

where the play, *Jodelet the Musician*, was to be performed.[305] I admired the ballet entr'actes, but the rest was poor stuff. The duchess showed me the splendid jewels she had inherited from her aunt, the queen of Poland, which I had already seen on the prince of Conti's coat. In the evening I supped in my antechamber with the duke of Enghien and the countess of Langeron.[306] The duchess did not sup with us, for they coddled her in the most extraordinary manner, allowing her to eat fruit but not meat. After supper we chatted for a long time, for the duke is a most agreeable conversationalist. The next day he showed me the park, which was in great disorder. I dined again with him, and then he conveyed me as far as St. Denis, where, after showing me the treasure, he returned to La Raincy and I to Maubuisson. He sent two men with me dressed in threadbare livery whom I took for guards until I was informed that they were pages, since princes of the blood have no guards.

On arriving at Maubuisson I heard to my joy that Madame was expected there the next day. She asked for relays of horses to hasten her journey, and I had them sent to her. She was delighted with them because they went so fast, but her attendants following on horseback failed to adapt themselves to this German fashion. Madame told me that the king had spoken of me in the highest terms and that Monsieur had been candid with the king about the shabbiness of His Majesty's present to me. The king, who had not seen it, seemed vexed and asked Monsieur's advice on the matter. Monsieur replied that I had seemed pleased with his present of diamond buttons to my daughter. After hearing this, the king ordered that a similar set be sent to me. This, though of course quite unnecessary, nevertheless redounded to my honor as proof of His Majesty's desire to please me. Madame also told me that the dauphin was to marry the princess of Bavaria and that

305. Jodelet was the stage name of an actor named Julien Bedeau (?–1660). His popularity was such that Paul Scarron wrote two plays for him, *Le Jodelet ou le Maître valet* and *Le Jodelet duelliste*, and Thomas Corneille another, *Jodelet prince*. Molière created an eponymous role for him, Viscount Jodelet, in *Les précieuses ridicules* (1659).
306. Claude Bonne Faxe d'Espeisses, countess of Langeron, one of the duchess of Enghien's ladies-in-waiting (Sophia, *Mémoires*, 161).

they meant to marry Mademoiselle to the elector of Bavaria.[307] This deal seemed to console Madame for the failure of her earlier pet project of arranging a marriage between my daughter and the dauphin. After my departure, however, it became known that the elector would not hear of having a French wife, and this brought Madame back to her original plan. The princess Palatine also persuaded Monsieur to recommend my daughter to the king, but just as he was about to do so he learned from the king himself that it was too late. Madame wrote to tell me the same thing when I reached Germany. Never, however, can I forget Madame's kindness to me at Maubuisson. Though by nature averse to convents, she stayed with me there for two days. Her farewell was very affectionate, and we parted with much regret.

Madame returned to Fontainebleau to go hunting with the king, and I went on to Asnières-sur-Seine to see the princess Palatine, whom I found confined to her bed, sick in body but healthy in mind. There were many things she wanted to talk to me about, but her physicians forbad it and hustled me out of the room without giving me the time to tell her all that was on my mind. Having been invited by the duke of Enghien to dine with him at de Gourville's house, I went there and met the duchess of Mecklenburg and the countess of Chavagnac. The dinner was worthy of the company, being both delicious and well presented. When it was over, the duke of Enghien provided me with relays which took me to Chimay that same day. The duchess of Mecklenburg honored me with her company for part of the way. Parting from this excellent princess, whose amiable temper enhances every pleasure, caused me a keen pang of regret.

After losing sight of her and of all I had enjoyed in France I was seized with such impatience to see my husband again that the carriage could not travel fast enough for me. On the next day, September 29, I slept at La Ferté-sous-Jouarre, on the 30th at Estoge, on October 1 at Châlons. From there we traveled by St. Ménehould, Verdun, and Mabatour to

---

307. Maria Anna Christine of Bavaria (1660–90) married the grand dauphin by proxy on January 28, 1680, and arrived at Saint-Germain on March 18 of the same year. She became a good friend of Madame. The marriage between Mademoiselle and Elector Maximilian of Bavaria never took place. She married Victor Amadeus II, duke of Savoy, in 1684.

Metz, which we reached on October 5 and where an attorney kindly put me up for the night. The magistrates presented me with some excellent preserves and an oration no less sugary. Before leaving Metz I attended the Protestant church service, which so delighted the pastor and his little flock that they thanked me as if I had come for their sake and not His.

That day I embarked to sail down the Mosel, a venture I had good reason to repent, for the lodgings were very bad in the village where we docked that evening, and the danger of rocks made it too risky to travel by night. Yet I pressed on as long as we had daylight, not bothering to stop at larger towns and, as a result, often landing in poor accommodations. One night we stayed with a gentleman named Wilbret, who, though said to be very rich, was a true bumpkin. That day is impressed on my memory because we were forced to walk a long way through the mud in order to reach his palace. It is true that he offered to send a carriage to retrieve me at the river's edge, but I began to doubt whether he actually owned horses, for it grew late and no carriage arrived. His wife received us seated in an armchair, for an injury to her legs had rendered her immobile. Unable to command her legs to move, she seemed equally incapable of commanding her tongue to stop, for it never rested. She repeatedly offered us refreshments but never served them. Just as my cook was about to prepare some meat he had brought with him, nearly all of it was carried off by Mr. Wilbret's famished greyhounds. Our meal was consequently on the light side. The chatelaine talked incessantly of the good wine in her cellar and of her desire that we taste some, but unfortunately, she said, the servant who knew where to find the good cask was himself nowhere to be found. She made a great fuss about searching for him, but he never appeared. This I did not mind. But I confess to having been somewhat surprised when they showed us whole hillsides clad with vines and yet did not offer us a single grape. They were kind enough to allow me to put up my bed in their chapel, with the altar serving as a dressing table. The holy place was decorated with their genealogy, proving the legitimacy of the nobility so conspicuously absent in their manners. As an additional proof of their lineage, the master of the house attended our departure the next day in a gold-laced coat, which was evidently a relic of his ancestors. I have no recollection of the other places we passed through, for I was too impatient to see my husband again to notice anything.

At Cologne I transferred to a very small boat, since no other was for hire. A strong headwind spun the boat in circles without allowing us to make any headway. My women began to scream, but I kept on playing cards. We finally managed to sail down the Rhine as far as Duisburg, much to my relief, for it was very cold on the river. To my great surprise, however, it was a French garrison that welcomed us on what was the elector of Brandenburg's territory. For the elector had signed a miserable treaty, ceding to the French Duisburg and other fortified towns of his western dominions.[308] My husband had kindly sent a carriage and enough relays of horses to carry me to Osnabrück in a single day. My own carriages arrived in Duisburg the same day I did, proving that I had made no better progress by water than they had made by land.

---

308. Peace of St. Germain between Brandenburg and France.

Eighteenth-century print of Sophia as a widow

Chapter 7
Osnabrück, Nykøbing, Hanover (1679–80)

Words fail to describe my joy on seeing my husband again. He, for his part, was pleased with how I had conducted myself at the French court and thought that the whole affair had come off very well.[309] My joy was soon dampened when I heard that he was planning a trip to Italy and was still considering a marriage between my oldest son and Sophia Dorothea of Celle. A devoted father, he believed that the alliance would secure his children's future, fearing that they might be left in an untenable position was he by mischance to die before his brothers. Hammerstein came to Osnabrück to negotiate the matter, but the Celle party was so utterly unreasonable that the negotiations were broken off, by no means to my regret, nor to that of Duke John Frederick either. For I would infinitely have preferred my son to marry his daughter, who was by birth my son's equal, if the match had offered any advantages. But this good duke did not expect to die any time soon and consequently hesitated about the terms of the wedding contract. He asked us to come and see him at Linsburg before his departure for Italy and after his wife's for France.[310] We went there and were most kindly received by this good prince, who warmly encouraged me, as he had already done several times by letter, to join the dukes on their Italian tour. But having been there once I had no desire to return and left it to my husband to arrange their rendezvous in Venice. At Linsburg I took leave of Duke John Frederick, little imagining that it was for the last time. He started for Venice by way of Augsburg, while my husband took the route through Basel.

---

309. Sophia's husband had actually wanted her to stay at Maubuisson the entire time, presumably in order to avoid touchy protocol issues at the French court (Sophia, *Mémoires*, 250). As was seen in the previous chapter, his fears were unfounded: Sophia's treatment by the French royal family and court was markedly more deferential than was required by French protocol.

310. Duke John Frederick had a country house in Linsburg near Nienburg, which is located on the Weser River approximately fifty miles northeast of Osnabrück. His wife Benedicta Henrietta, the daughter of the princess Palatine and Sophia's brother Edward, was likely traveling to France to visit her mother.

After both were gone I heard that my sister Elizabeth, the abbess of Herford, was dangerously ill and desired to see me. I lost no time in hastening to her. Her joy at my arrival was indescribable. It was as if an angel had come down from heaven to cure her. She was surrounded by people whose gloomy piety tormented and bored her. They had deprived her of all amusements, including music, although she needed something to take her mind off her malady, incurable dropsy. At the start of her illness, although she suffered much, she was quite composed, saying that she thanked God for sixty years of health, that we all have to die eventually, and that we arrive at death through disease. With the utmost calmness she had made out her will and ordered her coffin. I noticed, however, that her mental powers ebbed with her physical strength. As the disease grew worse she lost her senses and believed that she was fully cured, although, with her stomach horribly distended and the rest of her body resembling a skeleton, death was close at hand. I was mortified to witness her piteous state and to realize that the sister I knew had already left her body. Heartily as I dislike sad scenes, I could not leave her side, for she clung with passionate tenderness to me. She often expressed her anxiety for my children's future should their father die before his brothers.

One day, when I least expected any news, Miss Gheel came in during my toilette to announce the arrival of Major Jordan from Hameln. I did not hurry getting dressed, since I did not believe that his message could be important. When ready, I desired him to meet me in my sister's room. Handing me a letter from Major General Öffener, he informed me that Duke John Frederick had died at Augsburg after two days' illness.[311] The shock was so great that I myself turned deathly pale. Though deeply lamenting the loss of so dear a friend, I had cause to thank God for delivering my husband and my children from their enemies, which at that time consisted of the entire Celle court. My poor sister shared my sentiments regarding this unexpected event and was sad to see me depart for Osnabrück after we had bid each other farewell for the last time.

---

311. John Frederick died on December 28, 1679.

The courier dispatched to my husband found him in Switzerland. He returned at once to Osnabrück, arriving a few days after me. Shrugging his shoulders, his first words to me were, "I'm glad I'm not the one who's dead." Nevertheless, he deeply felt the loss of his beloved brother and resolved to do all in his power to live at peace with the one he still had. He decided, therefore, to grant out of generosity that which he would never have done out of fear. Lady Harburg's conduct toward him had not entitled her to expect such kindness. Nevertheless, for his brother's sake he consented, when least called on to do so, to recognize her as duchess of Celle. However, he stipulated that the emperor must ratify a new contract between the brothers regarding the succession in case Lady Harburg bore a son. Three weeks after my husband's return, the sad news arrived that my poor sister the abbess of Herford was dead.[312] I felt the blow acutely and was still full of grief when my husband went to Hanover to take possession of the duchy and to bury his late brother, whose obsequies were celebrated with great pomp and pageantry, half according to Lutheran and half according to Roman Catholic rites.[313]

Some time after these events the queen of Denmark invited us to visit her at Nykøbing, her dower house, which had been built by my ancestress Queen Sophia of the House of Mecklenburg.[314] We set off in high spirits and with a large retinue, though I was accompanied only by my daughter, Madam von Harling, Miss Gheel, and, for gentlemen, High Bailiff Grote, Chevalier von Sandis, and Mr. Klencke.[315] The queen had

312. Elizabeth died on February 11, 1680.

313. Duke John Frederick had converted to Catholicism in 1651; the state religion was Lutheranism.

314. Nykøbing is on the Danish island of Falster, which, together with its neighboring island, Lolland, was the traditional dower estate of Danish queens. The queen dowager was the royal administrator of the two islands and of her estates in Ibsholm and Dronninggård.

315. Otto Grote (1636–93) had served the Danish royal family for three years as tutor of their second-oldest son Prince George (who subsequently married Anne of England) before entering the service of the Brunswick dukes in 1665 as a privy councilor to Duke John Frederick; he was later Duke Ernest Augustus's minister of war and high bailiff of the duchy of Grubenhagen. He was married to Anna Dorothea von Ahlefeld, one of Sophia's ladies-in-waiting.

sent us a pinnace to Heiligenhafen so that we could travel by water.[316] Fortunately, the sea was so calm that no one got sick. But what wind there was blew against us, and my husband, unwilling to spend the night at sea, made us land, hoping to find a vehicle that would take us the rest of the way. We walked for a long time, however, and none was to be seen. At last we spied men rowing a little boat who offered to transport us to where the queen had carts waiting to take us to Tolhus, where we were to spend the night.[317] Worn out by our walk we were only too thankful to get into the boat, which brought us to the spot where the carts awaited us. I had never before seen people of quality make use of such conveyances, which were like hay carts, except without any hay to make them comfortable. I had a little box put in for me to sit on. My daughter sat in front of me, and Chevalier von Sandis behind. One of the queen's footmen acted as coachman, and a little boy rode the lead horse as postillion. Without knowing the way they set off at full speed, for it was already very dark. At a place where the road was submerged, the little boy led us off the track, and the cart tipped over in the water. We all would have drowned quietly had the footman's shouting not attracted the attention of my husband, who was with the other carts high above us on the right road. Perceiving our danger he was very uneasy and sent men to our rescue. They waded into the thigh-deep water and carried us to land. With great difficulty the cart was righted, and we had no choice but to get back in. It was the most uncomfortable of vehicles, but nothing else was to be had because we had left our carriages at Heiligenhafen. Near Tolhus we had to cross a stream again, but this time on a pontoon bridge. Mr. Schwarz was waiting on the other side to welcome us in the queen's name. To my profound joy he ushered us to a carriage, which, however, turned out to be even more primitive than the carts. After we had arrived at our resting place for the night, I was delighted to learn at supper that Danish victuals are better than Danish vehicles.

---

316. Heiligenhafen, a seaside resort on Fehmarn Sound, is located in the present-day German state of Schleswig-Holstein.

317. I can find no Tolhus on the island of Lolland, which is probably where the duke ordered the sailboat to land. Perhaps the town is Toreby.

The next day, after breakfast, we went straight on to Nykøbing, although we had to cross another pontoon bridge to get there.[318] Awaiting our arrival on the other side was the queen, her daughter the electoral princess of Saxony, her son Prince George, and her whole court.[319] Her Majesty, embracing us most affectionately, gave us the kindest of welcomes. She desired my husband, her daughter, and me to get into her own carriage, seating my husband beside herself and her daughter beside me. On reaching the palace Her Majesty did me the honor of accompanying me to my room and remaining there for some time to talk to me. When she wished to return to her own apartments, I wanted to escort her as etiquette demanded, but Her Majesty would not permit it. Nothing could exceed the kindness the amiable queen showed us.

The amusements arranged by Her Majesty included two hunting parties for my husband, in which she herself took part, driving in an open cart, though it was raining hard. We all went along, in fact, even down to the footmen and boys, who each had his own cart and thus traveled in the same royal Danish style that we did. In a long procession of more than one hundred carts we went to the places where the peasants had amassed large quantities of hares for us to shoot. The queen hit some, and my husband killed more than thirty. The queen, who wanted me to enjoy the hunt too, insisted that I should try a shot. As chance would have it I hit a hare the first time I ever fired a gun, a feat of arms that earned me much unmerited praise. When Her Majesty was not hunting she played cards. The electoral prince and Prince George sometimes persuaded me to join them in country dances. As the queen was a person of singular goodness and merit, for whom I

318. Here Sophia draws attention to another unpleasant consequence of her husband's decision not to sail all the way to Nykøbing. Taking the pontoon bridge from the island of Lolland to the island of Falster involved crossing about a third of a mile of the Guldborg Sound on wooden planks secured to a string of boats. It was doubtless a dyspeptic experience.

319. Anna Sophia (1647–1717), wife of John George III (1647–99), the future elector of Saxony. Prince George of Denmark (1653–1708), afterward duke of Cumberland and consort of Anne of England (1665–1714), who in 1702 became queen of Great Britain and Ireland.

have the greatest affection and esteem, I gladly did all in my power to please her.

After eight highly enjoyable days we were obliged to leave. Her Majesty, with extreme kindness, insisted on accompanying us as far as Tolhus, where we said adieu and where she spent the night. The next day, while we were at dinner, the queen graciously surprised us by reappearing, refusing to budge until she had seen us embark and watched us sail out of sight. Was I to praise this virtuous queen as she deserves, I would never come to the end. She is the dukes' sister, and that says everything. The wind was favorable for our voyage, but after crossing the sea we were forced to take to our carts again, to which I was beginning to get accustomed. Indeed, I could hardly object to them after having seen so great a queen and her royal family make use of the same conveyance. On reaching a wretched inn toward nightfall we found that our cooks had not arrived yet. This mishap, however, caused no distress, since everyone insisted on taking part in preparing the meal. But when bedtime came, my husband and I were the only ones who enjoyed any comfort: our beds had arrived, whereas the others could not even find straw to lie on. Nevertheless, everyone was in excellent spirits as we made our way back to Hanover.

My joy, however, was of short duration. For a few days after our return, just as I was least prepared for such a blow, I learned that I had lost my brother the elector, who had been carried off by a weeklong fever.[320] My grief surpasses the power of words to express. He had always loved me as a daughter and did me the honor of making me his confidant and writing me by every mail, in a style of such fire and charm that this correspondence had formed one of the chief pleasures of my life. This loss has so increased the pain in my spleen that it constantly reminds me that I am now fifty years old and must soon follow my sister and brother. Besides the deaths in my family, my husband's absence would have driven me to desperation had I not occupied my mind with other thoughts in order to divert it from these triste topics.[321] Thus it comes

320. Charles Lewis died on August 28, 1680.

321. Shortly after receiving the oath of allegiance from his estates on October 23, 1680, Ernest Augustus had departed on his nearly annual trip to Italy.

to pass that I have amused myself by describing the past, an endeavor in which I would doubtless have succeeded better had I been in a more cheerful mood, free from sad reflections and melancholy. I hope that my husband's return, which is expected in a few days, will fully restore me so that I do not soon go the way of all flesh.

Hanover

February 25, 1681

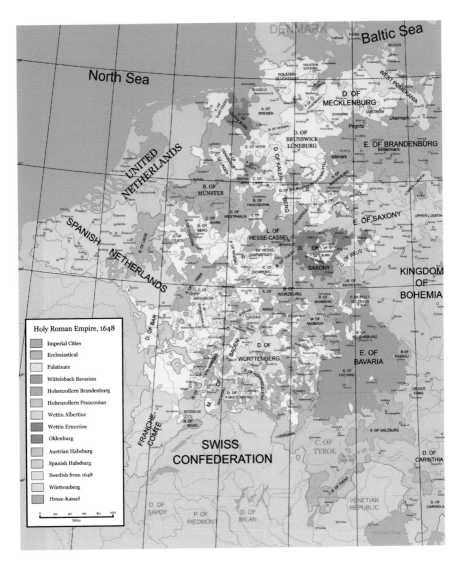

Holy Roman Empire, 1648

House of Orange

William I (1553–84)
("*The Silent*")
Stadholder of the Netherlands
m. 1575 Charlotte of Bourbon (1547–82), mother of Louisa Juliana and Elizabeth
m. 1583 Louise de Coligny (1555–1620), mother of Frederick Henry

Louisa Juliana (1576–1644)
m. 1593 Frederick IV (1574–1610)
Elector Palatine

Elizabeth (1577–1642)
m. 1594 Henri de La Tour d'Auvergne
(1555–1623), Duke of Bouillon

Frederick Henry (1584–1647)
m. 1625 Amalia von Solms-Braunfels (1602–75)

Frederick V (1596–1632)
Elector Palatine, King of Bohemia
m. 1613 Elizabeth Stuart (1596–1662)
Daughter of James I of England
Sophia's parents

Henri de La Tour d'Auvergne
(1611–75), Viscount of Turenne
Marshal General of France
Sophia's great-uncle

Louisa Henrietta (1627–67)
m. Frederick William (1620–88)
Elector of Brandenburg
("*The Great Elector*")

William II (1626–50)
Stadholder
m. 1641 Mary Stuart (1631–60)
Daughter of King Charles I

Frederick I (1657–1713)
Elector of Brandenburg, King in Prussia
m. 1684 Sophia Charlotte (1688–1705)
Sophia's daughter

William III (1650–1702)
Stadholder, King of England
m. 1677 Mary (1662–94)
Daughter of James II of England
Queen of England

Frederick William I (1688–1740)
King of Prussia
m. 1706 Sophia Dorothea (1687–1757)
Sophia's granddaughter by her son George Lewis

Frederick II (1712–86)
King of Prussia
("*The Great*")

This table does not show all issue. King of England, Scotland, and Ireland has been shortened to King of England.

House of Stuart

James VI and I (1566-1625)
King of England
m. 1589 Anne of Denmark (1574-1619)

Charles I (1600-49)
King of England
m. 1625 Henrietta Maria of France (1609-69)

Elizabeth Stuart (1596-1662)
m. 1613 Frederick V (1596-1632)
Elector Palatine, King of Bohemia
Sophia's parents; for the other
children besides Charles Lewis,
see below

Charles Lewis (1617-80)
Elector Palatine
m. 1650 Charlotte of
Hesse-Kassel

Elizabeth Charlotte (1652-1722)
m. 1671 Philippe I (1640-1701)
Duke of Orleans
Court title: "Monsieur"

Elizabeth Charlotte (1676-1744)
m. 1698 Leopold (1679-1729)
Duke of Lorraine

Charles II (1630-85)
King of England
m. 1662 Catherine
of Braganza (1638-1705)

Philippe II (1674-1723)
Duke of Orleans, Regent of France
m. 1692 Françoise Marie
de Bourbon (1677-1749)
Legitimized daughter of Louis XIV

Henrietta (1644-1670)
m. 1661 Philippe I (1640-1701)
Duke of Orleans
Court title: "Monsieur"
Brother of King Louis XIV

Marie Louise (1662-1689)
Court title: "Mademoiselle"
m. 1679 Charles II (1661-1700)
King of Spain

Anne Marie (1669-1728)
m. Victor Amadeus II
(1666-1732), Duke of Savoy,
King of Sardinia

Mary (1631-60)
m. 1641 William II (1626-50)
Stadholder of the Netherlands
See House of Orange table
on previous page

James II (1633-1701)
King of England
m. 1660 Anne Hyde (1638-71)

Anne (1665-1714)
Queen of England
m. 1683 George of Denmark
(1653-1708)

William (1689-1700)
Duke of Gloucester

Frederick V and Elizabeth Stuart's other children besides Charles Lewis and Sophia: Frederick Henry (1614-1629), Elizabeth (1618-1680), Rupert (1619-1682), Morris (1620-1652), Louisa Hollandina (1622-1709), Lewis (1624-25), Edward (1625-1663), Henrietta Maria (1626-1651), Philip (1627-1650), Gustavus Adolphus (1632-1641).

This table does not show all issue. King/Queen of England, Scotland, and Ireland has been shortened to King/Queen of England.

House of Brunswick-Lüneburg (Hanover)

George (1582–1641)
m. 1617 Ann Eleanor of Hesse-Darmstadt (1601–59)

Christian Lewis (1622–65)
m. 1653 Dorothea of
Holstein-Glücksburg (1636–89)

George William (1624–1705)
m. 1675 Eleanor d'Olbreuse
(1679–1722)

Sophia Dorothea (1662–1726)
See George Lewis at right

John Frederick (1625–79)
m. 1668 Benedicta Henrietta of
the Palatinate (1652–1730)
Sophia's niece by her brother Edward

Ernest Augustus (1629–98)
Elector of Hanover
m. 1658 Sophia (1630–1714)
For their other children besides
George Lewis and Sophia
Charlotte, see below

George Lewis (1660–1727)
Elector of Hanover, as George I
King of England
m. 1682 Sophia Dorothea, div. 1694

Sophia Charlotte (1668–1705)
m. 1684 Frederick I (1657–1713)
Elector of Brandenburg, King in
Prussia

Sophia Dorothea (1687–1757)
See Frederick William at right

George Augustus (1683–1760)
Elector of Hanover, as George II
King of England
m. 1705 Caroline of Ansbach (1683–1737)

Frederick William I (1688–1740)
King in Prussia
m. 1706 Sophia Dorothea

Frederick Lewis (1707–51)
Prince of Wales
m. 1736 Augusta of Saxe-Gotha (1719–72)

Frederick II (1712–86)
King of Prussia
("The Great")

George III (1738–1820)
Elector of Hanover, King of England

Ernest Augustus and Sophia's other children besides George Lewis and Sophia Charlotte: Frederick Augustus (1661–90), Maximilliam William (1666–1726), Charles Philip (1669–90), Christian Henry (1671–1703), and Ernest Augustus (1674–1728).

This table does not show all issue. For simplicity's sake, the succession of the Brunswick-Lüneburg dukes (Christian Lewis et al.) to the family's duchies (Calenberg, Lüneburg) is omitted. King of England, Scotland, and Ireland has been shortened to King of England.

Bibliography

Primary Sources

Anonymous. *La vie de Lazarillo de Tormès. La vida de Lazarillo de Tormes.* Translated by Alfred Morel-Fatio. Paris: Aubier, 1988.

Arnauld, Antoine, and Claude Lancelot. *General and Rational Grammar: The Port-Royal Grammar.* Translated and edited by Jacques Rieux and Bernard E. Rollin. The Hague: Mouton, 1975.

Die Briefe der Kinder des Winterkönigs. Edited by Karl Hauck. Neue Heidelberger Jahrbücher 15. Heidelberg: G. Koester, 1908.

Byron, George Gordon. *Beppo, a Venetian Story.* Boston: Monroe & Francis, 1818.

Campion, Henri de. *Mémoires.* Edited by M. C. Moreau. Paris: Jannet, 1857.

Charles Lewis, palsgrave of the Rhine and elector Palatine. *Schreiben des Kurfürsten Karl Ludwig von der Pfalz und der Seinen.* Edited by Wilhelm Ludwig Holland. Bibliothek des literarischen Vereins in Stuttgart 167. Tübingen: Litterarischer Verein, 1884.

A Collection of Original Royal Letters. Edited by Sir George Bromley. London: John Stockdale, 1787.

Descartes, René. *A Discourse of a Method for the well guiding of Reason, and the Discovery of Truth in the Sciences.* London: Thomas Newcombe, 1649.

_____. *The Philosophical Writings of Descartes.* Translated by John Cottingham, Robert Stoothoff, and Dugald Murdoch. 2 vols. Cambridge: Cambridge University Press, 1985.

Elizabeth, consort of Frederick V, king of Bohemia, elector Palatine. *The Letters of Elizabeth of Bohemia.* Edited by L. M. Baker. London: Bodley Head, 1953.

Elizabeth, countess Palatine. *The Correspondence between Princess Elisabeth of Bohemia and René Descartes.* Translated and edited by Lisa Shapiro. Chicago: University of Chicago Press, 2007.

Elizabeth Charlotte, duchess of Orleans. *Elisabeth Charlottens Briefe an Karoline von Wales und Anton Ulrich von*

Braunschweig-Wolfenbüttel. Edited by Hans F. Helmolt. 1789. Reprint, Annaberg: Grasers, 1909.

English Historical Documents, 1660–1714. Vol. 8. Edited by Andrew Browning. New York: Oxford University Press, 1953.

Ernest Augustus, duke of Brunswick-Lüneburg and elector of Hanover. "Briefe des Kurfürsten Ernst August von Hannover an seine Gemahlin, die Kurfürstin Sophie." Edited by Anna Wendland. *Niedersächsisches Jahrbuch* 7 (1930): 205–64.

Evelyn, John. *The Diary of John Evelyn*. 2 vols. London: J. M. Dent, 1950.

Heywood, Thomas. *A Marriage of Triumph*. 1613. Reprint, London: Percy Society, 1842.

I Ciarlatani. *Fly Cheerful Voices: The Marriage of Pfalzgraf Friedrich V & Elizabeth Stuart*, recorded June 13–15, 1997, Christophorus, 77214, 1998. Compact disc.

Leibniz, Gottfried Wilhelm, Freiherr von. *Correspondance de Leibniz avec l'électrice Sophie de Brunswick-Lunebourg*. Edited by Onno Klopp. 3 vols. Hanover: Klindworth, 1874.

Mancini, Hortense and Marie. *Mémoires d'Hortense et de Marie Mancini*. Edited by Gérard Doscot. Paris: Mecure de France, 1965.

———. *Memoirs*. Translated and edited by Sarah Nelson. Chicago: University of Chicago Press, 2008.

Montpensier, Anne-Marie-Louise d'Orléans, duchess of. *Memoirs*. Translated by Philip J. Yarrow, edited by William Brooks. London: MHRA, 2010.

Penn, William. *No Cross, No Crown: A Discourse Shewing the Nature and Discipline of the Holy Cross of Christ*. Philadelphia: Collins, 1853.

Schmidt, Friedrich. *Geschichte der Erziehung der pfälzischen Wittelsbacher*. Monumenta Germaniae Paedagogica 109. Berlin: A. Hofmann, 1899.

Sophia, electress, consort of Ernest Augustus, elector of Hanover. *Memoiren der Herzogin Sophie nachmals Kurfürsten von Hannover*. Edited by Adolf Köcher. Publicationen aus den K. Preußischen Staatsarchiven 4. Leipzig: Hirzel, 1879.

———. *Briefwechsel der Herzogin Sophie von Hannover mit ihrem Bruder, dem Kurfürsten Karl Ludwig von der Pfalz, und des*

Letzteren mit seiner Schwägerin, der Pfalzgräfin Anna. Edited by Eduard Bodemann. Publicationen aus den K. Preußischen Staatsarchiven 26. Leipzig: Hirzel, 1885.

_____. *Memoirs of Sophia, Electress of Hanover, 1630–1680.* Translated by H. Forester. London: Richard Bentley & Son, 1888.

_____. *Briefe der Kurfürstin Sophie von Hannover an die Raugräfinnen und Raugrafen zu Pfalz.* Edited by Eduard Bodemann. Leipzig: Hirzel, 1888.

_____. *Die Mutter der Könige von Preußen und England. Memoiren und Briefe der Kurfürstin Sophie von Hannover.* Translated and edited by Robert Geerds. Munich: Langewiesche-Brandt, 1913.

_____. *Mémoires et lettres de voyage.* Edited by Dirk Van der Cruysse. Paris: Fayard, 1990.

_____. *Leibniz and the Two Sophies: The Philosophical Correspondence.* Translated and edited by Lloyd H. Strickland. Toronto: CRRS, 2011.

Sophie Charlotte, queen, consort of Frederick I, king of Prussia. *Briefe der Königin Sophie Charlotte von Preussen und der Kurfürstin Sophie von Hannover an hannoversche Diplomaten.* Edited by Richard Doebner. Leipzig: Hirzel, 1905.

Strozzi, Barbara. *Opera Ottava: Arie & cantate.* La Risonanza. Conducted by Fabio Bonizzoni. Glossa 921503, 2001. Compact disc.

Treaty of Westphalia. avalon.law.yale.edu/17th_century/westphal.asp.

Secondary Sources

Allgemeine Deutsche Biographie. Edited by the Historische Commission bei der Königlichen Akademie der Wissenschaften. 55 vols. Leipzig: Duncker & Humblot, 1875–1910. Cited from www.deutsche-biographie.de.

Anonymous. "The Electress Sophia," *Quarterly Review* 161 (1885): 172–203.

Anonymous. *The Life and Amours of Charles Lewis Elector Palatine.* London: Thomas Nott, 1692.

Aretin, Karl Otmar Freiherr von. *Das Alte Reich 1648–1806.* 4 vols. Stuttgart: Klett-Cotta, 1993–2000.

Barine, Arvède. "Une princesse allemande au XVIIe siècle." *Revue des deux mondes* 50 (1882): 203–13.

Beasley, Faith E. "Altering the Fabric of History: Women's Participation in the Classical Age." In *A History of Women's Writing in France*, edited by Sonya Stephens. Cambridge: Cambridge University Press, 2000, 64–83.

Belgium and Holland including the Grand-Duchy of Luxembourg. Handbook for Travellers. 15th ed. Leipzig: Karl Baedeker, 1910.

Benger, Elizabeth Ogilvy. *Memoirs of Elizabeth Stuart, Queen of Bohemia, Daughter of King James the First*. 2 vols. London: Longman, 1825.

Beugnot, Bernard. "Livre de raison, livre de retraite." In *Les valeurs chez les mémorialistes français du XVIIe siècle avant la Fronde*, edited by Noemi Hepp and Jacques Hennequin, Paris: Klincksiek, 1979, 47–64.

Bodemann, Eduard. "Herzogin Sophie von Hannover. Ein Lebens- und Culturbild des 17. Jahrhunderts." *Historisches Taschenbuch* 7 (1888): 27–86.

Briot, Frédéric. *Usage du monde, usage de soi: Enquête sur les mémorialistes d'Ancien Régime*. Paris: Seuil, 1994.

Brocher, Henri. *À la cour de Louis XIV. Le rang et l'étiquette sous l'Ancien Régime*. Paris: Félix Alcan, 1934.

Cholakian, Patricia Francis. *Women and the Politics of Self-Representation in Seventeenth-Century France*. Newark: University of Delaware Press, 1990.

Duggan, Josephine N. *Sophia of Hanover: From Winter Princess to Heiress of Great Britain, 1630–1714*. London: Peter Owen, 2010.

Elias, Norbert. *Die höfische Gesellschaft: Untersuchungen zur Soziologie des Königtums und der höfischen Aristokratie*. 1969. Reprint, Frankfurt: Suhrkamp, 1994.

Feder, Johann Georg Heinrich. *Sophie Churfürstin von Hannover im Umriß*. Hanover: Hahn, 1810.

Feuerstein-Praßer, Karin. *Sophie von Hannover (1630–1714): "Wenn es die Frau Kurfürstin nicht gäbe."* Regensburg: Pustet, 2007.

Gibson, Walter Brown. *Hoyle's Encyclopedia of Card Games*. New York: Doubleday, 1974.

Green, Mary Anne Everett. *Elizabeth, Electress Palatine and Queen of Bohemia.* London: Methuen, 1909.

Gumbrecht, Hans Ulrich. *The Powers of Philology. Dynamics of Textual Scholarship.* Urbana and Chicago: University of Illinois Press, 2003.

Hauck, Karl. *Karl Ludwig, Kurfürst von der Pfalz (1617–1680).* Forschungen zur Geschichte Mannheims und der Pfalz 4. Leipzig: Breitkopf & Härtel, 1903.

Havemann, Wilhelm. *Geschichte der Lande Braunschweig und Lüneburg.* 3 vols. Göttingen: Dieterich, 1853–57.

Knoop, Mathilde. *Kurfürstin Sophie von Hannover.* Hanover: Lax, 1964.

Köcher, Adolf. "Denkwürdigkeiten der zellischen Herzogin Eleonore, geb. d'Olbreuse." *Zeitschrift des historischen Vereins für Niedersachsen* (1878): 25–41.

———. *Geschichte von Hannover und Braunschweig, 1648 bis 1714. Erster Theil (1648–1668).* Publicationen aus den K. Preußischen Staatsarchiven 20. Stuttgart: Hirzel, 1886. Reprint, Osnabrück: Zeller, 1966.

Kroll, Maria. *Sophie, Electress of Hanover: A Personal Portrait.* London: Gollancz, 1973.

Motley, Mark. *Becoming a French Aristocrat: The Education of the Court Nobility, 1580–1715.* Princeton: Princeton University Press, 1990.

Oman, Carola. *Elizabeth of Bohemia.* 2nd ed. London: Hodder and Stoughton, 1964.

Schnath, Georg. *Streifzüge durch Niedersachsens Vergangenheit: Gesammelte Aufsätze und Vorträge.* Hildesheim: Lax, 1968.

———. *Geschichte Hannovers im Zeitalter der neunten Kur und der englischen Suzsession 1674–1714.* 4 vols. Veröffentlichungen der Historischen Kommission für Niedersachsen und Bremen 18. Hildesheim: Lax, 1938–82.

Sellin, Volker. "Kurfürst Karl Ludwig von der Pfalz: Versuch eines historischen Urteils." *Schriften der Gesellschaft der Freunde Mannheims und der ehemaligen Kurpfalz* 15 (1980): 1–24.

Smith, George Charles Moore. *The Family of Withypoll: With Special Reference to Their Manor of Christchurch, Ipswich and Some*

Notes on the Allied Families of Thorne, Harper, Lucar, and Devereux. Letchworth: Garden City Press, 1936.

Sperling, Jutta Gisela. *Convents and the Body Politic in Late Renaissance Venice.* Chicago: University of Chicago Press, 1999.

Spittler, Ludwig Timotheus, Freiherr von. *Geschichte des Fürstenthums Hannover seit den Zeiten der Reformation bis zu Ende des siebenzehnten Jahrhunderts.* 2 vols. Göttingen: Vandenhoeck, 1786.

Ward, Adolphus William. *The Electress Sophia and the Hanoverian Succession.* London: Goupil & Co., 1903.

Wilson, Peter H. *The Holy Roman Empire 1495–1806.* London: MacMillan, 1999.

Name Index

Adolphus John I, palsgrave of Zweibrücken-Kleeburg, 65–68, 65n76, 67n82

Ahlefeld, Anna Dorothea von (one of Sophia's ladies-in-waiting), 97, 100, 104, 113, 181n315

Alexander VII, Pope (Fabio Chigi), 2, 110nn170–171

Amalia, princess of Orange-Nassau (née princess of Solms-Braunfels, wife of Prince Frederick Henry), 45–47, 46n32

Amalia Elizabeth, landgravine of Hesse-Kassel (wife of Landgrave William V), 61, 61n65

Anna Dorothea, duchess of Württemberg (née princess of Salm, wife of Duke Eberhard III), 60, 60n63

Anna Johanna, princess of Württemberg, 60–61

Anna Juliana, palsgravine of Zweibrücken, 80, 80n105

Anna Sophia, electoral princess of Saxony (née princess of Denmark), 126, 193

Anne, queen of Great Britain and Ireland, 1, 12, 183n319, 195

Anne of Austria, queen of France, 105

Anne Eleanor, dowager duchess of Brunswick-Lüneburg (née princess of Hesse-Darmstadt, Sophia's mother-in-law), 82n108, 93

Anthony Ulric, duke of Brunswick-Wolfenbüttel, 83, 130, 137–38, 141, 145, 163n284

Antonia, princess of Württemberg, 60–61

Armagnac, count of (Louis de Lorraine), 166

Artale, Giuseppe d', 99, 102, 116

Augustus Frederick, prince of Brunswick-Wolfenbüttel, 130n211, 137, 146n242

Augustus William, duke of Brunswick-Wolfenbüttel, 164n284, 166n293

Auriga, Countess, 98

Avaux, count of (Jean Antoine de Mesmes), 150

Aveiro, duke of (Raimundo de Alencastro), 61

Azzolino, Decio (cardinal of Fermo), 110

Barlow, Lucy (née Walter), 49, 50n41

Benedicta Henrietta, duchess of Celle (wife of Duke John Frederick of Celle, palsgravine of the Rhine, Sophia's niece and sister-in-law), 74n244, 179n310, 196

Beser (Hanoverian courtier), 113

Béthune, marchioness of (Marie Louise de La Grange d'Arquien), 165

Béthune, marquis of (François Gaston), 135, 136n231

Blanche de Castille, queen consort of France, 153n258

Bonstetten, baron von (Franz Ludwig von Bonstetten), 84, 118

Bonzi, Piero de, 101

Bouillon, cardinal of (Emmanuel Théodose de la Tour d'Auvergne, duke of Albret), 160

Brahe, count of (Peter), 65n77

Brionne, count of (Henri de Lorraine-Armagnac), 166n292

Philippe II, duke of Chartres, later duke of Orléans and Regent of France, 166, 167n294, 171, 195
Pibrac, seigneur de (Guy du Faur), 36
Platen, baron von (Franz Ernst, later count of Platen-Hallermund), 113, 113n176
Platen, baroness von (Clara Elizabeth, later countess of Platen-Hallermund), 7n10, 10n18, 113n176
Plessen, Kunigunde Charlotte von, 36
Plessen, Wollrad von, 36n6
Plessis-Praslin, countess of (Colombe le Charron), 156
Poitiers, Madam, 163
Poitiers, Miss, 163, 167
Pomponne, marquis of (Simon Arnauld), 160
Pomponne, marchioness of (Catherine Ladvocat), 166
Pozzo, Count Gabriel, 98
Princess Palatine, *see* Gonzaga, Anna
Puyguilhem, marquis of (Antonin Nompar de Caumont, later duke of Lauzun), 164

Quadt, Marie von (Sophia's governess), 36, 44
Quinto, Count, 102

Raison, Michael, 116n184
Rákóczi, Prince Sigmund (Sophia's brother-in-law), 24, 59
Rosen, Mr. von, 149, 166
Rudolf Augustus, duke of Brunswick-Wolfenbüttel, 130n211
Rupert, palsgrave of the Rhine and duke of Cumberland (Sophia's brother), 4, 12, 24–25, 38n13, 48–49n39, 49n41, 71–72, 195

Sacetot, Catherine de, 149
Sandis, Wilhelm, Ritter von (known as 'Chevalier von Sandis'), 97, 102–03, 149, 158, 181–82
Savoy, duchess of (Anne Marie d'Orléans, prior to her marriage known at the French court as 'la petite Mademoiselle'), 154, 160, 160n277, 195
Schütz, Johann Helwig Sinold, Baron, 130, 137, 145
Schwarz, Mr., 182
Serini, Countess, 100
Somerset, earl of (Robert Carr), 49n39
Sophia, countess of Hohenlohe-Neuenstein (née princess of Birkenfeld), 35, 35n4
Sophia Amalia, queen of Denmark (née princess of Brunswick-Lüneburg) 126–27, 126n200, 129, 131, 181–84
Sophia Charlotte, electress of Brandenburg and later queen of Prussia (née princesss of Brunswick-Lüneburg, Sophia's daughter), 9, 129n207, 132n219, 149, 151, 155, 157, 159, 163, 166–74, 181–82, 194, 196
Sophia Dorothea, princess of Brunswick-Lüneburg (Sophia's niece and daughter-in-law), 8, 10, 125n197, 130, 131n212, 132, 137–38, 142, 145–47, 146n242, 179, 196
Sophia Eleanor of Saxony, landgravine of Hesse-Darmstadt (née princess of Saxony, wife of Landgrave George II), 82, 82n109
Sophia Hedwig, countess of Nassau-Dietz, 35n4
Soranzo (procurator), 100
Staunton, Lady Phlippina, 49, 50n41